Surviving Transformation

Original art by Sheryl Barabba.

Also by Vincent P. Barabba

Meeting of the Minds

Hearing the Voice of the Market
(with Gerald Zaltman)

The 1980 Census: Policymaking amid Turbulence
(with Ian Mitroff and Richard Mason)

Surviving Transformation

Lessons from GM's Surprising Turnaround

Vincent P. Barabba

OXFORD
UNIVERSITY PRESS

2004

OXFORD
UNIVERSITY PRESS

Oxford   New York

Auckland   Bangkok   Buenos Aires   Cape Town   Chennai
Dar es Salaam   Delhi   Hong Kong   Istanbul   Karachi   Kolkata
Kuala Lumpur   Madrid   Melbourne   Mexico City   Mumbai   Nairobi
São Paulo   Shanghai   Taipei   Tokyo   Toronto

Copyright © 2004 by Oxford University Press, Inc.

Published by Oxford University Press, Inc.
198 Madison Avenue, New York, New York 10016

www.oup.com

Oxford is a registered trademark of Oxford University Press

Library of Congress Cataloging-in-Publication Data
Barabba, Vincent P., 1934–
Surviving transformation : lessons from GM's surprising turnaround /
Vincent P. Barabba.
p.   cm.
Includes index.
ISBN 0-19-517141-1
1. General Motors Corporation—Management—Case studies.
2. Automobile industry and trade—United States—Management—
Case studies.   3. Organizational change—United States—Case studies.
I. Title: GM's surprising turnaround.   II. Title.
HD9710.U54 G3726   2004
658.4'06—dc22   2003022678

9   8   7   6   5   4   3   2   1

Printed in the United States of America
on acid-free paper

This book is dedicated to the GM employees who, during the period 1992 to 2002 when it was being predicted that GM would be dethroned as the market leader of the domestic automotive industry, transformed GM business practices to make them more consistent, creative, robust, and systemic. Their immense effort contributed to the early stages of GM's turnaround. Although their accomplishments do not guarantee success, they have positioned GM, led by a newly formed team, to build on that effort in its quest to be great, again!

The book is also dedicated to Russell Ackoff and Peter Drucker, who pioneered most of the theories and applications that form the basis of this book and took the time to teach me about them — not in their classrooms but in the world of business and government.

Foreword

C. K. Prahalad

Harvey C. Fruehauf Professor of Corporate Strategy
The University of Michigan Business School

The focus of this book is "how to think" about large-scale business transformation: not just to survive a large-scale transformation, but to start, sustain, and thrive in a world of continuous change. The setting is the largest manufacturing company in the world, a century-old business (automotive), global operations, and a rich heritage of leadership. But leaders can become complacent and lose their edge. This is the story of how General Motors (GM) is regaining its lost luster. But it is not "about" GM: It is, rather, about how any organization that wants to transform itself can use the lessons from GM's transformation to guide the process.

The book deals with the central role of legacy mindsets, skills, and management processes in impeding the revitalization of an aging firm. The book is also an insider's view of that transformation—that of a detached and involved, analytical and thoughtful insider. It is the combination of these factors—size and complexity of the company, the nature and size of its problems, the legacy systems to be transformed, the financial stakes in question, and the credibility of the storyteller—that makes this a compelling read.

The transformation is described in three parts. The first part deals with the changing nature of interactions between the company and its customers. It is described as the changing nature of business models, from "make-and-sell," to "sense-and-respond," toward "anticipate-and-lead." The second part is about the impediments such organizations face in changing the way the company thinks and acts. The third part is about building a new approach—a "state of mind" that balances creativity and intuition with analytics and science. This presents a unique and interesting progression of ideas for thinking about the transformation of a large and established firm.

The critical starting point in the story is the changing nature of the customer-company interaction. The relative roles of the two are morphing and changing.

The grafting of the most advanced technology to the traditional automotive business creates a new relationship between the company and the consumer. The OnStar system becomes a "trusted friend in the sky" that makes "my trip" on the highway or in the neighborhood safer and more enjoyable. The ability of an individual consumer to interact with the largest company in the world—at his or her discretion—is quite revolutionary. This process of dialogue provides the company with unique insights into the way consumers use GM's products. For the first time, GM can have an ongoing relationship with consumers who ultimately use its cars and trucks. Before OnStar, the relationship was mediated by dealers and was at best episodic.

While OnStar changes the relationship between the consumer and the company after the purchase of the product, AutoChoiceAdvisor represents GM's approach in helping the consumer in his or her decision-making process. The AutoChoiceAdvisor provides a transparent and easy-to-use system for the consumer to identify the product that best suits his or her needs. The focus is not just on GM products but on the entire portfolio of products available to the consumer, including those of GM's competitors. This willingness to expose the entire choice in automobiles to the consumer is an act of courage. As the consumer starts to trust GM as a company that will do the best for him or her, GM also learns what consumers are looking for—an invaluable input to its own product development strategy. Both GM and the consumer benefit from this process of open access and transparency. This is an example of firms' voluntarily giving up the benefits of "asymmetric information" between the consumer and the company. In return, firms learn firsthand consumer preferences and competencies.

If GM did succeed in innovating at the consumer-company interface, then doing so must have been easy. Far from it. The second part of the book outlines the impediments. Transformations demand that managers accept that the existing ways of thinking and acting are dysfunctional. Large systems such as GM are complex. Given the multiple "perches" that managers occupy—functional, regional, and business unit—their perspectives on problems can be very different. The old saying "What you see depends on where you sit in the organization" holds true even today. Therefore, making assumptions explicit is critical for an effective dialogue and arrival at "consensus about practice." In large organizations, compliance is easy to get, but commitment based on a clear and unambiguous set of assumptions about the future and opportunities is difficult.

Managers are also socialized to think in some predictable ways. The dominant logic is like the genetic code. The discussion in part II focuses on the nature of complex problems and the implications of misspecification in transformation. This is a critical part of the overall thesis of this book. The type III errors (solving the wrong problems) and type IV errors (behaving as if we understand the problem when the environment is in flux and the problem is also evolving) and the examples that go with them are fascinating. The most telling story in the book is about the manager who thought that the dimensions on a chart represented 120 days when they really represented 120 months (chapter 9). The nature of complexity and interconnectedness of problems—short-term lease for luxury cars and the overhang of good-quality used cars competing with the market for new cars—is a great story. This obviously leads to part III.

Part III moves the reader into an important domain, one not well dealt with in management literature: the subtle mixture of intuition and imagination with analytics and information—the art and science of managing. The idea of a data-driven, analytical orientation runs throughout the book. But this is not about a mechanistic approach. Human creativity and intuition are a critical part of it. Whether it is Corvette, Cadillac, or Hummer 2, individuals make a difference in how data is interpreted and extended. Strategy is, as my colleague Karl Weick would say, "disciplined imagination." The author provides enough evidence of how disciplined imagination can work in a large firm.

This book is about transformation. It tackles transformation from a unique angle. It is not about restructuring and performance evaluation or training programs: it demonstrates that by changing selectively how we do business—by changing our interactions with customers, by changing the way we formulate problems internally, and by changing the way we imagine a future—we can make a difference. The caselets, drawn mainly from GM, illustrate the specifics of the argument.

The author combines a deep understanding of analytics, systems thinking, and organizational insights to build a theory of transformation that is refreshingly new. The focus on "how managers think and formulate problems and how this process impacts what they do" is well illustrated. One is left with a hunger for more detail about every case discussed in the book. The purpose of the caselets, however, is to illustrate the concepts, not to provide a "how to do it."

The book is rich in theory and practice. The author acknowledges his own intellectual debt to others, especially to Peter Drucker and Russ Ackoff—good company to keep. Mr. Barabba has been the conduit for translating good theory into good practice, and GM has been the beneficiary of this translation. Now all of us are the beneficiaries of Barabba's willingness to share his experience in facilitating the transformation of GM, the largest manufacturing company in the world. This is a serious book, and I do hope that leads to a serious and involved discussion of an elusive topic: the role of senior managers in the transformation and revitalization of their companies on a continuing basis.

Preface

This book describes some of what was learned from General Motors's experiences in its attempt to transform itself between 1992 and 2003. A legitimate question is, Why should a reader who is not in the automobile business expect to learn from the GM transformation experience? The answer is simple: GM has had a long history with a prolonged era of success. Today, it appears to be coming out of a phase of diminished expectations. GM's actions during this ten-year period have resulted in significant improvements: Profits went from a negative $4.8B to a positive $3.5B; productivity measurements went from among the least productive to among the most productive; measurement of customer perception of quality went from below industry average to above industry average; share of market went from continuing losses to market share increase; and approach to innovation went from acquisition of technology firms Hughes Electronics and EDS to introduction of new business designs (OnStar, Downstream Revenue, and AutoChoiceAdvisor) and renewed leadership in vehicle design and development.

Learning *what* went right or wrong during this period is valuable. Revealing *why* events went right or wrong adds to that value. The learning process is as important as the outcome, because most enterprises are facing significant changes in the environments in which they operate. For most enterprises, relying on what worked in the past or waiting for change to occur is a strategy for possible disaster. It is no longer a question of whether these environments become more complex or whether the rate of change accelerates. It is only a question of the extent and nature of the increased complexity and the rate of acceleration of change. In today's world of accelerating change, those interested in staying ahead of problems cannot afford to wait until what looks like a good idea is finished before they try to learn from it.

Why not focus on companies with proven success records rather than on one in transition? Attempting to understand and apply what successful firms, based on their past performance, may have in common assumes that what generally contributed to the success of this selected group of firms will work for any specific firm. The approach also assumes that what worked in the past for a particular enterprise will continue to work in the future. Despite these questionable assumptions, this type of study can still be valuable. Several books based on this approach contain meaningful insights that led to some of the ideas found in this book.

This book assumes that enterprises facing difficult times are more likely than currently successful companies to see opportunities for changing the way things are done. The premise underlying this assumption goes beyond the advice Wayne Gretzky's father gave the great hockey player when he said, "Go to where the puck is going, not where it has been." The advice to the reader is to accept the premise: "Firms who have learned from their mistakes may find it easier to move the puck away from where it is and get the puck to where *they* want it."

The book describes how organizations can start the strategy development process with their destination clearly understood and accepted, using GM as a case in point. This message applies whether the enterprise is large or small, public or private, currently successful or in trouble. Starting with your destination inspires employees to avoid limiting their aspirations because of the current enterprise trajectory, and helps them steer clear of actual and perceived constraints of the encompassing environment.

This is not a book for someone looking for "seven quick steps to transformation." Although time is short, successful transformations that last do not take place overnight, and transformation will be different for each enterprise.

The insights gleaned from GM's journey to its destination provide a deeper understanding of the following:

1. Minimizing or avoiding the "zone of discomfort" felt by employees when your enterprise is required to change from where you are to where you need, or want, to be
2. Thinking about your current business as the extended enterprise system it has the potential to be — starting with your destination
3. Getting to a destination after you have determined where it is
4. Developing an effective dialogue with selected customers, using the latest technology
5. Staring a complex and uncertain future directly in the eye — and developing a business design that increases the chances of favorable future conditions

6. Creating and nurturing a strong and effective relationship between and among information providers (market researchers) and information users (decision makers)
7. Identifying "the right problem" to be working on rather than finding out later that you solved the wrong problem
8. Developing teams that sort out the conflicting issues underlying the multiple perspectives of functional organizations
9. Creating awareness of the interaction of the parts of the system, in order to anticipate whether the outcomes of decisions will differ from initial expectations
10. Understanding the encompassing environment in which your enterprise operates and determine how you want to interact within that system
11. Revealing the implicit assumptions of your plans and how you can assess the likelihood of their actually occurring
12. Ensuring that the knowledge of what is known (and what is unknown) by your enterprise is made available to all who need access to it
13. Determining your destination in the face of an uncertain future and identifying ways to think about getting your enterprise to that destination

Background

In one of his many compelling books on systems thinking, C. West Churchman, made "one further remark about the coming pages" that may be helpful: "The underlying imagery of the book is that of a voyage, with pathways and concomitant dangers and joys. The writer is simply a guide." Churchman then went on to point out that the reader has "every right to know something about the guide—and at least to know how he comes to think he's professionally capable of the job."[1]

In this spirit, the reader should be aware that the content of this book is drawn from experiences seen and heard through the eyes, ears, and mind of a very interested and involved observer. That the effect of these experiences on what is seen, heard, and remembered cannot be precisely measured does not mean the effect does not exist. As such, what follows are experiences of the author, experiences most relevant to the mental model from which this book was written.

---

1. C. West Churchman, *The Systems Approach and Its Enemies* (New York: Basic Books, 1979), 8–9.

From the Schoolroom to the Back Room

Like many business school students in the 1960s through the 1980s, I was taught in a manner that led me to believe that the world of business was a predictable place. I believed that since all the pieces to the puzzle were available I had simply to lay them out to find the single answer to the problem.

At that time, disciplines like operations research were being heralded as an effective approach to solving many of our very complex problems. Additionally, national and local economies were being described and forecasted from what appeared to be very accurate econometric models. Fifteen years later, I would discover that some thoughtful people had been challenging these approaches even as I was being taught to accept them. In 1999, one of the principal contributors to systems thinking, Russell L. Ackoff, was feted at a festive eightieth birthday celebration. Among the many tributes he received that evening was a special note from Peter Drucker recalling a 1950s experience:

> I was then, as you may recall, one of the early ones who applied *Operations Research* and the new methods of *Quantitative Analysis* to specific BUSINESS PROBLEMS—rather than, as they had been originally developed for, to military or scientific problems. I had led teams applying the new methodology in two of the world's largest companies—GE and AT&T. We had successfully solved several major production and technical problems for these companies—and my clients were highly satisfied. But I was not—we had solved TECHNICAL problems but our work had no impact on the organizations and on their mindsets. On the contrary: we had all but convinced the managements of these two big companies that QUANTITATIVE MANIPULATION was a substitute for THINKING. And then your work and your example showed us—or at least, it showed me— that the QUANTITATIVE ANALYSIS comes AFTER the THINKING—it validates the thinking; it shows up intellectual sloppiness and uncritical reliance on precedent, on untested assumptions and on the seemingly "obvious." But it does not substitute for hard, rigorous, intellectually challenging THINKING. It demands it, though —but does not replace it. This is, of course, what YOU mean BY system. And your work in those far-away days thus saved me—as it saved countless others— from either descending into mindless "model building"—the disease that all but destroyed so many of the Business Schools in the last decades—or from sloppiness parading as "insight."

My own experiences had led me to believe, as Drucker and Ackoff had discovered decades earlier, that many—though certainly not all—the approaches to decision making I was taught were flawed. The basic flaw was that many of them required that I simplify, or hold constant, much of the contextual complexity surrounding the problems I was attempting to solve. My attitude toward these limitations developed over a seven-year period in which I participated in seventy political campaigns. In these campaigns, rapid and dynamic change in the business, political, and social climate made uncertainty the only certainty. The campaigns included city, state legislative, gubernatorial, congressional, senatorial, and presidential elections, and several public initiatives. The work took me to nearly every state and provided the opportunity to directly engage with the great diversity of thinking and ideas found in local officials and community leaders throughout the country. During this period, I often found it more important to get those involved in implementing the strategy to agree on the alternative that would allow them to work, as a team, to achieve a successful outcome. Russ Ackoff later brought clarity to my experiences in describing his view of developing a consensus: "The nature of consensus is not understood. It is complete agreement, not in principle, but in practice. It is this distinction that is not widely grasped."

In short, the type of work I was doing was not at all like solving jigsaw puzzles. It was more like trying to understand the interaction between the atomic elements of a molecule, where a change to any one element could cause the composition, properties, and identity of the molecule to change. And when new elements are added, their interaction creates a new dynamic that impacts the nature and outcome of the whole. Changes in the environment within which the molecule is contained can also affect the structure. Problems, I found out, were not solved well by attempting to make them appear simpler than they were.

Over the next twenty-five years, I would move from the world of politics to industry. I served twice as director of the U.S. Bureau of the Census, appointed by Presidents Richard Nixon, Gerald Ford, and Jimmy Carter. I also served as manager of market research activities at the Xerox Corporation and as director of market intelligence at Eastman Kodak Company at a time when both enterprises were beginning to feel the effects of offshore competition in their home markets. I eventually came to General Motors as director of marketing research and planning in 1985, just as the enterprise was beginning to acknowledge the realities of its worsening market position. In 1990, Richard Wirthlin, the noted political and strategic researcher, and I were in the GM boardroom. I had asked him to work with GM on a very complex problem. For years, GM's leadership role in the auto industry had been slipping. At the same time, management had been denying that this trend would persist and bring the company to the brink of financial disaster. Finally, emerging from a sustained period of denial, some members of the management team wanted to understand what had happened and what it would take to reverse the downward spiral. In fact, the worst was yet to come. Two years later, GM would face the possibility of bankruptcy.

While the meeting's chair completed the introductions and other formalities, I recalled a political activity in which Richard and I had participated nearly twenty-five years earlier in Flint, Michigan, the birthplace of GM. In 1966, while employed by the California political consulting firm of Spencer-Roberts, I was contacted by Donald Riegle (then a Republican), who was attending the Harvard Business School and had decided to return home to run for Congress in Michigan's Seventh Congressional District—a traditionally Democratic "safe" district. Given the political heritage of the Democratic-leaning district and its history of election outcomes, the incumbent congressman and his supporters had no reason to expect a Republican, much less a young Republican from the Harvard Business School, to present any serious threat. Had they not been so confident of their past successes and their belief that the district would behave in the future as it had in the past, they would have recognized how the autoworker's changing social values could affect his traditional attitude toward political campaigns and candidates. They were about to find out about these changes the hard way. The Riegle campaign had started with a destination: a congressional district with changed political behavior. The campaign team had spent a significant portion of its budget developing an in-depth understanding of voters in the district, finding out what issues mattered to them. The team also tried to find out which of the candidate's positions might resonate with, and lure away the votes of, those Democratic and Independent voters who were not fiercely loyal either to the incumbent or to his party.

On Election Day, contrary to conventional wisdom, pundit predictions, and virtually all expectations, Riegle emerged with a narrow upset victory. The defeat of the district's established political machine came as a surprise to everyone except the newly elected congressman and his forward-thinking staff. Two years later, using improved techniques and what was learned from the previous election, Riegle won again, this time with a more comfortable margin.

From the Back Room to the Boardroom

With this memory in mind, I was struck by the irony that here we were, twenty-two years later, in the boardroom of the world's largest manufacturing corporation, addressing a very significant set of problems. These problems had come to pass because leaders of the firm, much like the leaders of the local Democratic party in Flint, had failed to accept that change was occurring and that the practices that had worked so well in the past were no longer sufficient to maintain the growth and viability of the enterprise. Sitting next to Richard, I leaned over and said that, although it was only 40 miles away, we had come a long way from the *back room* of the political campaign in Flint to the *boardroom* of the General Motors Corporation. We both smiled. The journey that had led us from back-room strategy sessions in Flint had taught me that, whether the issue was political campaigns, public policy making, or significant business decisions, the world was rapidly changing and had grown more complex. What had not changed, however, was the need to solve problems by making good decisions. The last eighteen years have allowed me to develop additional understanding and insight while leading a group of talented people who supported GM leaders as they developed their strategy and made key decisions contributing to GM's move from the brink of disaster back to a point where it is positioned, but not guaranteed, to be *great again*.

The insights gained from these observations have not resulted in a series of static proclamations developed by observing from afar. Rather, the insights come from the experience of being there and understanding not only the rational and emotional dimensions behind what actually was decided—including decisions *not* to take action—but also how the decisions were made. The observations provide a framework for the stories contained in each chapter. Consequently, the observations presented are limited in terms of breadth of examples, but they are deep in their understanding of what actually happened.

Before coming to GM I had often used the saying "I can provide you with information that is fast, accurate, or cheap—take two!" After arriving at GM, I soon learned that, although the phrase was catchy and clever, it was not a sufficient answer for an enterprise that was going through a wrenching transformation. I have come to understand that it is not about one *or* the other, but about one *and* the other. For example, if those who provide information do so in a manner that encourages enterprise decision makers and analysts to work with them to improve their ability to anticipate the knowledge required to support them, then the information providers will be able to say, "I can give it to you fast enough, accurately enough, *and* at a price you will value."

To its credit, GM management allowed me to explore the periphery of these ideas and experiences, and to experiment when conditions allowed. It has also encouraged my writing and speaking on these topics, thus allowing the opportunity to explore and discuss their application within GM with the academic community, as well as with leaders in other enterprises.[2]

I also benefited from working at the U.S. Census Bureau early in my career. Before working for the Census Bureau, I came from a small company where, at least in my own mind, I was capable of doing every job in the company almost as well as anyone else could. As the director of the world's largest statistical agency, I soon found out that, in every department for which I was responsible, there were several people who knew far more about that area than I did. This led, by necessity, to the awareness of the importance of managing the interaction of the departments—and of not trying to manage them separately.

Earlier, others like Drucker and Ackoff were working within businesses in a similar vein to expand academic theory regarding organizational behavior, systems thinking, and strategic decision making. Eventually our paths would cross, and I was provided the opportunity to glean insights from what they had learned as critical observers and participants. We also found that common principles and pursuits carried over from the political sphere and academia to the arena of government and the corporate world.

Leo Grebler, one of my professors at the University of California, Los Angeles, once opened a graduate seminar by stating he did not intend to cover all aspects of the subject of the course, but to uncover those aspects with which his students were not familiar. In many ways, this is the plan for this book. Even if

---

2. Vincent P. Barabba, "Understanding the Enterprise as a System," in Jay Chatzkel, ed., *Knowledge Capital* (New York: Oxford University Press, 2003); "Revisiting Plato's Cave: Business Design in an Age of Uncertainty," in Don Tapscott, Alex Lowy, and David Ticoll, eds., *Blueprint to the Digital Economy* (New York: McGraw-Hill, 1998); *Meeting of the Minds* (Boston: Harvard Business School Press, 1995); "Market Based Decisions," in Sidney Levy et al., eds., *Marketing Manager's Handbook* (Chicago: Dartnell Press, 1994); "The Market Research Encyclopedia," *Harvard Business Review* (Jan.–Feb. 1991); Vincent P. Barabba, with Gerald Zaltman, *Hearing the Voice of the Market* (Boston: Harvard Business School Press, 1991).

I wanted to, there would be no way to completely cover the distinctions between "make-and-sell," "sense-and-respond," and the emerging concept of "anticipate-and-lead" as an aid to gaining your destination. Nor could I address all of General Motors's attempts at applying these concepts. There are, however, some aspects worth uncovering so learning can take place, aspects not everyone is aware of. In this case, it is not only the specific uncovered events or activities but the manner in which they interact that may ensure the whole of the enterprise is greater than the sum of its parts. It is hoped that the same will be said of this book.

Acknowledgments

Many academic and business colleagues spent considerable time reviewing early drafts of the manuscript and made significant contributions to the final effort. Without their actions and support, the content of this book would have been primarily theoretical. Those who contributed the most were: Sean Baenen, Odyssey; Charles Babcock, GM; Osvald Bjelland, Synecta Ltd.; Robert Bordley, GM; Jeff Hartley, GM; Bill Kenney, Sears; Ian Mitroff, University of Southern California; Chunka Mui, Diamond Exchange Fellow; Jim Mullin, Market Insight Corporation; Andrew Norton, GM; Mark Paich, Decisio Consulting; Johnnie Pourdehnad, University of Pennsylvania; C. K. Prahalad, University of Michigan; Nick Pudar, GM; Phil Samper, Gabriel Venture Partners; Adrian Slywotzky, Mercer Management; Richard Smallwood, Market Insight Corporation; Glen Urban, Massachusetts Institute of Technology; Ramasamy Uthurusamy, GM; Lyle Wallace, Decisio Consulting; and Jerry Zaltman, Harvard Business School.

Susan Knoppow helped tremendously in the initial organization and drafting of the manuscript, and Julie Curtis contributed to earlier drafts of the section on problem solving. Jim Dolot, Lori Kneisler, and Joyce Salisbury made sure I had my facts on GM correct. Steve Leslie helped with many of the graphics, and Patricia Hawkins made sure that several of the projects described in the book were implemented well. Herb Addison, as acquiring editor for Oxford University Press, did an incredible job of asking the tough questions and offered organizing recommendations that led to greater clarity and consistency. Heather Hartman and Jenny Foerst and the entire production team at Oxford University Press paid attention to detail while keeping the big picture in mind. My wife Sheryl not only contributed the beauty of her artwork for the cover, but also kept saying, "Don't make it any more complicated than it needs to be." I am sure the work could be more straightforward than it is, but thanks to her it is far less complicated than it might have been.

Contents

III MARKETING AS A STATE OF MIND

Surviving Transformation

1 Setting the Scene

The following story represents thirty years of practical experience and observation. It reveals several major issues faced by any enterprise trying to transform itself so that it can grow and increase its operating margins and services to society. It also sets the stage for thinking about how to start with your destination.

Traditionally, there have been two primary approaches used in attempting to grow and increase margins: (1) improving the manner in which the enterprise is currently doing business, or (2) moving into promising areas of new business. This story focuses on the interaction between the two traditional approaches and describes demonstrated processes for addressing the interactions of both—doing one *and* the other versus doing one *or* the other. The story also identifies the manner in which strategic thinking procedures, including creating an idealized design of what you want to be, can assist leaders interested in transforming the enterprise—without destroying it in the process. The story is hypothetical, but most readers will have experienced something like the "problems" the participants face, though perhaps not the outcome.

The ABC Company

The chief executive officer (CEO) of the ABC Company has called a meeting of his senior management team. A respected market analyst from Smith & Jones Investment Company has just issued the following summary of ABC.

> Investment in the ABC Company appears less than exciting. Its prospects for revenue and profit growth seem adequate at best. It operates in an extremely competitive industry, in which the pricing environment offers little or no opportunities for generating acceptable levels of growth or even significant improvement in its profit situation. It is the best-managed company in an uninspired market and is expected—at best—to increase its rate of growth incrementally. Assum-

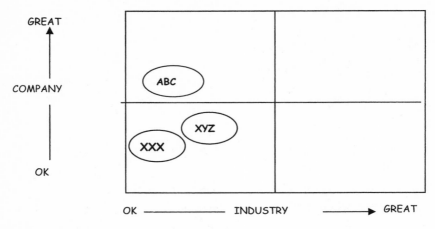

Figure 1.1 ABC's market position.

ing, of course, that it does not simply hold to its current level or, worse yet, actually suffer a decline.

The CEO generally agrees with this assessment and has been considering transforming ABC into some new and potentially promising areas of business. At the beginning of the meeting with his leadership team, he draws a chart to describe why he feels the financial markets do not see ABC as a stock in which to invest (fig. 1.1).

He points out that by just doing competitive assessments and benchmarking of the best practices in its industry, ABC has fallen into the trap of being the best of a dying breed. That its industry is not growing implies that the only way for ABC to grow is for it to gain a greater share of a pie that, though large, is not getting any larger. Traditionally, this strategy has led to very competitive industry actions that result in inevitably diminishing profit margins. The CEO states that he believes the existing business design for the industry is not sufficient to warrant continued investment. He also states that he does not want to wait until it is too late to take constructive action. To drive home his concerns, he begins drawing another chart (fig. 1.2).

Before he can finish drawing the curve, he senses deep apprehension in the room and decides to open the topic up for discussion. The chief financial officer (CFO) starts out. "Your curve is too optimistic!" she says. "If we do not immediately get costs under control, you can expect your chart to look quite different." She goes to the board and modifies it (fig. 1.3).

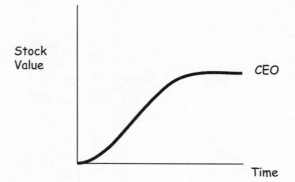

Figure 1.2 CEO's initial position.

The vice president of marketing scoffs: "It is not solely about costs! If you could acquire operating capital, at the right price, and let the company develop and deliver the product portfolio we've been asking for — at the right price — we could really turn this thing around!" He strides to the board and makes his own modification (fig. 1.4).

The vice president of engineering stands up and grabs his own marker. He crosses out the words "Marketing and Sales" and replaces them with "Engineering" (fig. 1.5).

"I agree with your chart," the engineering vice president explains to the marketing vice president, "but your belief that we can sell our way out of this problem is all wrong. If we could just make fewer products, and make them very well, we wouldn't need to spend so much on marketing. Engineering fewer, but really great, products — that's where we need to invest our limited resources."

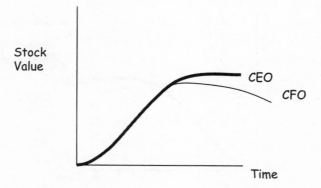

Figure 1.3 CFO's position.

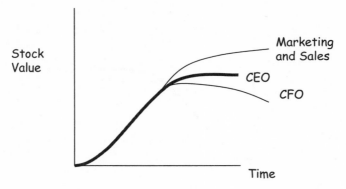

Figure 1.4 Marketing vice president's position.

The chief information officer (CIO), sensing an opportunity, stands up and offers an opinion: "You're both right! But the solution is to invest in information technology and systems. That way we can reduce the cost of marketing by creating an improved customer-relationship management system and reduce engineering costs by updating and automating all of our current processes to speed up development."

The director of a new division, moving into a new market, smiles at the traditional combatants, each trying to increase his or her allocation of the existing resources, and calmly walks to the board. "We have to think out of the box," she says. The operating managers glance at each other and smile as if to say, "Here we go again with that 'out of the box' stuff." Undaunted by the operating management's reaction, she continues: "Let's face it, the market analysts are right.

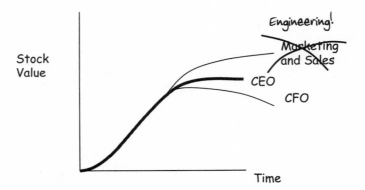

Figure 1.5 Engineering vice president's position.

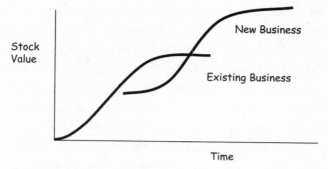

Figure 1.6 Director of new business's position.

We are in a terrible industry. We cannot make a sufficient return on the capital we ask our shareholders to provide us. That's why our stock has not appreciated at the same level as that of companies in other industries. We need to get into a new business!" She modifies the chart (fig. 1.6).

Exasperated, the senior chief operating manager of the existing business jumps out of his chair and exclaims, "What box is it that you want to get out of? Who is going to fund the development of the new business? If you take resources from the existing business, you will make the situation worse than it already is! If you want to think out of the box . . . then get out of my box. And, if your idea is so good, go get your own money—don't mess with mine. I need all of it to stay alive! Just remember, if I don't exist . . . neither will you!"

As tensions mount, a senior advisor senses the CEO's frustration over how the meeting is disintegrating. She walks up to the chart and adds a circle, which she labels "Zone of Discomfort" (fig. 1.7).[1]

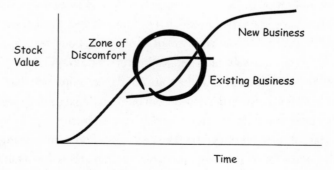

Figure 1.7 Senior advisor's position.

"We're all approaching this problem from the narrow perspectives of our functional responsibilities. This type of discussion has been going on for over five years, and our situation is not any better than when we started. We need to step back and look at the problem from a broader company perspective." After a moment, the senior advisor continues: "In that Peter Drucker article that our CEO distributed last year, Drucker took the position that every enterprise has three essential dimensions: the traditional business, in our case the one for which we are all concerned; the transitional business, the one that our CEO has decided we should look into; and the transformational business, which we never get to because we can't get past our own parochial interests! This is a classic problem that occurs when companies try to move into new areas of business. Naturally, no one is comfortable while 'switching gears,' but we have to trust one another and begin moving in the right direction for the entire company."

The CEO thanks the advisor and suggests they start over, and the team reflects on what has occurred. In the ensuing dialogue, the CEO asks the team if anyone has any suggestions on how to get around their inability to think about the business in a more holistic way. The vice president of engineering has just attended an executive seminar at the University of Pennsylvania's Wharton School, which introduced him to Russell L. Ackoff's concept of systems thinking and idealized design. At the time, he had been intrigued with the approach but had a hard time determining how he might implement it at ABC, because the approach was not limited to improving the engineering department: it called for re-creating the entire enterprise.

"Today's 'discussion,'" he points out to the group, "was the beginning of what Ackoff would describe as 'formulating the mess.' That is, if we would all step back and consider what each of us was saying, we would see that we revealed three issues: first, what problems and opportunities we face individually; second, an indication of the extent to which they interact; and, third, the obstructions to and constraints on our ability to do something about them.

"I now appreciate the reality and implications of what Ackoff said to our seminar: 'There are as many realities as there are minds contemplating them.' Each of the problems that we have described from our functional vantage points co-produce the mess that the company is currently experiencing.

"I also started to better understand an analogy Ackoff used to bring home the meaning of the mess: 'Problems are to reality what atoms are to tables. We experience tables, not atoms. Problems are abstracted from experience by analysis. We do not experience individual problems but complete systems of those that are strongly interacting. I call them messes.' As I think about what was going on today, including my own comments, it becomes clear that what we are experiencing is a dynamic situation consisting of a complex system of problems. The weakness of our approach is that we are thinking of them as individual or isolated problems (atoms), when, in systems thinking terminology, what we are really experiencing is a 'mess,' that is, the interaction of the problems leading to the way others see our enterprise (the table)."

The VP of engineering goes back to the chart where he "corrected" the VP of marketing: "What we've been doing is using a reference projection; that is, extrapolating the past into the future. We in essence have been arguing over projections, on the false assumption that 'what was past will be prologue.' Who in this room believes that the environment in which we have done business will be the environment in which we will do our business? The VP of marketing and I were trying to make the current business better. Our differences were primarily based on different views of the business. Based on his experience and where he would like to see the company go, he really believes we need more products. Based on my experience and where I would like to see the company go, I think it would be better to have fewer products that are made really well. Instead of arguing from our functional points of view, we should have asked questions, such as how could we resolve our differences in the context of what's in the best interest of the customer and the company. Is there a way we can develop a product portfolio process that produces more products that are designed in a manner that allows me to make them with fewer problems? Perhaps the CIO has found a partial answer in the use of new technologies that we need to find the time to better understand in order to determine whether they may actually help. The director of new business development went further and gave her impression of what would happen if we were to get into an entirely new business.

"Instead of projecting what each of our individual approaches could accomplish, we, as a team, need to look at these historical trends and combine them with approximations of what external trends—trends over which we have little to no control—are likely to do. I would bet that if we did so we would see, as the CEO started to point out at the beginning of this session, that the mess we are in will result in a continued decline leading to disastrous consequences for the company, whether or not any of us improves the conduct of his or her functional performance. The CFO was also right in her assessment that our income and cash flow are likely to continue to drop. If that does occur, it will further erode the company's value and negatively affect the company's ability to provide a proper return on investment to the shareholders. We need to understand and come to agreement on the ramifications of our current behavior and the mess we are in so that we can focus on the changes necessary to avoid the mess."

The engineering vice president then retrieves copies of his seminar notes and shares with his colleagues the section on developing an idealized business design:

A bounded idealized design of a system begins with the assumption that the system involved was destroyed last night. It no longer exists, but its environment is assumed to remain as it was, untouched. Participants design the system they would ideally have right now if they could have whatever organization they wanted. This design should be subject to only three requirements.

First, the design must be *technologically feasible*. The intent of this requirement is to prevent the design from being a work of science fiction. It is important to note that this requirement does not preclude technological innovation—for example, invention of the fax machine or the videophone. There is no requirement that the design or any of its parts be economically feasible.

Second, the design must be *operationally viable*, capable of working and surviving in the current environment *if* it were brought into existence. However, it need not be capable of being implemented. This requirement removes the need to consider practicality, but it does mean that the system designed obeys relevant laws and regulations currently enforced.

Third, because any design is unintentionally but inevitably constrained by the designers' lack of at least some relevant information, knowledge, understanding, and wisdom, the system designed should be capable of "learning" from its own "experience" and adapting to internal and external changes. It should also be subject to change by internal and external agents. In other words, it should be ready, willing, and able continually to improve itself and be improved by others.

An idealized design is neither ideal nor utopian, because it is capable of improvement. It is the best (virtually unconstrained) design its designers can prepare now, but the design, unlike that of a utopia, is based on the assumption that nothing real can remain even approximately ideal for long. Therefore, the term "idealized" means the design is the best *ideal-seeking system* its designers can produce now.

In an unbounded idealized design of a system, the designers are permitted to change any of the containing systems, but only in ways that affect the performance of the system involved.[2]

Having listened intently and having observed the positive body language of his team members in response to Ackoff's ideas, the CEO speaks up: "The VP of engineering has made clear that we have become accustomed to incrementalism, to 'tinkering' with our business—and usually from our individual functional perspectives. Instead we should consider the prospects of large-scale reform and determine if we are missing great opportunities. We always try to improve the current systems by continued analysis of what we know, normally ignoring the fact that there is much we do not know. We need to develop the attitude and skills to consider the whole system and how the parts interact. If I can borrow from what we have learned about systems thinking—we need to design a business system that is greater than the sum of its parts. We must think big, and this requires discontinuous and creative thinking. We need to remember that the major advances in our company's history have usually resulted not from tinkering at the margins of existing operations, but from bold new ideas."

The CEO and the group discuss the merits of the idealized design approach and decide to give it a try, to conduct an unbounded idealized design session. They take the position that to get to the idealized design approach they need to start with the assumption of a nearly clean sheet; that is, the business as they know it no longer exists, but its containing environment is assumed to remain as it was.

With this agreement, the CEO addresses the group: "A conglomerate headed up by a corporate raider has just completed a hostile takeover of the ABC Company. The CEO has just returned from a meeting with the new owner, who has directed him to have the existing management team come up with a plan that creates a dramatically new ABC—not a plan that is focused merely on improving the existing company. If he is not satisfied with the creativity and aggressiveness of the plan, the current management team will be fired and a new team brought in. The new owner has assured the CEO he will have access to sufficient resources to implement whatever plan the team develops, so long as the expected return on the investment is 50 percent greater than ABC's current return. He wants to see a documented plan, with the supporting information and knowledge, in one week."

With the takeover story, the CEO has set the stage for the transition from the earlier arguments to the idealized design activity—specifically, by creating a "discontinuity" in the thinking processes of the participants.

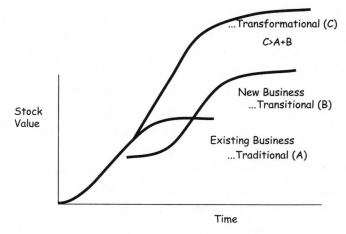

Figure 1.8 Senior advisor's idealized design representation.

The senior advisor who earlier introduced the notion of the zone of discomfort offers a description of a "destination," in which the "new" businesses provide growth not only by taking advantage of the existing customer base, but also by meeting the needs of new ABC customers, possibly enabling the growth of the traditional business and, if done properly, resulting in a transformation business greater than the sum of A + B. To illustrate her point, the senior advisor adds another curve to the earlier chart and adds Drucker's concepts from the article she mentioned earlier.

The VP of engineering comments that the senior advisor's idea, based on his seminar experience, could serve as an initial description of a possible idealized design from which the team's goals, objective, and ideals could be developed. It could also serve as a starting point from which the team could compare where the enterprise is now, so that gaps could be identified and closed, or narrowed, by the new plan.

Within hours, the team envisions a series of new businesses that make full use of the existing ABC customer base and also provide new services to people who are not ABC customers. The new businesses they develop are designed to create a customer experience so well received that the new enterprise eventually gains these customers' confidence. By gaining their confidence, the team will improve its chances of encouraging customers to try other current and future ABC products and services. The team embarks on an intensive series of discussions, attempting to establish a vision of what its members want their company to be and the gaps they must close in order to get there.

Once they have completed the gap analysis, they then create viable alternative strategies in order to realize the idealized vision through successive approximations. With these alternatives clearly on the table, they perform a side-by-side comparison of risk and return for each alternative. The approach is designed not to pick the best alternative, but to develop insight into the value embedded in each. As they begin to understand the alternatives, they gain additional insight into the situation as a whole. Before the final review of each of the alternatives, the group goes through an exercise to identify any possible "disruptive" ideas—that is, ideas that may address the consumer problems in an economically less expensive way.

With the situation more thoroughly understood, all the shared insights come together in the form of a new, hybrid alternative, which systematically combines the best elements of each of the initial alternatives, the underlying rationale for the new alternative, and the commitment to allocate resources to implement the hybrid strategy. By articulating the rationale for its decision, the group establishes a unifying vision that integrates the original conflicting points of view.

The CEO closes the final meeting with the following observation: "In our previous approach to planning, final decisions and implementation were limited by future estimates of future revenues and costs based on past experience— most of which many of us believed to be good guesses, at best. In this idealized design approach, we have enhanced our chances of success by engaging all the parts of the system and have ensured that, in addition to knowing what to do, we also understand why we are doing it. The revenue and profit targets we have set for ourselves are realistic; the assumptions upon which they are based are understood by all and will be tracked to make sure we are not surprised by unforeseen changes.

"After reading more of Ackoff's publications, we have come to epitomize what he describes as reaching a consensus, that is, 'complete agreement, not in principle, but in practice.' Based on what we as an interdependent enterprise value, this is clearly the best strategy for us to implement. Although it may not have optimized the situation for any one of the areas we each represent, we were able—once we were forced to think in an idealized way—to identify a solution that was best for the enterprise. We now need to implement the plan with the same energy and spirit with which we developed it. To do so will ensure that our company and our stockholders will benefit, which ultimately is in the best interest of each and every one of us."

The Architecture of the Book

The rest of this book discusses what is required of any enterprise, no matter its size or whether it is public or private, to prepare itself to address the kind of dire situation (mess) in which the ABC Company found itself. It is organized as follows.

Part I describes how GM determined its destination and provides four initial applications designed to transform the basic business as it moves toward its destination. The four examples demonstrate the need to fully understand the distinctions between three prototypical business designs, "make-and-sell," "sense-and-respond," and "anticipate-and-lead," and when to apply the advantages found within each of the different designs.

Part II presents five examples of GM's attempt to improve its ability to listen, learn, and lead in applying the attributes of "make-and-sell" and "sense-and-respond" business designs to its basic business—making vehicles. Part II also gives examples of the potential value of "anticipate-and-lead" in that business. These examples cover a full range of current problems and are presented within the context of a problem-solving framework.

Part III describes an approach to *thinking about the enterprise as a system of interacting parts*. It is a way of thinking some enterprises, including GM, are learning to apply to gain the benefits of the "anticipate-and-lead" business design. Given that the encompassing systems of most enterprises are becoming more complex and their rate of change is accelerating, systems thinking provides the equivalent of an advance base camp for individuals and organizations to prepare themselves for the next leg in their attempt to reach their destination. The systems thinking atmosphere provides the leadership of the enterprise perspective and an appreciation for understanding and managing the interactions of the parts of their enterprises rather than managing each part separately. It is the place where leadership also addresses the importance of knowing how the enterprise interacts with the broader system within which it operates. Thinking tools that address complex issues and problems are presented as interdependent elements that must be learned and systemically applied as travel guides for any journey that starts with your destination.

The book's ultimate objective is to provide the reader with the ability to not only address problems but to do so in a manner that turns what appeared to be a difficult situation into a positive opportunity. As the previous two decades have shown, even if a company is not in mortal danger, the future is inherently uncertain. Any enterprise must be prepared to move quickly and effectively, whatever its current situation.

APPLYING THE RIGHT
BUSINESS DESIGN

> There is a big difference between doing things right (efficiency) and doing the
> right things (effectiveness).

> —Peter Drucker

In a world of more fragmented markets, extensive social concerns, and digitally
accelerated opportunities, all elements of an enterprise must have direct access
to what the enterprise knows about its markets, its competition, and itself. Not
doing so lessens the possibility of the whole's being greater than the sum of its
parts. After all, an enterprise no longer has the time or the resources to operate
in a linear manner, one in which one group collects the information and another
group translates and presents the information to another group that then decides how to develop a product. This group eventually turns its outcome over to
another group to make the product, after which this group, in turn, releases the
product to yet another organization that then promotes and distributes the
product (or service).

Adrian Slywotzky, author of *Value Migration* and coauthor of *Profit Zone*, has
revealed that the primary driver of value growth in the 1980s and 1990s was
business design innovation: inventing and discovering new customer priorities,
new value propositions, new sources of profit, and new strategic control.[1] Slywotzky has provided a clear and succinct definition of business design:

> A business design is the totality of how a company selects its customers, defines
> and differentiates its offerings (or responses), defines the tasks it will perform
> itself and those it will outsource, configures its resources, goes to market, cre-
> ates utility for customers and captures profits. It is the entire system for deliver-
> ing utility to customers and earning a profit from that activity. Companies may
> offer products, they may offer technology, but that offering is embedded in a

comprehensive system of activities and relationships that represents the company's business design.[2]

The Range of Business Designs

Beginning with the start of the twenty-first century, digital opportunities have multiplied our options and created the possibility of a broader range of business designs within which innovation can take place.[3] This book will illustrate the current range of business design alternatives by positioning three prototypical designs to anchor the endpoints of the current range of thinking; its midpoint will offer an emerging point of view to distinguish the traditional approach from the more visionary possibilities. The characteristics of the three business designs are captured by three terms:

- Make-and-sell
- Sense-and-respond
- Anticipate-and-lead

The following descriptions of these business designs are illustrative and not meant to be fixed or comprehensive. For example, Stephan Haeckel, in *The Adaptive Enterprise*, provides a more complete description of, and broader insight into, the applications of a sense-and-respond business design than that which is offered in this book.[4]

Make-and-Sell

A *make-and-sell* design does just that: the firm predicts, according to its past experience and current market research, what the market will demand. Make-and-sell consists of providing goods and services that satisfy a need or desire consumers are currently aware of and that they have, or can acquire, the means to purchase, rent, or lease. The key to success is the ability to correctly predict demand over the period of time within which the enterprise expects to gain its expected return on the capital investment. The make-and-sell enterprise views itself as an efficient mechanism for making offers, relying primarily on interchangeable parts and economies of scale. It depends on learning curves and interchangeable people—people who execute defined procedures in accordance with a prescribed business plan. Performance measurements are gathered through benchmarking and "best practices" evaluation.

Industrious and dedicated, driven by their "psychological gyroscope," "inner-directed" producers manage a daily routine that focuses on doing what they have always done—only better.[5] Believing strongly that change will be evolutionary, they assure themselves of success by continual improvement in how they have conducted their business over the years. They challenge all claims of forthcoming radical change and possess interpersonal skills to persuade others they are on the right path. Others see them as conservative traditionalists.

Sense-and-Respond

A *sense-and-respond* design starts with the enterprise believing that the future is neither predictable nor controllable, and, therefore, it organizes itself to respond to what is actually happening, as opposed to what was forecasted to happen. Sense-and-respond seeks to provide products or services that satisfy needs or desires that customers are aware of and that are not being satisfied by the current market. This process starts by reaching out to selected markets and stating, in effect, "Help me to identify your needs, and let's work together to satisfy them." A sense-and-respond organization sees itself as an adaptive system for responding to an ever changing, ever widening range of requests. It is built around dynamically linked subprocesses and relies primarily on economies of scope, rather than economies of scale, to operate profitably. The people in a sense-and-respond environment are empowered and accountable, and spend their time producing customized outcomes in accordance with an adaptive business design. In a recent exchange of correspondence, Stephan Haeckel provided a performance metric: "Performance is measured by growth in net value created, which is the dollar value of the benefits realized by the customer minus the cost to the producer of providing the features that evoke those benefits."[6]

With their "psychological radar" always on, "other-directed adapters" recognize that, as the environment becomes increasingly unpredictable, it becomes necessary to give up control of procedures and processes, and instead to architect and control the organizational context within which empowered people improvise and adapt to changing circumstances.[7] Context consists of a declaration of purpose, bounds, and a high-level role-and-accountability design. These people make a very perceptive team that prides itself on knowing earlier and responding faster to changing customer needs. Alert and vigilant, they are at all times seeking to know the current needs of individual customers, and they invest in understanding the underlying values that drive customers. Like the bow-and-arrow game hunter, they aim just ahead of market, basing their aim on a pattern of emerging knowledge about customers, society, and business practice. Others see them as externally driven internal-change agents.

Anticipate-and-Lead

An *anticipate-and-lead* design assumes the future is largely determined by what the enterprise purposefully creates to change things—not how it responds to signals from the marketplace. The mindset is different from make-and-sell in that the anticipate-and-lead enterprise accepts that it cannot predict what the market is likely to want, whereas the make-and-sell mindset is to produce the product or service on the assumption that the predicted conditions will lead to the sale of the amount of product or service actually produced or provided. The anticipate-and-lead enterprise focuses on the future it wants to create. Once this future is determined, the enterprise attempts to lead the consumer to new ideas based on both articulated and unarticulated consumer needs. The deep understandings of these needs are sometimes gleaned from direct observation of the consumer's behavior, including what he or she would prefer that is not now available, as he or she chooses from among the existing list of current and future products and services. The ability to anticipate and lead is facilitated by emerging digital technologies. Observing real-time market and actual consumer behavior and tying these findings directly to the enterprise decision process enables timely and effective decision making. Although the techniques used may be similar to those used in the other business designs, the purpose to which they are used is profoundly different: to cause a future condition more favorable to the enterprise and the customers it chooses to serve. Performance is measured by the enterprise share of truly new and profitable products. Evaluation of best practices is replaced by the determination to develop the next practice.

Dominant Leadership Personality: Visionary Designers

Their broad interests in both topics and people help visionary designers draw seemingly unrelated things together, yielding unforeseen synergies. The manner with which they sense possibilities and how to address them makes them *enthusiastic* and *confident* about their solutions. They seize upon the most viable ideas and attempt to make them real. They possess a high degree of both introspective and interpersonal abilities and are comfortable both within the solitude of their own ideas and in the social world. They rely on their own judgment in the face of doubt from others, and it is the power of their convictions that gets them through even the rockiest of times. Others see them as adventurous inventors.

Tables I.1–I.3 illustrate further distinctions between make-and-sell, sense-and-respond, and anticipate-and-lead by detailing each in the context of the (1) enterprise's fundamental business design, (2) knowledge use practices and processes, and (3) information technology.[8]

Depending on the reader's responsibilities, experience, skills, and mental model, it is highly probable that one of these business designs will appear superior to the others. For example, someone with an interest in improving the efficiency of the manufacturing process would see efficiency based on the economies of scale associated with the make-and-sell business design as, on balance, more valuable than the other designs. On the other hand, someone whose focus is on quickly responding to changing customer requirements may see more value in the sense-and-respond design, because it demands that the enterprise respond to what customers want and relies on empowered workers—both good practices in an increasingly service-oriented economy. And, finally, someone who believes that the enterprise can come up with an entirely new approach to developing products that customers will want—even if customers cannot articulate their preferences—will see more value in anticipate-and-lead. Nevertheless, it would be a serious mistake to assume that one business design is inherently better than another. Depending on the business conditions that exist and the ability to think creatively, a hybrid model, taking advantage of the most appropriate traits of each design, is likely to be most beneficial.

The Importance of "And"

In the world of increased complexity and accelerated change, there is great peril in choosing one strategy *or* the other. Serious consideration needs to be given to whether there may be value in using traits of one strategy *and* traits of another. A classic example of this distinction is found in Nicholas Negroponte's pioneering book, *Being Digital*. At the time of its publication in 1995 Negroponte made a strong case for how the world would move from an industrial world of products made up of "atoms" to a knowledge-based world of products made up

Table I.1. Distinctions in Fundamental Business Design

Trait	Make-and-Sell	Sense-and-Respond	Anticipate-and-Lead
Attitude toward knowing the future	Over the period of time in which we expect to gain a profitable return on our investment, we can accurately predict what kinds and how many products and services we need to produce.	We cannot predict the future, so we must design our business to quickly adapt to changing conditions, which we will identify earlier than our competitors by continually assessing market conditions.	We cannot predict the future, but we can largely determine what it will be by what we do. We must anticipate what will be required that is currently not provided and do so in a way that is in the interest of the firm, its customers, and the containing system in which we operate.
Mental model and strategy	Business as an *efficient* mechanism for making and selling others to well-defined market segments with predictable needs	Business as an *adaptive system* for responding to consumer requests in less predictable environments	Creative approaches that lead to the development of entirely new products and services customers desire and believe to be a fair value
Basic metaphor	A *fixed-rail system* efficiently *scheduling* trains to stop at predetermined places along preplanned routes, based on predictions about where most people will want to go and where goods need to be shipped	A *taxi company* dynamically *dispatching* vehicles to pick up individual customers and take them where they want to go this time, allowing drivers the flexibility to position themselves where people may want them	A *molecular structure* in which every activity, operating as an element of a system, *interacts* with other relevant elements and the entire structure is sensitive to the effects of the environment in which it is encompassed
Profit focus	*Profit margins on products gained through economies of scale.* Make and sell as much of the same thing as possible to reduce the fixed cost per unit of production.	*Returns on investments and economies of scope.* Reduce cost of customized responses by reusing modular capabilities over a wide range of responses and customers.	*Gain high margins and profits by providing the newest, most innovative, and most wanted products.* License technology and intellectual property to other enterprises trying to catch up.
Market leader criterion	*Share of targeted market.* For example, share of mid-sized vehicles sold, personal computers sold, full-life policy premiums, and so on.	*Growth in net value created, coproduced with customers.* Share of value going to customer, and share to the firm is determined instance by instance when negotiating the price.	*Share of truly new and profitable products.* Acknowledged as the most innovative and imaginative enterprise.

Table I.2. Distinctions in Knowledge Use and Processes

Trait	Make-and-Sell	Sense-and-Respond	Anticipate-and-Lead
Process	*Mass production.* Emphasis on repeatable procedures, replaceable parts, and standard job definitions to efficiently mass produce products *defined by the company.*	*Selective customization.* Modular products and services, produced by modular capabilities, inside and outside the company, which are linked to create customized responses to requests *defined by customers.*	*Causing the future we want to create.* Determination of how to cause that future to occur; design and implement a plan of action to bring about the necessary changes as quickly and as innovatively as possible.
Know-how	*Embedded in products.* The expertise of designers, engineers, or actuaries is captured as a new service or product that is incorporated in an offer.	*Embedded in people and processes.* Know-why expertise is codified in systems designs; know-how expertise is codified in process designs and procedures, andexpertise is applied by accountable individuals. It is applied on demand to respond to implicit or explicit customer requests.	*Embedded in the intelligence of the interdependent network.* When know-how or know-why knowledge changes in either an element of the network or the environment in which the network operates, the enterprise identifies any opportunities caused by the change and takes actions to achieve the benefits.
Product and service design	*Design for consumers.* Intuition and market knowledge lead to products and services that satisfy enough targeted customers to meet investment objectives. Customer involvement is passive.	*Adaptive design.* Constant monitoring and surveillance of consumer attitudes and behavior leads to products and services designed for efficient adaptation to frequent changes in customer requirements. Customers can be active participants in the design of the changes.	*Design to cause change.* Design is idealized. It is based on intuition and market knowledge. Products and services are designed to cause selected customers to change from the accepted way of doing things to a better way of doing things. Interested customers can be actively engaged in the idealized design process.

Table I.3. Distinctions in Information Technology

Trait	Make-and-Sell	Sense-and-Respond	Anticipate-and-Lead
Information architecture	*Functionally managed*, for use by people in the function. Each function creates its own view of "what's going on out there" and has its own processes for "how we do things around here." Focus is on providing the information needed to execute the function's business plan.	*Enterprise management* of information to represent the current status of the environment and of organizational context. Supports decentralized decision making using role-specific manage-by-wire support based on common data storage and use.	*Web-based open system.* Enterprise and customer share access to what is needed for each to gain maximum benefit from the other. Transparency will require established privacy and security procedures acceptable to all parties.
Knowledge management	The most efficient knowledge management is to store precise measurements of what the enterprise knows and what it will need to know in an efficient and accessible warehouse.	Primary knowledge is know-why (systems knowledge) as opposed to know-how (process knowledge). It must be available to all those who need it.	The goal is not management: it is quick acquisition. The enterprise needs knowledge about the future it wants to create. Storing what worked in the past is less useful. Design a system that will adapt as strategy develops, based on prior success in changing the way things happen.

of "bits" of information.[9] Since that time, the remarkable growth and eventual decline of purely bits-based business has given way to the belief that opportunity is not a future world of solely atoms *or* bits, but a future world of atoms *and* bits.

The twenty-first-century challenge for the leadership of any enterprise is to create a business and organizational design that takes full advantage of the following:

- Digital infrastructure and technologies that were developed with astonishingly high levels of investment before the "high-tech" bubble came back to reality, because it is safe to assume that they will serve as the basis for new, even more revolutionary developments
- The growing portion of the population that has learned to use, and now expects to find, these new technologies in their everyday activities

Yesterday's Successful Functional Structure May Fail You Tomorrow

Unfortunately, many enterprises, like the ABC Company in chapter 1, are organized and managed in ways that create barriers to forming a rich and vivid picture of what customers would be willing to purchase or experience. This is particularly true of products and services not currently in the market but that, if made available to customers at a price they considered a fair value, would be desired. Knowledge and market information captured by one organizational function tends to be discussed, nurtured, and reinforced within that function, but it seldom enriches the market understanding of others important to its final implementation. These functional "silos" often exacerbate differences between internal organizations, which often leads to arguments about this approach or that approach instead of finding what combination of approaches would be seen positively by the ultimate consumer.

This problem is compounded by the fact that consumers are being asked to choose from among a vast array of existing products and services, all of which are competing for the consumer's attention and disposable income. Normally, this would be considered all good news. Not all, however, is good news:

- Consumers are finding it more difficult to find the time and energy to sort out which of the hundreds or thousands of products and services available they should consider and which they should avoid.

- Enterprises are finding that direct and indirect competitors are finding alternative ways (sometimes using surprising and "disruptive"[10] technologies) to meet the needs of traditional customers, ways that have increased pressure on profits right at the time when enterprise needs additional resources to develop new and innovative responses to the competitive threats.

Under these changing conditions, management must lead the enterprise to fulfill its purpose of "creating a customer" by adopting a strategy that, when appropriate, has the appropriate mix of make-and-sell, some of sense-and-respond, and some of anticipate-and-lead. To accomplish this, leadership must adapt its business design to more effectively create a dialogue with its chosen customers so it can successfully compete in the business and social environment.

Adapting to and Changing the Environment

In nature, species that survive do so because they are formed to meet the challenges of their environments. Humpback whales survive because their mouths have baleen, fibrous strainers that catch the tiny krill and plankton that fill vast parts of the sea. Hawks survive because their combination of vision, soaring wings, and talons helps them prey upon the small birds and mammals that live in open fields and meadows. These animals have evolved in a way that allows them to respond to the challenges they face every day. If their environments change faster than they can biologically evolve, however, they are out of luck. Few animal species have the capacity to adapt to accelerating rates of change.

Human beings and their organizations are quite different. Although they, too, must adapt themselves to the environment, they also have the capacity to *change* the environment. Jacob Bronowski describes this difference between human beings and other animals quite simply: "Man is a singular creature. He has a set of gifts which make him unique among the animals: so that, unlike them, he is not a figure in the landscape—he is a shaper of the landscape. In body and in mind he is the explorer of nature, the ubiquitous animal, who did not find but has made his home in every continent."[11]

In the foreword to Haeckel's *The Adaptive Enterprise*, Adrian Slywotzky addresses the issue of adaptation in business designs: "Adopting a sense-and-respond orientation produces multiple benefits for an organization. I'd like to point out three benefits over and above those articulated by Haeckel: new business building, solving the medium-term growth crisis, and preempting future competitive opportunities."[12] After elaborating on the first two benefits, Slywotzky addresses the third benefit as follows: "The third benefit grows out of the second. Playing sense-and-respond reinforces itself. Once a company gets into a dynamic mindset, it learns, it gets better. Its know-how extends beyond archery, aiming at a static target, to include skeet shooting, taking on a moving target. As the company develops its sense-and-respond skill set, it elevates sense-and-respond from listen and comply to anticipate and preempt."

Slywotzky further points out the timeliness sense-and-respond fosters: "Sense-and-respond helps us be on time—on market time. Very good sense-and-respond helps us be early. But a superior ability to sense and interpret signals about changing customer needs before they mature into formal requests helps us get there sooner still, soon enough to preempt the next major opportunity and to create an unassailable leadership position."[13]

The four chapters that follow show how GM, primarily a make-and-sell enterprise, attempted to operate with some of the traits found in sense-and-respond and some found in anticipate-and-lead business designs. The examples reveal how GM developed decision processes to improve the chances of working on the right problem and addressed rapidly changing consumer and market conditions by causing changes in those conditions that were more favorable to the enterprise.

Part I explains how one large, ponderous organization was able to introduce new product and service concepts by challenging the limitations of working solely with the traits found in the make-and-sell business design. Part II will look in more detail at how the organization actually took the daunting initial steps of transforming the organization in preparation for the more profound changes described in the following four chapters.

2 Creating an Extended Customer Relationship Business

Metamarkets: Markets in our minds. Metamarkets are clusters of related activities that consumers engage in to satisfy a distinct set of needs. Boundaries of Metamarkets are derived from activities that are closely related in the minds of consumers. They are not created or marketed by firms in related industries. Metamarkets can be organized around major assets, major interests, major life events, or major business processes.

—Mohan Sawhney

Markets are . . . created . . . by businessmen. The want they satisfy may have been felt by the customer before he was offered the means of satisfying it. . . . But it was a theoretical want before; only when the action of businessmen makes it effective demand is there a customer, a market.

—Peter Drucker

If you are focused on finding differences, the two statements that open this chapter may appear to be in conflict. Sawhney makes the point that a certain type of market is not created by firms; Drucker, that only firms can create markets. If you are focused on understanding the effect of complex and rapidly changing conditions on strategy development, these two statements can be seen as both being right. That is, it is not about one *or* the other; it is about one *and* the other. To fully appreciate the world of *and* versus the world of *or* requires an understanding of changing business conditions. This chapter and the three that follow begin with an explicit statement of the old and the new competitive worlds of doing business.

The Old Competitive World

The old competitive world was epitomized by fixed boundaries: country markets; industrial classification of businesses; and the choice to be (1) low-cost producer, *or* (2) specialized in specific products and services, *or* (3) focused on meeting specific customer needs for specific purchase occasions, *or* (4) focused on customers who can be reached through specialized distribution channels. The enterprise distinguished itself from its competitors by how well it managed (1), (2), (3), or (4).[1]

The basic premises under which this condition operated required a world of predictable consumer needs and consistent industry structures in which change, too, was slow and predictable. Additionally, the ability to identify and maintain a primarily vertical value chain of activities and a firm's profits was limited to its share of the total profits available from the industry in which it operated. It was in this old competitive world that the make-and-sell business design was developed and has flourished for a long time.

Under this condition, Sawhney's concept of a consumer metamarket is less likely to be served by a single firm and, therefore, is more likely to require an intermediary to bring customers their desired bundle of services.

The New Competitive World

The new competitive world is epitomized by few boundaries: global markets; difficulty in classifying businesses; and (1) attempting to be most efficient and effective producer, *and* (2) providing the range of products and services required by customers, *and* (3) being focused on meeting customer needs for specific purchase occasions more efficiently and effectively than any competitors, *and* (4) being focused on customers and on reaching them in ways they want to be reached. The enterprise distinguishes itself from its competitors by how well it manages the interaction of (1), (2), (3), and (4).

The increased complexity compounded by the rapidly expanding rate of change that characterizes the new competitive world requires management to find an appropriate balance between *make-and sell*, *sense-and-respond*, and *anticipate and lead*.

As valuable as the contribution of concepts like value chain analysis were to the old competitive world, where the chain was primarily defined by the industry in which one operated, the new competitive world reduces, but does not eliminate, its value. The new competitive world allows the enterprise to seek profits where they can be found—by putting together the bundle of services sought by the consumer, including the creation of products and services that could alter the customer's want for the original bundle. The new competitive world requires the enterprise to understand that it is a system within a broader system and it is in the larger system that potential profit opportunities exist.

The new competitive world also offers the enterprise the choice between using an external intermediary to provide a broader range of services to meta-markets, or directly using its own trust-based intermediary.

In his 2000 book *How Digital Is Your Business?* Adrian Slywotzky (with coauthor David Morrison) updates his previous definition of business design with a cogent twenty-first-century definition of business design in a digital world, with its potential to facilitate strategies capable of preempting the competition: "*Digital Business Design* is the art and science of using digital technologies to expand a company's strategic options. DBD is not about technology for its own sake; it's about serving customers, creating unique value propositions, leveraging talent, radically improving productivity, and increasing profits. It's about using digital options to craft a business model that is not only superior, but *unique.*"[2]

As GM approached the end of the last millennium, it became quite clear that the rapid rate of change in the world was making it much more difficult to predict customer requirements. In addition, improved methods of knowledge creation through electronic methods of data collection and analytic tools would cause significant differences between the way business was currently conducted and the way it would be conducted in the future.

Late in the 1990s, there was much gnashing of teeth in traditional "brick and mortar" companies over their possibly being "dis-intermediated" by the dot-com companies. There were daily stories about how dot-com companies would use the Internet to persuade customers to order products through these intermediaries and bypass the traditional distribution system. This shift would force manufacturers to meet dot-com terms, or, since these intermediaries "owned" these customers, the dot-coms would move "their" customers to someone else who would.

A more balanced view is presented in table 2.1, adapted from a prophetic 1999 report, *The Incumbent Response*, by the Corporate Strategy Board.[3]

Table 2.1.   Competitive Distinctions Between Dot-coms and Incumbent
Business Firms, 1999

Competitive Drivers	Dot-Com Entrants	Incumbent Firms	Advantage
Value proposition	Currently support Internet channel only Highly responsive, able to enhance value proposition as needed	Customers can utilize well-integrated, multichannel access to optimize transaction and service needs	Incumbent
Cost structure	High market valuations provide access to cheaper capital Lower cost structure than most traditional competitors High customer acquisition and marketing costs	Can transform existing sales and fulfillment assets to meet click and mortar demand Can share marketing, distribution, and overhead cost among channels	Incumbent
Customer base	No established customer base Currently attract profitable customers—affluent, loyal, valuing convenience, etc. Over time, may attract price-sensitive, bargain hunters	Established customer base Own extensive knowledge of customer preferences Uniquely positioned to observe and learn from customer self-selection among channel alternatives	Incumbent
Brand	Incur high cost of establishing new brands Not encumbered by existing brand image Benefit from free marketing, media coverage, IPO hype	Established brand names Existing brand image may not be relevant to new business	Incumbent
Human resources	Equity options and growth potential attract talent Younger staff generally more comfortable with new technology and rapid change	Even generous compensation packages unlikely to match potential upside of dot-coms Mature workforce is better trained and highly skilled	Dot-com
Organizational alignment	Pure play focus increases likelihood that incentives are well aligned Performance metrics (e.g., site traffice, page views) closely aligned to drivers of success	New business objectives and existing performance metrics and incentives are likely to be misaligned Employees resist change	Dot-com

Toward an Anticipate-and-Lead Business Design

As it has turned out, even the two areas in which the dot-coms were believed to
have an advantage are less clearly their advantages today.

Understanding the strengths and weaknesses of its position as summarized
in *The Incumbent Response*, GM determined that, instead of building barriers in
an attempt to "keep the dot-coms out," which is to say, instead of creating a business design *around* the existing technology, it would engage the dot-coms to
determine whether the technology could be used *within* GM's current business

design. By experimenting with different concepts, GM gleaned a deeper understanding of the change occurring in business and market conditions. This
deeper understanding gave insight into how customers would react to the functionality provided by these new technologies. Given what it learned, GM is now
positioned to use its existing business competencies and resources to lead by introducing a business design that improves the customer-relationship experience
with GM products and services. Interestingly, when the Corporate Executive
Board's assessment was originally published, some observers claimed it was too
heavily biased in favor of the incumbent firms. Time, however, has reaffirmed
the value of the incumbents' existing assets.

For example, GM has

- A base of over 30 million customers with which to communicate on a personal and frequent basis
- Access to a distribution channel that has allowed fulfillment of customer requests for products and services, with the existing franchise distribution system also serving as a barrier to entry, since state franchise laws protect it
- The ability to integrate some of the electronic customer requirements directly into the operation of the vehicle, which has been demonstrated with
  the OnStar mobile communication system
- Very well known brands for its vehicles, parts, and financial services

Experimentation and improved understanding of the true value of GM assets
and capabilities in taking advantage of these developing technologies has led
to the belief that these new technologies enable GM's decision makers, in Slywotzky's terms, "to craft a business model that is not only superior, but *unique.*"

Anticipating Customers' Need for an
Improved Experience

In 1995, GM was a part of a consortium that hired Wirthlin Worldwide to study
the key factors that consumers reported drove their buying decisions. The study
measured both the importance consumers placed on these factors and their current level of satisfaction with how these factors were being addressed in the marketplace.

The results revealed twenty-six key factors that affected consumer decision
making. Figure 2.1 displays how consumers rated these drivers on two dimensions: *importance* on the horizontal dimension, and their current *satisfaction* on

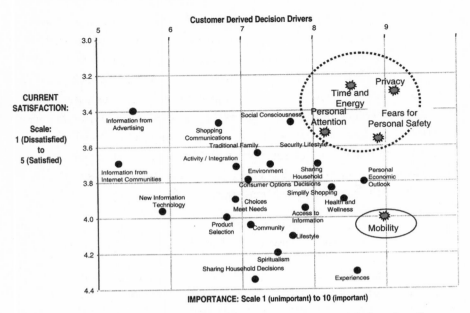

Figure 2.1 Customer decision-making factors, 1995. Published by the Quest Group. Study conducted by Wirthlin Worldwide.

the vertical access. Because GM was interested in identifying important areas in which customers were dissatisfied, the vertical scale puts dissatisfaction at the top of the vertical axis. For example, consumers' attitude toward *privacy*—the ability to keep information about their lives and affairs private—is positioned as both the most important driver and the one about which customers were least satisfied.

During the GM review of this information, it became clear that the position of five of the factors, when considered in relation to each other and to all the other factors, revealed a potential unarticulated consumer need.

The first of the five selected factors was *mobility* (being able to go where you want to go, when you want to go). This factor is at the heart of GM's traditional business. Located in the lower right-hand corner, it was rated very high in importance by consumers, who also indicated their satisfaction with the manner in which their requirements were being met in the marketplace. GM was not surprised by this positioning, because in most of North America the ability to get where you want to go when you want to go is quite good.

Under the old competitive world, GM's view would have been, "We have done a very good job in meeting customer requirements in our industry, so let's stay focused on what we are currently doing—because it works. If it's not broken, don't fix it!"

However, the following four factors (located in the upper right-hand corner of the figure)—also among the most important but, compared to other consumer needs, not well served—caused further investigation:

- *Personal attention* (being able to get friendly and helpful attention from companies and stores)
- *Time and energy* (being able to find time and energy needed to meet all of your demands in life)
- *Privacy* (being able to keep information about your life and affairs private)
- *Personal safety* (being able to walk alone at night in your neighborhood without feeling afraid)

These observations reinforced earlier thinking that GM would benefit greatly if, in addition to satisfying the mobility decision driver, it could also create a relationship, through well-managed everyday experiences with customers, that would provide *personal attention* and save *time and energy* while guarding *privacy* and *personal safety*. It was concluded that, if this relationship were created and customers experienced the benefit, GM could increase not only its market share but also its share of the disposable income of these customers.

The Future Destination

GM's vision statement reads, "To be the world leader in transportation products and related services." The "and related services" part of the statement has been, from its inception, tempered by the need to stay focused on the basic business. It was, therefore, critical to tie any new business strategies specifically to improving the experience of the automotive consumer. This behavior on the part of senior management sent a strong message to operating management that GM's leadership was not taking its eye off the basic business—one of the concerns that led to the zone of discomfort between operating management and the new business management in the hypothetical account of chapter 1. In describing the strategy as illustrated in figure 2.2, Rick Wagoner, GM's CEO and president, made sure that everyone understood that any new business would be based on the relationship with existing and potential automotive consumers. During a global leadership meeting, he made it very clear that, if GM were to be successful in convincing customers that it could provide the "and related ser-

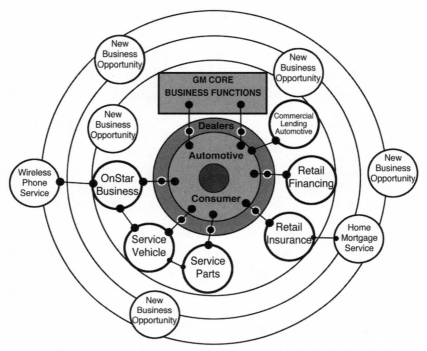

Figure 2.2 Extended customer-relationships business design.

vices" portion of its mission, it would have to do so with customers who were very satisfied with GM's handling of "transportation products." A discussion of how GM worked to ensure customers were sufficiently satisfied with GM's transportation products is presented in part II.

With this commitment to basing any new business on the existing relationship with the automotive consumer, the following statements served as the operating principles by which GM would develop and grow new business in its attempt to lead customers to GM's "transportation products and related services."

- New business opportunities closest to the basic business would be included in the "core business" if they offered higher margins or the ability to directly improve the automotive consumer's experience with GM. For example, OnStar (discussed in chapter 3) improves the customer experience by providing safety and security features, *and* personalized service for hotel and restaurant reservations. It has also extended the relationship by providing hands-free mobile phone services, and, since its electronic architecture is integrated into the vehicle's electronic systems, other services, such as onboard diagnostics, are now possible.

- Business opportunities furthest from the basic business would bear a heavier burden of proof that GM should own, versus partner with, existing or potential new services. OnStar would be owned, but wireless service would be provided through a partnership relationship. Home mortgages, which is an extension of General Motors Acceptance Corporation's (GMAC) competencies in making loans to automotive dealers, fits nicely into GMAC's competency and allows GM to develop superior service to the customer by managing both automotive and household financing.
- Part of the consideration for engagement would be a determination whether or not the new business would help reduce the likelihood that market leaders from other sectors would attempt to enter GM's business. For example, the fact that OnStar is a factory-installed rather than a dealer-installed feature, coupled with its direct integration into important vehicle services (e.g., airbag deployment, emission sensors, fuel and oil gauges, and the like), allows GM to provide a safe and secure software operating system. This competency positions GM to require those in telecommunication and "infotainment" industries with designs on accessing GM's core customers to work through the demonstrated benefits of GM's operating system. GMAC also provides increased understanding of financial service firms that target GM's core customers or business.

The last of these points was designed to minimize, to the extent possible, any unforeseen threats to the automotive business from all forms of other businesses, threats including Clay Christiansen's concept of a competitor's introducing disruptive technologies that might attract the automotive consumer.

To effectively conduct such a competitive assessment, GM must remain sensitive to its ability to compete in the adjacent areas of business where it is likely to run into leading companies of these areas. GM needed to develop strategic alliances or acquisitions (or both) to minimize the ability of others to move into its business space.

The Economics of the Extended Customer-Experience Initiative

The GM extended customer-experience initiative illustrated in figure 2.2 has the potential to increase both revenues and profits, as well as reduce operating costs.

First, the cost of acquiring new customers is increasing. Media fragmentation makes it extremely expensive to reach the mass audience of potential GM buyers in vehicles, mortgages, insurance, and communications (media frag-mentation is discussed further in chapter 4, which describes GM's AutoChoice-Advisor). Businesses that can leverage their existing customer bases and lower customer-acquisition costs for new services can significantly increase prof-itability.

Second, conserving an individual's time for the important activities of life is an important consumer decision driver. Services presented as a menu from which to choose, rather than as a locked-in bundle, reward the consumer with time savings, improved service, and saved effort, while allowing the enterprise the resources and capability to increase personal attention.

A simple example illustrates the power of the extended customer-experience initiative. The example is typical of business designs when the interactions of re-lationships are tracked over time. Consider two businesses, each with its own customer base. The businesses are managed and rewarded as independent busi-ness units, and each has its own acquisition costs, retention rates, customer service costs, and contribution margin. Neither business has a large share of the market, and both have potential for growth. The levels of price and marketing spending that generate the highest profit for each business are developed inde-pendently.

Now, consider managing the two businesses as a system in which only their *combined* profitability is important. Experience with contemporary customer-relationship management suggests the possibility of several direct improve-ments in the combined business system.

- Customer acquisition costs for each business should fall. It is easier to sell an additional service if the consumer already has a trusted relationship with the firm.
- Customer retention rates should increase. Customers are less likely to churn if they buy several products from the same provider. This is especially true if the consumer receives a discount, enhanced customized services, or other incentives for buying additional products.
- Customer service costs should decrease. The incremental customer service cost of an additional service is low compared to the initial setup cost for the first service.[4]

These three improvements are well understood and have demonstrated they can improve profitability. What is not as well understood is that often most of the benefit from extending the business relationship comes from changing price, changing marketing spending, and changing other marketing decision variables to the new profit-maximizing levels implied by the combined system. In the example given, when the two businesses are managed as a combined system, the following can be said.

- In order to attract customers, the price for the first service can be set very competitively. The price on the second service can be increased slightly, but, because the acquisition costs are reduced, margins will be much higher. The customer who buys both products benefits, because the combined price is lower. In essence, the seller is sharing a portion of the reduced acquisition costs with the customer.
- Because of the lower combined costs, the retention rate of existing customers is higher, resulting in a greater number of customers who have both products.
- Overall system profitability increases significantly.
- The combined business system can be unique. Competitors find it difficult to replicate the model, because they must be in both businesses to compete and it is prohibitively expensive to build both installed bases. Generally, complementary products and services designed for the customer of the basic business—the same attributes that help avoid the zone of discomfort—also make imitation by others more difficult.

This extended customer-experience initiative builds on GM's ability to satisfy targeted customer or market segments through innovations that create or meet existing demand with unique combinations of products, features, and services, all of which still require innovative development, manufacturing, and marketing approaches to create a "superior and unique" customer experience. As an example, GM could include bundled and unbundled services to allow the customer access to different vehicles or services on demand, as well as different methods of choosing and purchasing their vehicles.

Additionally, some of the services can complement GM's vehicle business during economic conditions that discourage the purchase of new vehicles. OnStar's onboard diagnostic and emergency services may be perceived as more valuable by someone driving a car older than they normally drive, because they may be more anxious about the potential for unexpected breakdowns. In the early part of 2003, GMAC's mortgage business took advantage of current economic conditions, which led to increase in mortgage refinancing and generated significant profits. These same economic conditions had caused the vehicle business to face diminished margins because of extensive incentives to maintain high levels of industry sales and market share.

The strength of any business design like that which GM is developing—regardless of industry—is that it allows the enterprise to stay focused on the current business while allocating an appropriate amount of its scarce resources to gain incrementally higher margin revenue on services that, in turn, improve the customers' experience. It avoids the zone of discomfort sometimes experienced as an enterprise moves into new, less familiar areas of business.

The design is driven by an enterprise-wide vision of a system in which each area of the extended enterprise has the following: a defined purpose; identification of the interactions between areas; negotiated commitments between areas that interact; and identification of the ways the enterprise will sense, interpret, decide (allocate resources), and implement decisions in response to opportunities and threats. The primary sources of profits are periodic transactions and annual revenues generated from customer-experience-based products and services. Both forms of revenue are generated through long-term customer-experience-based relationships.

The next chapter discusses a business opportunity that provides an improved customer experience, which in turn generates revenue over the life cycle of the product.

3 Creating the Business You Want

If a man will begin with certainties he will end with doubts, but if he will be content to begin with doubts he shall end in certainties.

—Sir Francis Bacon

Chapter 2 described GM's strategy for extending its relationship with the automotive consumer. The announcement below is an indication of the benefits to the customers when GM initiates new applications of that strategy as well as the benefits to GM. It is a tangible example of moving from the old competitive world to the new competitive world.

January 28, 2004

GMAC Insurance And Onstar Create Innovative Insurance Products

Detroit, Michigan—GMAC Insurance and OnStar are partnering to create new and innovative insurance products for their joint customers. Under the collaboration, GMAC Insurance will utilize the capabilities of OnStar's in-vehicle safety and security system to offer OnStar subscribers unique insurance products and significant premium discounts.

   "We're extremely excited to be able to announce a great new set of additional benefits that will now be available to OnStar subscribers as a result of our partnership with GMAC Insurance," said OnStar President Chet Huber. "We're proud of the level of service OnStar delivers to its 2.5 million subscribers," said Huber, "and having those benefits recognized by the insurance industry, with tangible savings for our customers, is a great next step."

   This announcement is another step in the growing partnership between OnStar and GMAC Insurance according to Gary Kusumi, president of GMAC Insurance Personal Lines. "There are synergies among our services that naturally give rise to new products and services that empower consumers," said Kusumi. "This type of innovation arises from the power of two best-of-breed players working together with consumers in mind. There will be additional innovations from this partnership."

OnStar's unique technology and broad range of existing safety and security services are at the core of the insurance benefits from GMAC Insurance. Responding to airbag deployments, roadside assistance situations, in-vehicle emergencies, stolen vehicle location assistance, or helping subscribers with remote vehicle diagnostics, all work to fundamentally improve the driving experience. OnStar's hands-free, voice activated cell phone capabilities are recognized as providing a safer alternative to hand-held devices when calls must be made or received while driving.

The new evolving GMAC Insurance products include the following:

OnStar Subscriber Discount—GMAC Insurance will begin rolling out a special subscriber discount for OnStar customers in several states, with plans for national expansion. The discount is the result of research that recognized the safe driving habits of OnStar subscribers. This is in addition to the enhanced safety discount given when vehicles are equipped with the OnStar system and together premiums are adjusted accordingly with discounts up to 20%.

Mileage-Based Insurance—GMAC Insurance and Onstar will pilot a new mileage-based consumer insurance concept beginning in February. The program will offer discounts to eligible subscribers in three states as part of a test program to validate feasibility and customer appeal. Eligible customers must have an active OnStar subscription and drive a qualified GM vehicle since OnStar's vehicle connectivity provides the basis for this service. With the customer's permission, OnStar will verify mileage on the vehicle twice during the policy period. Because of the ability to cost effectively gather actual mileage readings, discounts can range up to 40%. The lower the vehicle mileage, the more significant the discount.[1]

The Old Competitive World

The automotive manufacturer developed the basic vehicle with integrated functionality, such as radios, and received all of its remuneration (including a markup on the parts acquired from suppliers) at the time of the consumer's transaction with the dealer, who eventually sold the vehicle to a consumer. The manufacturer's contact with the buyer during the period of ownership was primarily indirect, occurring only if it handled the financing or when the vehicle came in for repairs under warranty.

Belief in the value of the "old" world is alive and well in the hearts and minds of many associated with the automotive industry. Keith Crain, the respected publisher of *Automotive News*, for example, wrote an editorial in the August 12, 2002, issue: "Consumers like their cars; in many cases, they feel passionate about them. But they don't want all the ideas that auto companies offer. The manufacturers, it would appear, have discovered that telematics isn't something they can add to their vehicles and make an instant $100 a month extra. It sounded good, but no one asked the customer. I think the jury is still out on On-Star and satellite radio. It remains to be seen whether the customer will feel any great need for those services."[2]

The New Competitive World

The automotive manufacturer, in addition to receiving most of its remuneration at the time of transaction, invests in embedded technology that allows the customer to activate specialized services paid for over the entire ownership experience. The embedded technology stays with the vehicle so that it is possible to earn revenue over the entire lifetime of the vehicle. Under this condition, the manufacturer stays in continual contact with the owner of the vehicle and must demonstrate that the value of the services provided by the embedded technology is greater than the associated fees.

The new competitive world is best described in an article written by Todd Lappin for the July 1999 issue of *Wired*:

> If you haven't kept your eye on the horizon, you might think General Motors is only involved in the old-fashioned business of making and selling automobiles. Cars are still what the company does best, of course: One of its vehicle lines alone—the GMT 800, a full-size truck sold as the Chevrolet Silverado or GMC Sierra—will generate roughly $18 billion in revenues this year, making it a bigger enterprise than Microsoft.
>
> But for GM, the future is just as much about serving the driver as it is about selling the ride. The 500 million hours a week that Americans spend in their cars represents a huge audience of consumers. And that explains why capturing subscribers, not harnessing horses, is the hot new motor trend, as an emerging constellation of automakers, electronics manufacturers, and telecom providers convert transportation platforms into communications platforms that connect the driver, and the vehicle itself, to the rest of the datasphere.[3]

The Customer Benefit

In June 1996, shortly after GM made the decision to develop OnStar, a vehicle sent an emergency telephone message for the first time. The message was sent by an OnStar-equipped Cadillac to the OnStar call center because the vehicle had been involved in an accident and the air bag had been deployed. It was the first of thousands of calls to alert the call center that there was a high probability that someone in the vehicle required help. The ultimate customer benefit comes when lives are saved:

> On March 30, 2003, OnStar helped save two lives in Rockingham County, N.C. It all started when the driver fell asleep and drove off the road with his 2001 Chevrolet Tahoe. The vehicle traveled off U.S. 220 on the grass median, hit a guardrail, ran into a bridge, plummeted down an embankment and landed upside down on railroad tracks. The crash trapped the driver and 1-year-old grandson, killing the driver's wife. After the vehicle's airbags deployed, OnStar answered the emergency call and notified Rockingham County 911 of the vehicle's location. The OnStar advisor honked the horn and flashed the lights so the rescue team could easily find the vehicle. Emergency personnel contacted a Norfolk Southern Railroad dispatcher, who was able to stop a train before it crossed the accident site. Rockingham County 911 said that OnStar was the only one to report the crash. "OnStar gave us the general location," said 911 Supervisor Frank Moore. "They have helped us a number of times before."[4]

Background

In 1993, planners presented a business proposition to GM to develop a microwave-transmission–based mobile communication system that would be the basis for reliable wireless two-way voice and data services to a moving vehicle.[5]

At the time the proposal was made, GM was in its "stop the bleeding" and survival mode. This period was marked by continued market share erosion's increasing competition and very poor financial performance. Although there was a desire for new growth opportunities, the enterprise's tolerance for additional initiatives that required significant capital investment was very low.

Under these conditions and on preliminary review and financial evaluation, management rejected the proposal, primarily because of the large amount of investment capital needed to build the microwave tower infrastructure required to support a national service. The team doing the evaluation, however, was impressed with the possible revenue opportunity and possible operating cost savings associated with mobile communications and noted that, if there were a way to do it with reduced upfront capital investment, the idea had merit. A few years later, planners proposed using existing cellular technology and a global positioning satellite (GPS) system to record latitude and longitude information, in place of the more expensive microwave technology infrastructure.

In early 1995, after an extensive review of several alternative approaches to building a business using the cellular and GPS approach, GM's managers decided to take advantage of the lower investment costs associated with the existing infrastructure. They believed that, by using GM's size and market access, combined with aggressive market pricing, the enterprise could establish a large consumer base while ensuring that upfront capital investment was kept low. The expected sales volume would permit GM to negotiate favorable hardware prices and realize scale economies. Management also felt that GM's knowledge of vehicle electronic systems could lead to a broad range of vehicle integrated services that a non-automotive company would find difficult to match in a timely manner.

Underlying the decision to go forward with OnStar was management's desire to begin "growing the business" (as discussed in chapter 2) in areas of higher potential profit margins and opportunities that not only took advantage of GM's market position with the automotive consumer, but enhanced the experience of those consumers as well, and with minimal capital investment.

Frame the Problem Right—The Old World Approach: Beginning with "Certainties"

The initial evaluation of the OnStar business opportunity was primarily framed as a capital budget decision. In the capital budgeting frame, GM's decision was whether or not to allocate additional capital to the development of a mobile communications system. In the capital budgeting framework, the task is to *forecast* the penetration rate, which in this case is the fraction of GM car buyers who choose to subscribe to OnStar. Usually, the forecast will result from a combination of historical analogy, market research, and managerial judgment. Practically, the penetration forecast will be expressed as a growth curve over time and entered into a spreadsheet model—and for the eventual decision this forecast will be accepted as being *real*. Indeed, several consulting and investment banking firms recently framed what is now termed the "telematics" opportunity in exactly this way. A recent *McKinsey Quarterly* article concludes that the returns on telematics investments have been low and that automobile manufacturers are better off investing in new vehicle programs. According to the article, vehicle original equipment manufacturers (OEMs) would be wise to limit their telematics investment and focus on a few services closely connected to the vehicle, such as safety and security. After stating their conclusion, the authors concede that their projections, especially on the revenue side, are highly uncertain and that sensitivity analysis has revealed that telematics *could* be very profitable if subscription rates and fees prove higher than expected.[6]

Frame the Problem Right—The New World Approach: Beginning with "Doubts"

Idealized design is all about *creating change*. The initial OnStar business design did not benefit fully from an idealized design. It was not until the idealized approach to strategy was better understood inside GM that it was used to assess the full value of the OnStar opportunity. As we have seen, the idealized design framework attempts to design a system that will achieve particular operating goals. The goals could be financial, such as return on investment, but also more qualitative, such as developing more frequent relationship experiences with customers. A basic tenet in idealized design is to conceptualize the system that managers want, without initially being constrained by current organizational or financial constraints.

The idealized design framework poses a very different question than capital budgeting analysis. Capital budgeting asks whether or not a business is profitable, given a set of operating assumptions. Idealized design asks how we can create an operational system that generates the outcomes we want. In capital budgeting, the operating characteristics of the business are assumptions to be debated. In idealized design, the operating characteristics are the result of a conscious design process.

In the OnStar case, the analysis of the expected penetration rate illustrates the difference between the capital budgeting and the idealized design points of view.

In the idealized design framework, the task is to *design a process* that will cause the enterprise to reach the penetration rate necessary for OnStar to be viable. The traditional forecasted penetration rate is determined largely by the services we can think of now. Market research is extremely helpful in determining short-term penetration rates; however, in the long run, the penetration rate will be driven by applications we cannot even think of today. This insight was supported from discussions with Chunka Mui, one of the authors of *Unleashing the Killer App*, and his colleagues during a Diamond Exchange, an executive forum sponsored by Diamond Cluster.[7]

The discussion made clear that, in developing digitally based new products, the theories, hypotheses, and practices underlying traditional measures needed to be complemented by alternative methods supported by new theories and hypotheses. Soon, terms like *Moore's Law* (every eighteen months, chip density would double while costs remained constant, leading to ever more powerful computing devices without raising their price) and *Metcalf's Law* (that networks dramatically increase in value with each additional node or user) were being included in presentations. Most important, planners eventually accepted that forecast applications of the new idea could not even be thought of until eventual third-party participants thought the OnStar service valuable enough for them to apply their capability and thinking to making such an idea even better — none of which could be forecasted with traditional methods.

Above all, OnStar's mission was to develop a viable business based on its services. To ensure they focused their attention on creating a business that was attractive to customers, planners were not allowed to use revenue assumptions based on forecasted incremental vehicle sales made by GM solely because of OnStar. Not only were these assumptions difficult to prove, given the profits on incremental sales, only a small number of these sales (whether they eventually occurred or not) would justify almost any program.

Planners even raised the possibility that OnStar would eventually improve GM's market value. This possibility was evaluated through two interdependent influences on market capitalization.

The first influence was the amount of annual annuity-based revenues and profits that would eventually be included in GM's total revenue and profits. This was presented as an important influence on market value in that it addressed the automotive market's sensitivity to changing economic conditions. It was believed that, although small in comparison to total revenues, the profit contribution in a down economic period would be more meaningful.

The second influence was OnStar's ability to improve the customer experi-

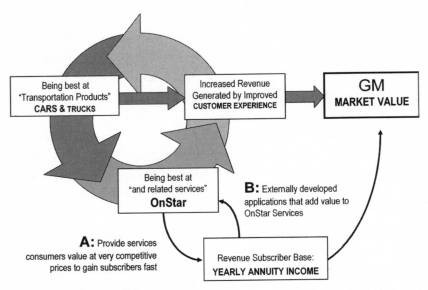

Figure 3.1 OnStar's virtuous circle.

ence of GM new-vehicle buyers. In this instance, OnStar was the beneficiary of GM's large annual share of automotive consumers. The idealized plan was to get as many of these new-vehicle purchasers as possible to subscribe to OnStar. Once this objective had been established, the concept of a "virtuous circle" was used to identify actions for GM to take to effect the objective. Figure 3.1 illustrates how the approach was described. Activity A, "provide services consumers value at very competitive prices to gain subscribers fast," was instituted to encourage GM vehicle customers to subscribe to OnStar. It would do so by attracting them with services market research had indicated they would value at option prices ranging from free to relatively expensive. The hypothesis was that the large subscriber base would attract activity B, "externally developed applications that add value to OnStar services," by third-party application and content providers. Businesses would partner because they believed forming an alliance with OnStar was the most effective and efficient way to reach large numbers of automotive consumers of mobile services.

To test the hypothesis underlying the idealized plan, GM management took an option on potential future business opportunities via the following important actions:

- To provide these new services at prices low enough to attract a large subscriber base, GM would be required to factory install the hardware in nearly all of its vehicles—knowing that not all consumers would subscribe.
- To encourage development of third-party applications, GM would create within OnStar the resources to encourage and develop alliances with third parties.
- To maximize the use of the OnStar call centers and to maintain consistency in the manner in which mobile services were being provided throughout the industry, GM would encourage other OEMs to provide the OnStar service.
- To ensure the electronic protocols that were being developed would be accepted by the automotive industry (including suppliers), GM and Toyota would take the lead to form the Automotive Multimedia Interface Consortium.

The idealized design framework augmented managerial attention on financial forecasting with an understanding of what it would take to design a system that would meet financial objectives. This difference led GM to make decisions very different from those that would have been made if only financial analysis had been used. The following summary compares what GM has done to what Chatterjee et al. recommended in their *McKinsey Quarterly* article regarding the evaluation of telematics:

- The idealized design framework recommended that GM factory install OnStar in every vehicle, whereas the capital budget framework would recommend that OEMs take a conservative approach.
- The idealized design framework encouraged GM to create the OnStar telematics platform, scaled for millions of subscribers, and to offer it to other OEMs, whereas the capital budget framework would recommend that platform development be left to others, such as telecommunication companies.
- The idealized design encouraged GM to orchestrate the creation of a complete package of telematics services, whereas the capital budget framework would recommend that OEMs focus on a few services.

Although it is still too early to make any definitive statement, the hypothesis underlying OnStar application of the idealized design, in this instance, seems to be proving itself correct:

- GM's subscriber base as of April 2004 was more than two-and-a-half million customers.
- OnStar is the provider of 85 percent of vehicles using embedded wireless services.

- There are five OEMs offering the OnStar system: Honda (Acura), Toyota (Lexus), Subaru, Volkswagen, and Audi. Combined with GM, this group conducts 45 percent of new-vehicle sales—all potential OnStar customers.
- OnStar is the largest reseller of cellular phone time in North America.
- There are over fifty companies aligned with OnStar, providing applications and content to OnStar subscribers. They include

  - Verizon Wireless
  - EDS
  - NAVTECH
  - SpeechWorks
  - Fidelity
  - Weather Channel
  - *Wall Street Journal*
  - Disney

- On a monthly basis, OnStar

  - answers 250,000 routing calls
  - answers 16,000 roadside assistance requests
  - performs 30,000 door unlocks
  - responds to 800 air bag deployments
  - responds to 800 stolen-vehicle location requests
  - runs diagnostic checks on 20,000 vehicles

Although these preliminary statistics are impressive, a story helps illustrate the potential of what lies ahead:

In the not too distant future, a couple and their two kids are driving to Florida for a family vacation in their OnStar-equipped Chevrolet TrailBlazer. The wife has used the OnStar concierge service to plan this trip. Therefore, an OnStar advisor has planned the family's itinerary. The advisor has also received the family's permission to track them on this journey and provide services to make their trip safer and more pleasant.

Halfway to their destination, the TrailBlazer's onboard diagnostic system communicates to the OnStar advisor that the car's emission sensor is about to indicate a problem and will illuminate the "Check Engine" message on Driver Information Center. The advisor, using the diagnostic information from the emission sensor and other sensors related to engine performance, determines that the sensor may be malfunctioning and that the engine may not be emitting emission above the limit.

Since the OnStar advisor knows where the family is going, the advisor per-

sonally calls them in their vehicle and informs them that the vehicle's "check engine" light will soon go on. The advisor reassures the family that, given where
they are, they can safely finish their trip to Florida. However, since either the
sensor needs to be replaced, or the car's emissions control system needs servicing, the advisor offers to schedule a convenient service appointment with a
dealership near the family's final destination. With the family's permission, the
advisor contacts the dealer near their lodging, makes the appointment, and determines that the dealer does not have the necessary parts available. The advisor, working with the dealer, makes sure that the service parts organization
arranges to have an oxygen sensor available at the dealership before the family arrives for service.

Meanwhile, the kids are enjoying the ride, because they have just downloaded a movie from a DirecTV satellite to their onboard personal video recorder.

Managing the interaction of the parts rather than managing the parts separately is the key to making this solution possible—the integration of the car's
onboard computer, the OnStar system, the dealer service facility, and the service parts organization. The family sees GM, the enterprise, as providing far
more than the vehicle in which they are driving. The parents, who have previously experienced a vacation delayed because of unanticipated problems, now
have experienced a relationship that is far greater in value than simply the sum
of the value of each part.

For GM, managing the interaction of the parts provides a powerful opportunity to create a positive experience that deepens and broadens its relationship
with the customer. Additionally, it has avoided a more expensive warranty repair cost by preventing the driver from having the vehicle towed to a service facility unnecessarily.

OnStar offers an excellent example of GM's ability to take advantage of
make-and-sell economies of scale and learn to build an adaptive capability as
it both senses and responds to changing market opportunities; it also shows
the emergence of the ability to anticipate by translating unarticulated needs
into a real product and service and lead by developing new ways to earn an
annuity-based revenue stream and to reduce warranty costs by avoiding them.
It also illustrates the importance of framing the problem correctly through an
idealized design. It is one of the first examples of how an "atoms-based" company enhanced its value by incorporating a "bits-based" business into its
strategy.

Chapter 5 provides an example of thinking beyond today's consumer's mental models and applying GM's creative and technological competencies to design a new and compelling product and service concept that can position the enterprise in a leadership position. But before we get to that story, the next chapter discusses the dramatic step of developing a transparent relationship with the consumer, and the trust upon which that relationship is based.

4 Transparency and a Dialogue with the Customer

Honesty and transparency make you vulnerable. Be honest and transparent anyhow.

—Mother Teresa

The Old Competitive World

Formerly, it was thought that the seller knew more than the customer about a product and its price. By bringing together all its knowledge about individual customers, the seller also knew more about the behavior of customers than did any one customer. The seller could reach large numbers of customers at the same time through mass media, efficiently and effectively.

GM and other large manufacturers helped create this paradigm and took full advantage of this condition. Chapter 2 pointed out that, in a world in which future behavior was somewhat predictable, a firm could take full advantage of economies of scale by designing, developing, producing, and selling products in accordance with estimates of future demand.

In North America, the customer's choice was limited to what North American manufacturers wanted to build. Information about pricing was closely held between the manufacturer and its distribution system. Most communication that took place between the manufacturer and the customer was impersonal and through mass communication. In the 1960s, given the number of women watching soap operas on television (e.g., *Love of Life*, *Search for Tomorrow*, and *Guiding Light*), a brand manager could reach approximately 80 percent of all women aged eighteen to forty-nine in a week with three minutes of daytime television. The 1960 cost of reaching these women, in today's dollars, was approximately $325,000.

More personal communication took place within the distribution system. In this world, the communication, with the exception of consumer research and limited dealer feedback, was one-way: from manufacturer to the customer.

The New Competitive World

Today, the individual customer is now capable of knowing as much (if not more) than any one individual seller about products and prices. Additionally, even if the brand manager were to stay with network broadcasts only, the cost would be approximately $15 million—forty-six times more expensive than in 1960. The promise of more targeted cable programming gives an indication of the value of targeting the right audience. By supplementing the more expensive network reach with two thousand spots in a carefully selected combination of daytime, early news, late night, and network morning shows, the brand manager could reduce the cost dramatically to approximately $5 million. Even with this more efficient placement, however, the cost would still be more than fifteen times that of 1960.

In the late 1990s, information technology and the Internet promised to change everything. But, given the reality of product and service fulfillment requirements (and state franchise laws in the case of automobiles), it did not change everything. It did, however, change a lot.

Today, nearly two out of three purchasers of new vehicles can get more information on the Internet about all vehicles in which they are interested in a fraction of the time it once took to watch the television shows whose commercials presented such information. They are, however, faced with an overwhelming array of products from which to choose.

As these consumers have come to understand the economics and the behavior of information providers, be they off-line or online, they have become more concerned and have raised questions about the value and the truth of information. A review of the customer decision drivers discussed in chapter 2 found that consumers did not rate information received through advertising or the Internet as important and were not satisfied with what they were receiving. These findings, and others, demonstrate that a case can now be made that customers are looking for information sources that not only are helpful in guiding decisions, but also can be trusted to provide unbiased information. Evidence is also beginning to come to light that enterprises can benefit from providing helpful and trusted advice.

Transparency and Trust

The 2002 Bank of Sweden Prize in Economic Sciences in Memory of Alfred Nobel was based on the work of three economists who were able to demonstrate that economic transactions are less efficient (in other words, somebody gets less value) when buyers or sellers have unequal access to key information. In essence, if customers do not know that you have exactly what they want, they may buy something less to their liking for a lesser price and possibly not from you. Also, if you do not know how to best serve your customers, it is more difficult to earn the right price for the products you do develop and, therefore, more difficult to achieve your growth and margin objectives. These scholars earned their prize for publishing convincing evidence of what some people had felt for a long time. The current term for these observations is *creating transparency*.

With AutoChoiceAdvisor, GM is creating transparency. The advice is totally unbiased, and the quality of outcomes when the customer goes through the process confirms its objectivity. Furthermore, unlike other, more commercially based sites that attempt to provide the same service, AutoChoiceAdvisor contains no unwanted solicitation (including intrusive pop-up and banner advertisements), and customer names are never sold or used without permission.

GM's understanding of trust—both its importance and how to nurture it—comes in large part from the work of Glen Urban and his colleagues at the Massachusetts Institute of Technology (MIT). Their pathbreaking research of the late 1990s contributed greatly to GM's eventual application of AutoChoiceAdvisor. In a project called *Truck Town* in the late 1990s, GM worked with Urban and his MIT team to test out a Web site featuring software-enabled advisors that mimicked the behavior of unbiased human experts.

In this study of trust-building practices, virtual "advisors" consulted with customers on purchasing decisions and provided honest comparisons of competing products. More than 75 percent of Truck Town's visitors said that they trusted these virtual advisors more than they trusted the traditional communication methods. As a result, GM concluded that honesty implied by the unbiased conduct of the virtual advisors would be a critical component in any Internet trust-building program.

Breaking Down Barriers

Mohan Sawhney's introduction of the metamarkets concept (discussed in chapter 2) also helped sharpen GM's thinking about trust. His observations grew out of his notion of "markets in our minds," clusters of activities that consumers engage in to satisfy a distinct set of needs, which can be organized around major assets, major interests, major life events, or major business processes.

Sawhney had contended that, in order to fully engage consumers, and to satisfy their needs within the metamarket, there needs to be a metamediary, a third party between companies and consumers that can gain the consumer's trust and help guide the consumer to the products and services he or she wants. Sawhney's concept seemed solid enough when GM first encountered it, but, upon reflection, it raised some very serious questions:

- Why did GM require a third-party metamediary?
- Why would GM deed its customer relationships to a third party?
- What would it take for GM to be seen as a trusted enterprise from which a consumer could expect unbiased information and a trusted relationship?

The issues raised by Sawhney led to an extensive internal discussion over what it would take to establish GM as "the site to go to" and whether GM could really deliver on the promise to provide objective data. The key question became, what would GM have to do to convince consumers that its products would be evaluated on the same basis as those of any other manufacturer? Planners decided to give the idea a try with AutoChoiceAdvisor, and in just one year GM built a site with the type of transparency a metamediary needs in order to be deemed trustworthy.

Gaining the trust of someone is very important. When you provide products and services that are very important to the well-being of the people who use them, trust is a critical attribute that is difficult to acquire and easy to lose. As with many of the examples in this book, the story of AutoChoiceAdvisor is neither flawless nor complete.

The Evolution of AutoChoiceAdvisor

It had become clear in the 1980s and 1990s that traditional methods of segmentation using age, income, and the like did not distinguish an individual's preference for a vehicle. Because of this condition and given GM's broad range of vehicles and services, GM developed a segmentation based on consumer needs, not demographics (as detailed in chapter 7). GM also believed that the Internet was a bona fide communication medium and that many consumers would integrate it into their auto-purchasing behavior as a source of information. The challenge was to find a way to bring these two observations together. The questions quickly became, *who* would use the Internet to gather information about his or her next new vehicle, and, importantly, *why* would they do so?

In many organizations, questions about who and why would be answered in the language of demographics (i.e., "women aged eighteen to forty-four") or, more recently, psychographics (i.e., "up-and-comers"). But GM knew, for example, that individuals who are quite similar demographically and psychographically often behave differently when it comes to a vehicle purchase, and express vastly different ideas, wants, needs, and concerns.

Although GM felt confident—with the use of its vehicle segmentation methods—about its understanding of purchasers of new vehicles, the project team for AutoChoiceAdvisor faced great uncertainty about how to design and execute an Internet site. Fundamental questions faced the team. For example, initial research indicated that the onsets of new media formats (Internet, personal video recorders, etc.) were not perceived by some consumers as simply extensions of older technologies. This of course raised a significant question: what was the value of understanding consumers' past use of traditional media as a method for understanding their future use of new media?

GM retained the services of Odyssey, an independent market research and market consulting firm based in San Francisco, to help find answers to these questions. Odyssey had found that, when it came to determining how consumers adopted and used different forms of media and services, their underlying attitudes—not traditional demographics—were better able to explain why they sought one form of information gathering over another. To evaluate the application of the Odyssey segmentation scheme, GM and Odyssey mapped the GM vehicle needs segmentation to the Odyssey consumer segments. This synthesis provided insight into a broader range of media habits for consumers in each of GM's targeted vehicle segments.

This earlier work revealed that there were indeed consumers in certain Odyssey segments who were more likely to purchase a new vehicle—because of who they were, not what they looked like or how much money they made—and who were also more likely to use online sources to gather information before vehicle purchases.

Armed with answers to the question *who* might come, GM knew if it built a site, there would be an audience. This left unanswered the second question, *why*.

The following six Odyssey segments were reviewed to determine the efficacy for this study.

- *New Enthusiasts.* These are the most upscale consumers, very interested in new products and willing to experiment, but they are extremely value oriented and will invest only in products and services that cater to their particular wants and needs. They will not be talked down to and are demanding and difficult consumers.
- *Independents.* These consumers are also upscale, but they believe above all in family, community, and responsibility. They are concerned about children and what children are exposed to in the media. Independents do not see technology as interesting or entertaining, but only as useful or not useful.
- *Surfers.* The third upscale segment, these consumers easily become bored and need to be stimulated and entertained. They see themselves as alienated from the mainstream, so they respond to products with a rebellious, cynical, or countercultural image. They are wary, distrustful consumers.
- *Faithfuls.* These consumers are the true lovers of television. Faithfuls are family oriented and middle-of-the-road in many respects, including income and education. They love celebrities and entertainment and want to be "with it," but only once doing so is safe.
- *Hopefuls.* These consumers share a number of attitudes with New Enthusiasts, but they are much more downscale in terms of income and education. Always discount their ability to step up with pocketbook and aptitude.
- *Oldliners.* Also a downscale segment, but much older than Hopefuls, these consumers are much less likely to have children at home. Everything that happened yesterday was better than what is happening today. Oldliners are heavy television viewers, even though they express concerns about inappropriate content.

Following a detailed review, it was determined that consumers classified as New Enthusiasts were the ones most likely to use newer media forms as part of their purchasing behaviors. The segment was sizable, representing roughly 18 percent of all households, and much more interested than other households in improving their home information experiences. Odyssey had learned over a decade of study that all of this stems from New Enthusiasts' deep-seated commitment to value. They do their homework before they buy. They push the purchase process to the limit in their search for value. At the same time, they are willing to pay to get what they want: they are not so much anti–high price as they are anti–bad value. Because they seek status through what they own, who they associate with, and what they do, members of this group would see a bad deal as insulting to their intelligence. What was important to the AutoChoice-Advisor team was New Enthusiasts' relentless appetite for information and that their desire for new information technology products and services had been tempered by services that overpromised and underdelivered. The team had identified its initial target for the design of AutoChoiceAdvisor and a goal: to make an achievable promise to New Enthusiasts and then overdeliver.

Creating a Service That Met Unspoken Requirements

Once it was determined that, in all probability, "if GM would build it, they (led by New Enthusiasts) would come," GM set the destination for AutoChoice-Advisor: to develop the leading online trust-based automotive consultative shopping tool, which would do the following:

- Provide an *unbiased* vehicle description based on the consumer's requirements and desires
- Establish a dialogue with online automotive consumers
- Gather quick feedback on consumer preferences

In essence, the objective was to create a site that would engender trust while improving communication between GM and consumers, and to simultaneously gather up-to-the-minute understanding of these consumers.

The trust-based approach of AutoChoiceAdvisor is quite simple: "By answering a few questions (which takes about 10 minutes) we will provide you with a list of 10 vehicles—each of which has a score based on how close the vehicles come to meeting your needs. The list will include vehicles from all manufacturers." Shoppers can access the site directly at AutoChoiceAdvisor.com, or they can enter through non-GM channels. Shoppers on National Public Radio's *Car Talk* Web site, and those accessing *Kelley Blue Book* online, both highly respected authorities on automotive shopping, have the option of linking to AutoChoiceAdvisor, as do visitors to NetZero and BlackVoices.com. Once they reach the site, shoppers answer a series of questions about their needs:

How will they use the vehicle? For commuting? For carpooling? To haul a trailer?

What is their price range? What body types and brands do they like?

What vehicle attributes do they prefer? Are they concerned about repair history? Fuel economy? Cargo capacity?

Once these questions have been answered, the AutoChoiceAdvisor asks users to rank their priorities. Do they care most about price range, or are other attributes more important? Is body style an important consideration, or would they prefer better fuel economy?

To guarantee an unbiased response to the shopper's answers, the measurable characteristics of each vehicle in the system (both GM's and competitors' products) come from independent sources that provide these services to the automotive industry. Furthermore, the information on vehicle quality comes from J. D. Power and Associates, one of the most noted independent market research companies specializing in measuring customer satisfaction.

Because GM knows trust is important, it does everything possible to ensure confidentiality. The site makes it clear that the information consumers provide will remain confidential. No GM representative will contact them about their responses unless they ask for the contact. GM also aggregates the information so that personal information is anonymous. The confidentiality process has been certified by TRUSTe, which requires GM to document what information is collected, how it is stored, who has access, and so forth. AutoChoiceAdvisor has no persistent cookies and requires no registration, which makes it even more trustworthy to users.

At any time, the customer can ask for the best recommendations from the current answers, whereupon AutoChoiceAdvisor matches the best estimate of the customer's preferences against a database of the more than 250 models currently on the market. After seeing the recommended vehicles, the customer can go back to the questions and answer additional questions or change responses to those already answered.

In a few minutes, the customer can address a complex issue by participating in simple dialogue with AutoChoiceAdvisor, investigating which vehicles should be considered for a wide range of underlying preferences—in effect, collapsing a time-consuming and expensive multiweek information gathering process into an approximately ten-minute Web site visit. GM vehicles appear in the consideration set only if they truly match the consumer's preferences. When no GM vehicle matches the customer's initial preferences, the respondent is offered an opt-in opportunity to view the GM vehicle that comes closest to his or her preferences. This option allows GM to ask, "What would make this GM vehicle more appealing to you?" The user also has the option to learn more about a given vehicle and even to link to its manufacturer's Web site. And if the user prefers, his or her input and search results are saved in a password-protected file so they can be reviewed at a later date.

The recommendation software provides quick and extremely relevant responses to the preferences submitted by consumers coming to the site. The approach is based on Bayesian statistical techniques that take full advantage of a database of prior customer preferences gleaned from thousands of consumers' responses collected during the development of the advisor. This approach allows the advisor to request a minimal amount of information from the customer, yet provide very specific responses developed by allowing the customer's responses to interact with a comprehensive and intelligent database.

The response has been positive. With more than thirty thousand visitors per month, GM can conclude that users have been overwhelmingly pleased with the results. Their comments give strong indications that they believe they are receiving unbiased, accurate information that will actually help them choose a new vehicle, regardless of make or model.

The Benefits of AutoChoiceAdvisor

AutoChoiceAdvisor has benefited GM in three important ways.

First, it has allowed GM to match vehicle products and services to individual customer preferences: By enabling customers to identify and match them with all vehicles currently in market, GM gains access to a continuous flow of customer preferences and understanding. This insight, combined with the creativity of GM's product development teams, offers the opportunity to introduce new vehicle concepts into the market to address unmet market needs. These observations do not replace all current market research methods, but they provide an additional approach that improves understanding of customers more likely to be "in market," along with more timely reports. In this sense, it complements

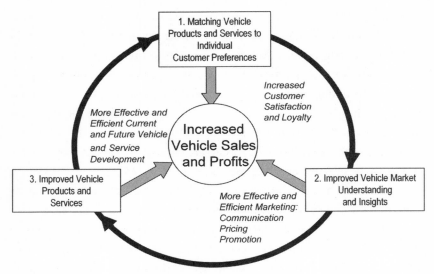

Figure 4.1 AutoChoiceAdvisor's virtuous circle.

traditional market research information that is collected by (1) prospectively asking what customers are likely to do before they are in the market, or (2) retrospectively asking customers to remember what they did and why when shopping for a vehicle they just purchased.

Second, it has given GM an improved understanding of the vehicle market: This insight helps the enterprise understand whether customers are not fully aware of GM products, or whether they are fully aware of what GM has available but are not interested. For example, if an analysis of the existing portfolio demonstrates that a product exists that would meet customer requirements to a greater extent than reflected in current sales, that insight provides a strong signal to those responsible for marketing communication to determine whether or not the existing communication program is achieving its objectives. If the product is seen as acceptable but not priced competitively, pricing actions can be taken. If customers are not fully aware of the benefits of new technology or the application of existing features, the enterprise can decide to increase its advertising or public communication programs to ensure the market is fully informed of the benefits.

Third, it has helped GM improve its vehicle products and services. Most significantly, if the company chooses to add or modify a vehicle, the minute that vehicle or modification is available in the market, it shows up in the desired characteristics of those customers whose requirements it meets.

To improve the chances the right product changes would be made, GM's vehicle-development systems engineering group played a major role in the early development of AutoChoiceAdvisor. Because the design team established a target that an AutoChoiceAdvisor session should not exceed ten minutes, engineers were forced to identify the absolutely essential information they needed. From the day AutoChoiceAdvisor went live, consumer information from Auto-ChoiceAdvisor has been fed directly into a simulation model developed by a team from engineering and market research. By analyzing the data, GM is able to determine whether there are segments in which they do not have an entry, or do not have an entry that competes in the mind of the consumer.

AutoChoiceAdvisor also provides designers and engineers of new vehicles with consumer preferences that are "always on and up-to-date" throughout the vehicle development process. This information allows GM to continuously measure consumer acceptance of its new vehicles as their designs evolve.

An Unexpected Benefit

By engaging in an online dialogue with the consumer, an enterprise has the opportunity to complement its traditional forms of communication by more personally informing the consumer about available products and services consistent with what he or she wants. All of this is possible because of Internet-inspired technology. Of equal importance, though, is the information it provides to refine other modes of communication, like advertising.

Bob Lutz, now GM's vice chairman of product development and North American operations, made the following observations in 1962 (well before he joined GM):

> Advertising, of course, attempts to furnish that information about the advertiser's product which will induce the consumer to buy the product. Two things work to prevent this from operating, however:
>
> 1. Other producers (advertisers) are deluging the consumer with counterclaims, creating some doubt, and destroying much of the impact of the first message.
> 2. The consumer may have learned to take advertising messages with more than a grain of salt, being accustomed to the rather large

amount of distortion and "puffing" which is conceded to be the normal state in advertising.

Throughout all this, the consumer remains in an essentially ambiguous situation which produces some anxiety and tension, especially if the product concerned is an expensive durable. It is only natural that the consumer seeks something "concrete," something or somebody he can trust in helping him make his purchasing decision.[1]

AutoChoiceAdvisor provides marketing communication managers with insights into that something "concrete" and into ways of gaining the customer's trust in making a decision on buying an automobile.

Win-Win for Customers and GM

When GM proposed the Web site to consumer focus groups in 1999, their reaction was mixed—but predictably so. Participants who had been chosen because they were classified New Enthusiasts asked logical questions based on their attitudes: Why would a manufacturer offer a site to compare its own vehicles with competitive products? What's in it for GM? What would GM do with the information?

Once the site began, however, the company and the consumer quickly realized that AutoChoiceAdvisor was more than a shopping tool. First and foremost, it gathers information for product development and marketing, and, just as important, seeks to establish GM as the leading advisor in the electronic marketplace. It also puts GM vehicles onto the consumer's radar screen by establishing a communication channel with people who might never have intended to consider a GM vehicle because they were unaware of GM's range of products or performance and quality. It is also possible that one day the advice will extend to other areas serviced by GM, such as financing and insurance, as displayed in figure 2.2.

To broaden the application of the advisor technology, GM created a license agreement with Richard Smallwood, who developed the recommendation software for AutoChoiceAdvisor, to use the approach developed for GM in other product categories. That approach is now being used by the Market Insight Corporation in a broader-based product advisor site (MyProductAdvisor.com).

There is an emerging body of evidence that developing a continuous trusted relationship with the customer is of considerable value to almost every enterprise. For example, Glen Urban of MIT's Sloan School of Management has pointed out:

> Digital marketing is important because it revolutionizes almost all aspects of marketing. Digital technology (1) introduces an entirely new channel to sell and market products, (2) allows new pricing options and individual promotions to customers, (3) enables new hot media communication, (4) offers opportunities to find new product needs and launch new products, and (5) supports improved distribution and service. Even more important, the Internet has changed the balance of power. Across industries, consumers are gaining the upper hand. Customer power in this Internet era is driven by three factors: more options, more information, and simpler transactions.[2]

Chapters 2, 3, and 4 described how GM applied the mindset underlying both sense-and-respond and anticipate-and-lead business designs. The next chapter is an example of taking advantage of the strengths of all three business designs—the design and implementation of a next-generation transportation experience.

5 Finding the Right Mix of Business Designs

All truth passes through three stages. First, it is ridiculed. Second, it is violently opposed. Third, it is accepted as being self-evident.

Thus the task is not so much to see what no one yet has seen, but to think what nobody yet has thought about that which everybody sees.

—Arthur Schopenhauer

Today's World

Enterprises compete with each other for their share of known markets. The most successful firms have intelligent sensing systems that provide them early warning of changing consumer requirements and attitudes. The successful enterprises have designed adaptive product and service development processes that allow them to change their products and services efficiently and effectively.

An "Embryonic" Future Competitive World

Marketing, the creation of customers, is the responsibility of the leadership of the enterprise. True marketing is an enterprise mindset, not just the responsibility of a department, or function, within the enterprise. As such, marketing is accepted as a thinking process that brings together the whole business so that the enterprise's products or services are seen positively from the point of view of the consumer. The successful enterprise provides products and services that are accepted in the marketplace and are seen as responsive to community and societal interests. The most successful enterprises develop products that meet customer requirements in ways that were unforeseen by them, for "nobody yet has thought about that which everybody sees." The products create a customer experience that is positively memorable and that engenders respect and loyalty for its innovation and performance. Success in this future competitive world will require the leadership of the enterprise to accept more risk and encourage a more innovative and entrepreneurial spirit throughout the extended enterprise.

A 2004 report from Reuters exemplifies GM's innovation and entrepreneurship:

FREEPORT, Texas, Feb. 10 (Reuters)—General Motors Corp. and Dow Chemical Co. launched the world's largest commercial hydrogen fuel cell project on Tuesday in a bid to jump start development of the green power source.

Fuel cells have been touted as environmentally sound electricity producers that could replace fossil fuels such as coal, oil and natural gas as the world's primary energy source.

Fuel cells operate by generating electricity through a chemical reaction between hydrogen and oxygen that leaves water and heat as byproducts.

Secretary of Energy Spencer Abraham said the new project would help propel advances in technology and drive down costs so that mass productiion of fuel cell-powered automobiles would eventually be possible.

"It really helps us to demonstrate this isn't some esoteric, pie-in-the sky idea," Abraham told reporters at the project launch.

"Today we're one step closer to the hydrogen economy," Larry Burns, GM's vice president of research and development and planning, said in a speech.

Burning fossil fuels produces smog and heat-trapping greenhouse gases such as carbon dioxide that are blamed for boosting the planet's temperature.

GM, like many car makers, has sought to harness fuel cells to power automobiles, and hopes to launch the cars on the market by 2010.

However, fuel cell costs are currently about 10 times too high to use in commercial cars and must be reduced to about $3,000–$4,000 per 75 kilowatts, Dow and GM said in a release.

The companies declined to comment on the cost of the project at the Dow plant.

Spencer Abraham activated the project's first 75-kilowatt capacity cell, which is fueled by excess hydrogen produced at the 30-square-mile manufacturing facility about 50 miles south of Houston. Another 12 are expected to go on line later this year.

Eventually, 400 fuel cells are expected to operate at the peak of the seven-year project at the facility, Dow's largest manufacturing site. That would provide 35 megawatts of electricity, enough to power to supply about 25,000 households for a year, GM said.

At the peak, output would supply about 2 percent of the Dow's electricity needs at the plant, the company said.

Spencer Abraham said development of fuel cell technology for automobiles was critical to help reduce the country's dependence on oil imports, which are expected to rise to 70 percent of the total U.S. consumption in 20 years from 54 percent currently.[1]

Any enterprise wanting to develop an anticipate-and-lead business design will require this kind of thinking.

The Background

In 1992, GM's North American operations lost nearly $5 billion. In 1994, it had earned nearly $1.5 billion, and 1995 would turn in a profit of $2.5 billion. In 1994, the leadership of the enterprise indicated it was time for it to reengage its strategic development process. The process started with the development of four future scenarios that represented a full range of possible external environments that could affect GM. The eventual goal of the process was to evaluate the extent to which GM's long-term plans were sufficiently robust to make it profitably operate, if required, in any of the scenarios. With this assessment, management would determine the extent to which current long-term plans were sufficient and identify steps to lessen any weak spots. The four scenarios GM developed in 1994 follow.

- *Momentum.* The key assumption in this scenario is that mobility systems—in GM's case, automotive vehicles—and providers will operate unchanged for the next thirty years; only incremental change projects will have value. The basis for this assumption is that, historically, the future has been evolutionary. Only occasionally is it revolutionary.
- *Technology reigns.* The key assumption in this scenario is that society will come to expect all problems to be solved by technical innovations. "Highest tech" products will be customer valued, and any limitations of existing product producers will be expected to be overcome. It further assumes that environmentally friendly technical innovations in vehicles and the roadway infrastructure will lead to decreased travel time and improved satisfaction with vehicular travel—even with increasing numbers of vehicles on the roads.
- *Environmental domination.* The key assumptions in this scenario are that the generation of CO_2 emissions is socially unacceptable, and alternatives to fossil fuels have not proven feasible. It is further assumed that environmental scientists have demonstrated conclusively that the deteriorating condition of the environment is caused in part by CO_2 emissions. Further, medical research has demonstrated the harmful effects of pollution on human longevity.

- *Geopolitical realignment.* The key assumption in this scenario is that economic factors will have driven the formation of new geopolitical trading groups throughout the world. Further, the actions of national governments will be increasingly influenced by business and trade considerations.

To ensure that an external perspective was maintained, in 1995 GM invited five outside experts to participate in a discussion around the four future scenarios that GM had developed earlier. The outside experts represented a wide range of external interests and points of view: Neil Goldschmidt, former governor of Oregon and secretary of transportation; Professor Lester Lave, director of Green Design Initiative, Carnegie Mellon University; Amory Lovins, Rocky Mountain Institute; Professor Ian Mitroff, University of Southern California (who served as moderator); and Sara Little Turnbull, director of the Process of Change Innovation and Design Laboratory, Stanford University Graduate School of Business. The discussion among the panelists was designed to reveal what would have to be true for each of the scenarios to be realistic. The outside experts then reported their personal observations of the discussion to GM's main policy board, the President's Council (now called the Automotive Strategy Board).

Given the economic and social conditions of 1995, the management team raised the most questions around the viability of the Environmental Domination scenario, questioning whether it could actually occur. One of leadership team members, executive vice president Harry Pearce, in the spirit of the process, suggested his colleagues should, for the purposes of the strategic thinking process, assume that one of GM's most respected scientists had conducted experiments that proved conclusively that CO_2 emissions from vehicles was the primary cause of global warming. With this assumption, there would be no question that GM would act on the information. Once everyone caught the spirit of the process, they looked just as hard at the Environmental Domination scenario as at the others and found that, if this scenario actually occurred, the current long-term plan would leave GM vulnerable to competitors that were working on alternative solutions to internal combustion engines, and vulnerable to the implications of strong government intervention.

During this assessment period, GM was preparing to introduce an environmentally friendly electric vehicle—the EV1.

Introduced in the fall of 1996, the EV1 proved to be a technological marvel in addressing the emerging societal concerns about the environment:

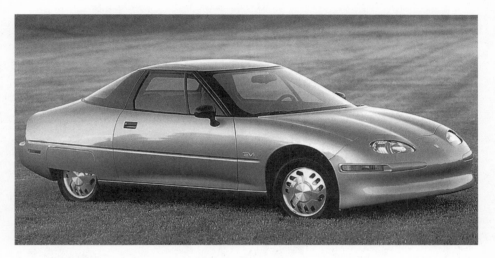

Figure 5.1 GM's EV1. Copyright 2003 GM Media Archive.

The EV1 had no engine because it didn't need one. No tailpipe because it had no exhaust. It had no valves. No pistons. No timing belts. No crankshaft. What did the EV1 have? Some remarkable electronics and a revolutionary new propulsion system. The most aerodynamic body shape of any production car, ever. One of the lightest, stiffest structures for a car its size. Super-low-rolling resistance 50 psi Michelin tires with wheels that weighed only 8.5 pounds. In addition to these innovations, the electric car also had an intelligent braking system that could regenerate energy and send it back to the batteries, a heat pump like the one used in some homes, and seven sophisticated on-board computers that controlled everything from the interior temperature to charging the battery pack.[2]

The GM experience with the EV1 is a story of how GM sensed and responded to a societal demand for an environmentally friendly vehicle. Although there were some customers who wanted a purpose-built environmentally friendly vehicle, GM could not, at the time, produce the vehicle with the driving range and functional characteristics that enough customers wanted and at the price they were willing to pay. As a result, the EV1, as presented, proved to be more of an important learning experience than a profitable and sustainable commercial endeavor.

Although not a humorous problem, the issue was captured quite well in the accompanying cartoon (fig. 5.2).

With the assessments made in the scenario process and the knowledge

Figure 5.2 Cartoonist's view of Ev1. Henry Payne reprinted by permission of United Feature Syndicate, Inc.

gained from developing the EV1 program, GM decided to take another step forward by making additional investments in projects that addressed alternative propulsion systems, new vehicle architectures, and "drive-by-wire" technologies (controls that are linked electronically, instead of mechanically, to the operating parts of the car), among others. As consumers' functional and performance requirements have come more into balance with society's environmental interests, GM's earlier investments, made in anticipation of possible societal calls for changes in vehicle requirements, have begun to bear fruit. In January 2002, at the Detroit International Auto Show, GM introduced the AUTOnomy—a new fuel cell vehicle. The AUTOnomy is a good example of an idealized design for future vehicle development. In this sense, it added the benefits of an anticipate-and-lead business design to the competency GM had gained in its initial sense-and-respond experiences.

By combining fuel cell technology with drive-by-wire concepts, GM developed a skateboard-like chassis topped by a body that can be easily interchanged with others (figs. 5.3 and 5.4). AUTOnomy represented a true reinvention of the automobile—and pointed the way to fuel cells' and advanced technology's taking the industry to clean, efficient, very compelling, and potentially much more

Figure 5.3 GM's AUTOnomy fuel cell concept car. Copyright 2003 GM Media Archive.

Figure 5.4 Fuel cell "skateboard" platform. Copyright 2003 GM Media Archive.

affordable vehicles. GM called the concept AUTOnomy because it builds on the personal freedom traditionally provided by the automobile.

AUTOnomy enhances this freedom because it holds the promise of eventually eliminating the automobile from the environmental equation and increasing energy independence. It also creates the pathway to renewable fuels, laying the groundwork for a future in which mobility is sustainable, in which the transportation needs of coming generations are not compromised by what we do today. The design concept of the AUTOnomy platform, in allowing different bodies to be used on the same platform, improves the enterprise's ability to determine a total number of vehicles without worrying about the demand for different body styles. This provides the opportunity for the AUTOnomy to take full advantage of the make-and-sell use of economies of scale.

Later in 2000, at the Paris Auto Show, GM introduced the Hy-wire ("Hy" for hydrogen and "wire" for electronic controls in place of conventional mechanical links).

If the AUTOnomy opened the door to some of the advantages of anticipate-and-lead business design, the Hy-wire truly represents a significant step across the threshold. Although GM has always tried to *anticipate* future needs, this time the company took on a *leadership* role in putting all the interdependent elements in place to make success more likely (fig. 5.5).

Customers did not ask for fuel cells in their vehicles. They did indicate desire for vehicles that would perform at a level similar to that of current vehicles with internal combustion engines (including relatively low operating expenses) but that would be more environmentally sensitive.

GM considered both the community and the customer in introducing the Hy-wire concept fuel cell vehicle. By thinking of the vehicle as part of the transportation system, including both customer and community, GM did not simply replace the internal combustion engine by dropping a fuel cell into a traditional vehicle.

Instead, GM developers took advantage of the enterprise's earlier efforts in fuel cell technology and electronic controllers to develop an entirely different kind of vehicle—the Hy-wire. It meets society's needs because hydrogen as a fuel is better for the environment. But, unlike GM's earlier all-electric vehicle, the EV1, the Hy-wire does not require that consumers sacrifice—for example, by enduring the limitations of battery technology—for environmental benefits.

Figure 5.5 GM's Hy-wire fuel cell vehicle. Copyright 2003 GM Media Archive.

Not only are fuel cells more effective in propelling the vehicle, but also the fuel cell operating platform of the Hy-wire can accept different bodies that perform different functions as required by the customer.

Because of the drive-by-wire technology, the body designers simply have to make sure the attachment points of the body match the attachment points of the fuel cell platform. This allows the vehicle designers much greater freedom to use the space that was taken by mechanical devices to improve customer functionality and convenience. Most important, since the platform can be designed to anticipate changing requirements, GM is able to predict with some certainty the number of these platforms required—given that changing preferences will be addressed in the attachable body. With this capability, the enterprise can design and develop the AUTOnomy platform in the context of a make-and-sell business design and gain the advantages of economies of scale, improved quality, and improved reliability, because of the reduced variations in the building process.

From a societal perspective, having learned from the EV1 experience, GM has taken the position that it will lead by focusing its resources not on being the first manufacturer with a fuel cell vehicle in the showroom, but on being the first to sell one million fuel cell vehicles.

GM has also pointed out to governmental and environmental leaders that, from the encompassing system's perspective, societal resources will have to be expended to make sure there is an infrastructure in place to distribute the hydrogen required by these fuel cell vehicles.

It is not reasonable to expect the customer (or narrowly focused vested interest groups) to have deep understanding of the economics of transportation, to enjoy the availability of energy resources (both renewable and nonrenewable), to know what is technically feasible, or to have a sense of what sufficient numbers of customers would want and be willing to pay for. It was up to GM and others to determine whether a fuel cell vehicle could meet customer and community needs better than other alternatives. Simply stated, it was up to the GM extended enterprise to start with the Hy-wire destination in mind.

What the Future May Hold in the Next Decade

A couple and their two kids are planning a family vacation trip to Florida, much like the family trip that was discussed in chapter 3. The difference this time is that this family is the owner of an OnStar-equipped GM Hy-wire vehicle. The wife contacts the OnStar concierge service to plan this trip, and, as in the previous story, OnStar services will have the family's itinerary and will also, with their permission, track them on this journey and provide services to make their trip safer and more pleasant.

There are, however, some very different services now. Since the family is currently driving a Hy-wire sport sedan, the OnStar concierge service offers to arrange for a different body style for the trip, because the trip will take several days and the family will be taking a considerable amount of luggage, including the family dog.

Using the My GM–Link Internet service, the family views several body styles that they can rent. They choose a very stylish multipurpose body style that comfortably seats four people and can accommodate their luggage, as well as safe storage of the dog's traveling crate. The concierge service makes arrangements with the family's local dealership to have the current body removed and temporarily replaced with the multipurpose body. Their current body will be stored and, at their request, refreshed, with several software upgrades included, while they are on their vacation. All of the reservations for hotel rooms, meals, and entertainment are made in advance. After the expenses for the trip are calculated, a debit card that will also keep track of all expenses is electronically downloaded from the family's account at GMAC financial services.

During the trip, OnStar forwards preselected electronic financial, personal, and weather information.

Oh yes! There are no emission sensors to alert the family that they are about to exceed the legal limit of exhaust emissions. With this vehicle's fuel cell propulsion system—*there are no emissions to sense.*

GM's forward-looking anticipate-and-lead design in developing completely new vehicles proves that even a large and inevitably bureaucratic enterprise can change direction if there is a willingness on the part of management to unleash the full imaginative skills and energy of its workforce to determine a future that works for the community, the customers, and the enterprise.

Part I has demonstrated the importance of starting with your destination and understanding the assumptions and distinctions that underlie the three business designs: make-and-sell, sense-and-respond, and anticipate-and-lead. In doing so, it has pointed out that the choice of business design is a function of the conditions within which the enterprise operates. It is not one *or* the other, but one *and* the other. Part II describes some of the actions taken by GM to position the enterprise to take the actions described in part I. It addresses the importance of integrating problem-solving approaches with relevant market information and developing the competencies to *listen, learn,* and *lead.*

LISTENING, LEARNING, AND LEADING

If a company is not operationally efficient, it cannot afford its strategy. On the other hand, if it is not strategically driven, the value that is created by operational efficiency could be wasted.

—C. K. Prahalad

In June 2003, GM introduced an advertising campaign under the headline, "The Longest Road in the World Is the Road to Redemption." The heart of the program is described in the following copy:

GM presents an overnight success story, a decade in the making.

Ten years ago, we had a choice. We could keep looking in the rearview mirror, or out at the road ahead.

It was the easiest decision we ever made.

The hard part meant breaking out of our own bureaucratic gridlock. Learning some humbling lessons from our competitors. And instilling a true culture of quality in every division, in every department, in every corner of the company.

Today, with quality at the core of our values, we're building the best cars and trucks in our history. GM is now challenging the automotive world in fuel efficiency, advanced emissions controls, styling and design, and manufacturing productivity.

It didn't start yesterday. And it doesn't happen overnight. But last year we launched over twenty new models on the way to posting our second straight year of market share gains. And a whole lot of you rediscovered that an American car can be a great car.

The road to redemption has no finish line. But it does have a corner.

And it's fair to say we've turned it.[1]

Part I provided four examples of GM's initial attempts to reach an idealized destination after it had passed through the period in which it faced near bankruptcy. The actions taken addressed rapidly changing conditions by causing changes in the market that were more favorable to the enterprise. They also involved learning how to apply the appropriate business design; that is, learning how to use one approach and the other rather than selecting one approach *or* the other.

Part II moves back in time, to before that period, to tell the story of what happened to position GM to think about an idealized destination. It addresses the importance of how organizations can take command of their functional bureaucracies and get them to adopt problem-solving approaches with relevant market information and develop the competencies to listen, learn, and lead.[2]

Background: Staring Disaster in the Face

In 1992, the GM Board of Directors installed a new management team, led by Jack Smith, a career GM employee who had earned a reputation for turning things around in GM's international operations. Smith and his new team faced the following conditions:

- Mounting corporate losses, an unprecedented third year of consecutive losses
- A significant gap between operating cash flow and cash required to cover interest and dividend payments
- "Downward spiral" generated by operating losses and need to fund product programs
- Almost half of the investment in the business was borrowed—additional outside borrowings and potential equity offerings severely limited
- North American Operations (NAO) as a key driver of corporate financial performance, a situation dictating that NAO become profitable on a "stand alone" basis
- An automotive market in recovery but trend growth expected to remain relatively flat
- Competitive intensity increasing—an anticipated 187 new competitive entries versus 46 for GM over the 1992–1996 time frame

Given the mandate by the GM Board of Directors to save the company, and faced with a severe financial situation, the leadership team focused most of its limited resources on a "stop the bleeding" set of initiatives to meet budget commitments for 1992 and restore North American Operations to profitability by 1993. This led to an operating plan to develop a more profitable product portfolio, reduce material costs, align production/capacity with demand, right-size the salaried workforce, and improve quality and reduce warranty costs. When the leadership had addressed these issues and returned North American Operations to profitability, they then developed, adopted, and published GM's vision and values statement in 1995. The statement was tightly focused but left room for further growth when the company emerged from the present economic crisis: "GM's vision is to be the world leader in transportation products and related services. We will earn our customers' enthusiasm through continuous improvement driven by the integrity, teamwork and innovation of GM people."[3]

The statement disappointed some people because it was neither exciting nor inspirational. But the decision to adopt it was not made out of lack of understanding or fear. The management team had undergone a deliberate process through which it gained considerable understanding of possible future conditions. Its members sensed the need to go beyond being just a transportation products company, but they did not want to confuse employees, suppliers, or customers. Even more important, they sensed that their current problems were not going away in the foreseeable future.

Given that GM's vision was "to be the world leader in transportation products and related services," the leadership of the enterprise sensed the need to avoid the zone of discomfort when considering new businesses like those discussed in part I. This concern required that GM stay focused on the basic vehicle business. GM President Rick Wagoner, who assumed the CEO position from Jack Smith in 2000, emphasized the importance of this issue by ensuring everyone understood that the relationship between the existing business and any new business required the existing customers to be really satisfied with the manner in which GM delivered "transportation products."

The examples presented in part II mainly typify, but are not limited by, the make-and-sell and sense-and-respond business designs. As was pointed out in the introduction to part I, any business design can be productive, depending on the context in which it is operating. In a world where the demand can be predicted for the period of the product's lifetime, the make-and-sell business works quite well. Sense-and-respond still requires the enterprise to make an assessment of future consumer behavior, but, because of expected rapidly changing conditions, accepts that the firm must build flexibility into its production and service delivery capability. This will be clearly demonstrated in the stories told in this part. A key component of success in these designs is to engage the customer in a dialogue to ensure that the enterprise earns its share of the demand for a particular category of product. For success in this design, collecting market research is a necessary but not sufficient endeavor. To be successful, the enterprise must have decision processes in place to ensure that the creative and technical product development designers make effective use of market research in determining the products and services the enterprise will develop. Then they must integrate the creative element that produces products that *anticipate* the market. To do otherwise courts disaster.

Asking the Right Question and Learning from Past Mistakes

In the late 1980s, when he was president of GM Europe, Jack Smith asked me whether the market research conducted in Europe was better or worse than the market research conducted in North America. My answer was that the market research conducted in Europe was well done, but that the effort in North America was more comprehensive and used more advanced techniques. The conversation concluded, however, with the observation that the information collected in Europe was used more effectively than the information in North America.

There were many unfortunate examples of not using information effectively. One particularly stands out:

> The Minivan: In the late 1970s GM had invested significant sums in a prototype concept called the multiple purpose car (MPC) which was designed to be built off of an existing front-wheel-drive vehicle platform. The research had indicated the potential for nearly a million units. Interestingly Ford market research had conducted similar research and found similar potential.
>
> Unfortunately GM management misinterpreted the consumer research findings, which indicated potential buyers came from virtually every existing segment of the market. Rather than recognizing an unmet need—the fact that many people were purchasing a wide variety of vehicles, none of which were fully satisfying—GM management interpreted the research to mean that there was no market for the concept. Additionally, GM had a significant station-wagon product lineup that some feared would be cannibalized by a minivan. For these and other reasons the program was stopped.
>
> GM was painfully reminded of its misinterpretation of the consumer research and the subsequent failure to go ahead in the production by a couple of lines in

the advertising script that introduced the very successful Dodge Caravan, six years later, in 1984: "Dodge Caravan, one vehicle that takes the place of an economy car, sporty car, station wagon and van. Dodge Caravan is a transportation revolution."[4]

The GM accounting system was able to book the savings of not producing the vehicle. The resulting "savings" contributed to GM's desire to meet its financial commitments in the period when the decision was implemented. As will be discussed in chapter 11, what the accounting system would not "account" for was the eventual revenue consequences of this action. Imagine the consequences if GM had produced the equivalent of a minivan six years before Chrysler.

Establishing the Relevancy and Reliability of Consumer Research

In 1992, when Jack Smith became GM's CEO and was presented the results of Vision 2000 (the process of which will be described in chapter 7), he said we had a lot riding on whether the market research was right. He asked what I could provide him to confirm that the market research underlying the proposed plan was correct. In response to his request, in May 1992, a thorough review of the research conducted before the introduction of eleven vehicle programs was compared with the actual sales results after the vehicles had been introduced. The summary of the report revealed sufficient evidence to warrant GM's acceptance of the research and set conditions upon which we could improve use of the research, saying, "If the research had been both available earlier and listened to, [it] could have improved our success rate with new product programs."[5]

The examples in part II demonstrate the importance of incorporating an understanding of what the enterprise knows (and does not know) into strategic decision-making processes, and the importance of the creative effort of product designers and developers. Part II begins with a chapter on different approaches to solving problems, approaches illustrated with "a matrix for framing the problem." This chapter is then followed by six important decisions that are related to the matrix. Although not all the examples presented operated as a seamless decision process at GM, the stories illustrate principles that apply equally to a wide variety of enterprises that seek to predict, sense, and anticipate the direction in which their markets are moving.

6 Solving the Right Problem the Right Way

Far better an approximate solution to the right problem, than a precise solution to the wrong problem.

—John Tukey

Doing nothing is better than to be busy doing nothing.

—Lao Tse

Anyone who has taken an introductory statistics course is familiar with Type I and Type II errors. A Type I error is a false positive, or the mistake of accepting a hypothesis as true when in fact it is false. A Type II error, on the other hand, is a false negative, or the mistake of rejecting a hypothesis when it is actually true. Ian Mitroff of the University of Southern California introduced me to Type III errors: *the probability of solving or working on the "wrong" problem when one should have worked on (attempted to solve) the "correct" problem.*[1]

This type of error leads us to believe we have solved the problem and can move forward, when in fact we are unenlightened about the real problem we needed to solve in the first place. For example, being mired in a fixed organizational mindset and not paying attention to changing conditions are two of the reasons that there are no photocopying machines bearing the International Business Machines (IBM) logo today. In 1958, IBM engaged Arthur D. Little to evaluate the market potential of two copiers (model 813 and model 914) developed by the Haloid Company (later to be known as the Xerox Corporation) Model 914 was to be a faster, more fully featured machine than competing products. Thus, it would carry a higher price.

The executive summary of the fifty-page final report clearly articulated how the existing structure and mindset of the client impacted the evaluation: "In considering this course of action IBM hopes to spread present selling costs over two product lines and to exploit more fully the office-equipment market coverage by its ET [electric typewriter] Division salesmen. We understand that selling costs in the division are now disproportionately high in some market territories outside of highly urbanized areas."[2] The report's executive summary concluded: "We do not believe the ET Division salesman is equipped to sell the model 914 as a systems machine. Specialists (systems analysts) and highly technical selling are required. IBM would therefore have to establish a separate sales force and systems training program to undertake the necessary market development program with a new product in this field." The report recommended that the "ET Division terminate considerations of the Haloid-Xerox model 914 as a new product opportunity for its sales force."

Thus, the model 914 was rejected, in part, because the perspective framing the problem was how well IBM's existing electronic typewriter sales force could handle the product. Had the problem been framed from the perspective of current deficiencies in office productivity and the role that improved distributed copiers could play in addressing that problem, as well as how a solution could lead to an entirely new business, the IBM decision might have been different and the subsequent success of the 914 might have been IBM's.

There were, of course, other reasons, based on current business practices, that contributed to IBM's decision to pass on the opportunity to gain access to the Haloid products. For example, the copy-volume estimates were based on the existing notion of making copies from an original. Even though IBM was developing typewriters that would produce originals of far greater copy quality than before, the analysis did not consider the impressive volume that could be driven by making copies of higher quality second-generation copies; therefore, they vastly underestimated demand. Another assumption was that customers would want to buy, not rent, the machines (much less pay for each copy from a leased machine).

Two years after IBM turned down the offer, revenues of the Haloid Xerox Company came to nearly $60 million. By 1968, sales reached $1.125 billion, and profits grew from $2.5 million to $138 million.

Obviously, business slipped from IBM's hands into those of others for many reasons. But focusing on the potential of the copying business as a way of exploiting an existing sales force started the decision-making process on a very narrow path. Today, IBM has demonstrated it is less likely to fall prey to missing opportunities by correctly solving the wrong problem. Xerox, on the other hand, subsequently has made decisions that suggest it did not learn from the IBM missed opportunity that gave Xerox its start.[3]

For example, in the mid 1970s, Eastman Kodak, to Xerox's surprise, introduced a medium-volume copier. The copier featured a recirculating document handler that allowed the customer to make multiple copies of complete sets, avoiding the space and time problem of having to collate after printing.

Before Kodak's introduction, Xerox's product planners assumed customers would be concerned over the possibility of damaging original documents by placing them into a recirculating document handler. Basing its moves on this assumption, Xerox had been developing an "escorted" document handler that virtually removed the possibility of damaged originals. The problem was that the cost of developing and manufacturing the "escorted" device was very high. Xerox conducted considerable market research to determine how much customers would pay to avoid damaging originals. Almost by chance, while conducting market research on the escorted document handler, someone asked a Kodak customer why he was not willing to pay much more for the safety of originals. The customer replied that the quality of the Kodak copies was so good that the organization always made a copy of the originals and then ran the *copy* through the document handler.

In this case, Xerox had been working on the wrong problem: developing a technologically complex device to guarantee the safety of originals. It failed to engage the customer in developing a solution, which in this case was to protect originals by running through copies that looked as good as originals. Working on the right problem would have avoided investment of significant development funds on an extremely complex and expensive "escorted" paper handler; instead, it would have dedicated those resources to improving copy quality.

Type IV Errors

Having worked with Russell Ackoff, Ian Mitroff, and others over the last twenty-five years, I have come to understand there is yet another type of error. A Type IV error sometimes occurs when one attempts to solve an ill-defined problem, set in a highly uncertain environment, while acting as if the problem is clear and the environment is understood.

The insidious problem with Type IV errors is that some academic disciplines have developed decision processes that avoid the complexity of reality by accepting "simplifying assumptions" designed to minimize uncertainty. For example, one of GM's very competent operation researchers had proposed to develop a model to optimize the results of new ventures that cut across the whole enterprise — that is, across the major subsidiaries that made up GM at the time (i.e., Hughes; Electronic Data Systems, or EDS; and GMAC). The individual had developed an elegant optimization model. Everyone agreed that the logic of the approach was flawless and that it was an inventive and relatively straightforward application of microeconomic theory based on quantitative data and assumptions about the future.

As this proposal was being reviewed to determine its application, GM was just completing a cross-company pilot project from which OnStar was eventually developed as discussed in chapter 3. Those who participated in the OnStar project indicated they could not have complied with any of the procedural and information assumptions that were explicitly stated as requirements to operate the optimization model. It was pointed out that no quantitative information existed, because this was an entirely new business, nor were there any similar businesses to provide surrogate data specifically of the type required. Additionally, all our assessments of the OnStar venture pointed out that every dimension of the business was extremely sensitive to a full range of alternative business and competitive assumptions, all of which had some likelihood of occurring in the future. In this instance, the optimization model was not accepted.

The limitations of the optimization approach used in this instance are described clearly by a group of distinguished professors, chaired by Herbert Simon of Carnegie Mellon University, in a report developed for the presidential White House science advisor by the National Science Foundation in 1986:

> Central to the body of prescriptive knowledge about decision-making has been the theory of subjective expected utility (SEU), a sophisticated mathematical model of choice that lies at the foundation of most contemporary economics, theoretical statistics, and operations research. SEU theory defines the conditions of perfect utility-maximizing rationality in a world of certainty or in a world in which the probability distributions of all relevant variables can be provided by the decision makers. . . . SEU theory deals only with decision-making; it has nothing to say about how to frame problems, set goals, or develop new alternatives.

> The descriptive theory of problem solving and decision-making is centrally concerned with how people cut problems down to size: how they apply approxi-

mate, heuristic techniques to handle complexity that cannot be handled exactly. Out of this descriptive theory is emerging an augmented and amended prescriptive theory, one that takes account of the gaps and elements of un-realism in SEU theory, by encompassing problem solving as well as choice and demanding the kinds of knowledge, consistency, and computational power that are attainable in the real world.[4]

Given the dominantly mechanistic mindset during most of the twentieth century and the simple machine view of the world that existed, we should not be surprised that many of our problem-solving techniques are based on the SEU approach: dissecting the problem, isolating its constituent parts, and exploring its behavior piece by piece. But, as the distinguished panel pointed out, this tradition of scientific inquiry has left us ill equipped to address highly complex, highly uncertain, and dynamic problems.

Many of the processes, techniques, and assumptions of SEU allow and even encourage us to sidestep complexities that are inherent in the problems we encounter. Sooner or later, our reliance on simplifying assumptions impairs our vision and comprehension of complex issues. Sooner or later, events take unexpected turns. Sooner or later, the answers do not come from taking apart the pieces, sorting things out, and putting them back together again. Sooner or later, we have to operate in the world as it is, not as we have set it up for an experiment.

The complexity of avoiding Type IV errors is compounded when participants in the conflict hold strong points of view on the subject. The hazardous problem of Type IV errors is that participants' failure to acknowledge or account for complexity and uncertainty leads to an enterprise's being ill equipped to anticipate unexpected outcomes, much less to effectively respond to them. And we are doing this to ourselves at a time of unprecedented change and uncertainty in the marketplace and societal environments in which we operate.

Avoiding Errors in Problem Solving

Avoiding errors in problem solving starts by asking the right questions during the framing of the decision to be made. Decision makers often spend too little time with this phase of the process, preferring instead to dash forward toward concrete action. But common sense cautions us otherwise: if you are asking the wrong question, there is no value in spending resources to get the right answer. If a problem well defined is half solved, then a problem ill defined is almost certain to be solved incorrectly.

How decision makers frame an issue shapes the way they will view the entire decision process. The framing must be broad enough to capture the entire scope of the issue. The framing must also be clear enough to alert decision makers to what they know about the issue, as well as to what they do not know and must learn in order to make wise choices.

Dealing with Problems

There are, of course, innumerable ways of addressing problems. Russell Ackoff has developed a taxonomy that distills all the alternatives into four possible actions:

- *Absolution:* To ignore a problem and hope it will take care of itself, go away of its own accord. More problems are treated this way than most of us would care to admit. To manage this way is to manage by default. This is attractive to many managers, because it is much more difficult to attribute responsibility for *not doing* something that *should have* been done than for *doing* something that should *not* have been done. The fact is that "letting well enough alone" sometimes works well.
- *Resolution:* To resolve is do something that yields an outcome that is good enough, that "satisfices."[5] Resolution involves a clinical approach to problems, one that relies heavily on past experience, trial and error, qualitative judgment, and so-called common sense. It focuses more on the uniqueness of a problem than on what it has in common with other problems.
- *Solution.* To do something that yields or comes as close as possible to the best possible outcome, something that optimizes. This involves a research approach to problems, one that relies heavily on experimentation, qualitative analysis, and uncommon sense. It focuses more on the general aspects of a problem than its uniqueness. Problem solving is a major occupation of the management sciences, which emerged in the military during World War II and whose use became the principal thrust of management in the 1950s and 1960s.
- *Dissolution.* To redesign either the entity that has the problem, or its environment, in such a way as to eliminate the problem and enable the system involved to do better in the future than the best it can do today—in a word, to idealize. Dissolution focuses equally on the generality and uniqueness of a problem, and it employs whatever techniques, tools, and methods—clinical or scientific—that can assist in the design process.

The difference between solutions and dissolutions is illustrated by the following very simple example: "Placing the instruction 'Close cover Before Striking' on the fronts of old paper matchbook covers, to prevent flying sparks from igniting the contained matches, constituted a solution to the problem — so long as everyone closed the cover before striking. When the abrasive was placed on the back of the matchbook rather than the front, the problem was dissolved."[6]

Somewhat in the same way, GM's development of the fuel cell vehicle, as described in chapter 5, provides an opportunity for dissolution of environmental concerns raised by the internal combustion engine, by simultaneously requiring efficient and effective means of personal and commercial transportation.

Framing the Problem: "What Is It That We're Trying to Solve?"

Framing is complicated by the fact that there are in reality the following two important and interdependent factors

- *Complexity* is the organizational, temporal, cultural, interpersonal, and logistical aspects of a problem.
- Different *individual perspectives* may or may not be consistent with each other and with reality. In other words, how stakeholders (those who affect or are affected by the outcome) perceive the problem may be inconsistent with reality. Likewise, different stakeholders may have very different perspectives on the issue.

In the process of framing, decision makers must assess to the best of their abilities both the complexity and various stakeholders' perspectives on the problem, in order to gain a comprehensive view of the challenge they will be facing. With this understanding, clarity is gained, and decision makers can identify the decision support tools and steps that will lead to an appropriate decision.

Contending with Complexity: The Nature of the Problem

The complexity of the issue tells about the nature of the issue, or, more specifically, the degree of complexity it entails in terms of organization, logistics, time, and certainty of desired results. Understanding the nature of the issue requires exploration of questions like the following:

- Is the issue self-contained or does it interact heavily with other issues that also need to be addressed? To what extent can we understand these interactions?

- Do decisions and actions regarding the issue take place within a single work group, or must they cut across multiple areas inside—or even outside—an organization?
- Are the timing and sequence for dealing with the issue clear and flexible, or are there other factors that introduce uncertainty, rigidity, or immediacy?
- Can we ascertain with confidence what will probably happen as a result of our decisions, or is there a great deal of uncertainty regarding how stakeholders may react? In other words, to what degree can we predict decision outcomes?
- Is the short-term effect of our planned intervention likely to be different from the long-term effect?

At one extreme are "simple" problems, which are self-contained within a single work team or organization, involving flexible timing and little uncertainty about expected outcomes. At the other extreme are "complex" problems, which intersect with many other challenges to affect stakeholders in multiple areas of an organization, involve difficult issues of timing, and are subject to highly unpredictable, volatile results from decisions.

As decision makers gauge the nature of an issue—its simplicity or complexity—they gain better perspective on the scope of the issue. This gauging also forces them to be explicit about the inherent types of complexity: Does it involve significant uncertainty about a sketchy future or organizational twists and tangles that make implementation a nightmare? Is the immediate issue only a symptom of something much larger and more dysfunctional in the enterprise as a whole? The answers to these questions direct us not only toward clearer and more accurate definition, but also toward which informational and decision support tools will provide the further guidance we need.

Contending with Perspectives: The Importance of a Shared Understanding of the Nature of the Problem

Attempts to identify different perspectives on an issue reveal the extent to which participants in the decision process see the problem differently, and reveal the degree to which they have a shared understanding of the nature of the problem. When stakeholders—those who affect or are affected by the decision to be made—share an understanding of what is involved, it is easier to find solutions that are satisfactory for everyone. To understand perspectives on an issue, decision makers must explore questions such as the following:

- How do various stakeholders inside and outside an enterprise view the issue, at both a rational level and an emotional level?
- Do stakeholders inside and outside the enterprise have well-formed ideas about the nature of the issue, or are their views only partially formed and impressionable?
- Do those involved hold very similar views about the nature of the problem, or are their perspectives varied and disparate?
- Do decision makers understand clearly the views of stakeholders outside the decision circle, who will be affected by outcomes (for example, customers, investors, constituents, or staff members)? Or, alternatively, are decision makers not sufficiently aware of these "external" audiences?
- Do the members of the decision team know each other? Or is this the first time they have worked together as a team?[7]

At one extreme in the realm of perspectives is a situation in which stakeholders have a consistent, closely shared understanding of what the issue entails and prospective solutions. The other extreme is a situation in which there are divergent understandings of the nature of the problem, a situation in which individuals come at the issue from their own angles, without agreeing on what the issue entails or appreciating others' perspectives.

Significantly, having a shared understanding of the issue does not mean stakeholders necessarily agree on what should be done about it. Rather, it means only that stakeholders comprehend and appreciate each other's views. Each person's view of the issue is potentially different, and out of these differences arise opportunities for learning. Additionally, without an understanding of various perspectives on an issue, decision makers cannot craft a solution that sufficiently accommodates everyone and ensures effective implementation.

Perspectives and Complexity: Implications for Framing the Problem

The interaction of perspective and complexity can be expressed in the form of a matrix, in which one axis considers the extent to which perspectives on the issue are the same, particularly as related to complexity. The other axis considers complexity, whether the issue is simple and straightforward, or complex. The matrix is a useful approach in defining the issue and the tools, principles, and techniques available to guide decision makers.

The matrix contains four dominant areas where issues cluster. Problems categorized into these areas present unique challenges to the decision maker and call for unique information and decision support tools to illuminate the prob-

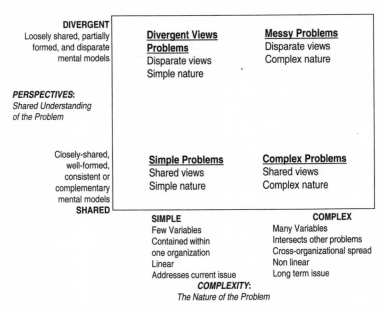

Figure 6.1 Matrix for framing the problem.

lem and guide those involved. Most issues do not fit "neatly" into one of the four types in the matrix; most real-world problems exhibit the characteristics of more than one type. However, characterizing the central challenge of a problem as closer to one type than to another points to approaches more likely to support the decision makers. Chapter 13 revisits this matrix and adds a third dimension addressing the importance of availability and access to quality information in the quest to choose the right decision process for the type of problem being solved.

Mind over Matrix

Decision makers sometimes find themselves at an impasse when they encounter highly complex issues. In such situations, an issue's complexity is its richness: without appreciating the complexity, we cannot solve the problem. But with complexity it is difficult to comprehend a solution, given the human mind's limitations. If we use simplifying assumptions or techniques—like dissecting the problem into constituent parts and addressing them separately—to bring the issue into the range of the human mind's capacities, we effectively "underrepresent" the true complexity. When this occurs, we are not dealing with the reality of the problem.

Because we cannot change either the capacity of the human mind or the complexity of the issues themselves, we must find a way to improve the interaction between the mind and the complexity of the problem in a way that preserves the reality of both original properties of each.[8] The matrix for framing problems is an initial step in this direction. It helps us begin to gauge the amount and type of complexity of issues likely to be encountered and to identify the process for addressing those issues.

Movement on the Matrix

After assessing the degree of complexity in an issue, as well as perspectives, or the degree of stakeholders' shared understanding of the nature of the issue, the issue can be positioned among the problem clusters on the matrix—as a simple problem, a divergent-views problem, a complex problem, or a messy problem—providing greater appreciation for the type of challenges it will present during the search for solutions.

Placing an issue on the matrix begins the process of striving for more clarity as a determination is made of how to approach the issue. Instinctively, most decision makers yearn for clarity: clarity in how people see the issue, what exactly it entails, what the optimal solutions are, and how to implement for optimal results. In terms of the matrix, the natural desire for clarity encourages decision makers to move an issue downward and to the left, toward the quadrant of simple problems.

This desire for clarity is plausible for the vertical axis, where a closely shared understanding of the problem among stakeholders will not only improve decision making in virtually every circumstance, but also greatly influence chances for a successful implementation of the eventual decision. A problem can be moved downward on the matrix by applying some of the following techniques:

- Consider measuring attitudes of those affected, to ensure understanding of their views, as well as how and why those views developed.
- Undertake a communications campaign to broadcast an "official" position and gain widespread support for it.
- Bring key people into a room and conduct a dialogue session to reveal and

test underlying assumptions and understand each other's mental models of the problem and its possible solutions.[9]

These steps typically increase clarity and consistency on the vertical axis, that is, increase a shared understanding and improve conditions for finding a consensus. Once people share the same perspectives on a problem, the right solution will be more evident and result in more effective implementation.

But the instinctual drive for clarity is not so well suited to the horizontal axis, where right-to-left movement affects the very nature, or complexity, of the problem. Moving a problem toward the "simple" quadrant along the horizontal axis would require one or more of the following:

- Reducing or eliminating intersections with other problems
- Reducing how widely the problem spreads across the organization, typically through structural change in the organization
- Reducing the effort to assess the number of unpredictable factors affecting the problem
- Holding constant as predictable some unpredictable factors affecting the problem

Understandably, decision makers may want to take these actions in the belief that doing so will clarify the problem, simplify it, and make it easier to solve. Driving toward this clarity is fine when it comes through research and genuine insight that reduce the uncertainty or unpredictability, or that increase understanding of the problem's logistics or organizational reach. But, in the drive toward clarity, too often decision makers use simplifying assumptions.

Decision makers in today's environment of rapid change and heightened complexity should beware of any attempt to address a messy or complex problem as if it were a simple problem just so they can "make a decision and get on with the business at hand." Instead, decision makers should avoid errors of the fourth type and seek out decision support tools that help them deal with complex issues in all their richness and reality; then they should find solutions that work in a complex, dynamic world, dissolving the problem to find the answer, as was the case with the Hy-wire vehicle and emissions solution described in chapter 5.

Simple Problems

In the matrix, the simplest problems reside in the lower left corner. Simple problems by their nature are the easiest to solve. Stakeholders share common, well-formed views of the issue, which is generally self-contained within a single organization. Decision makers also have some assurance about how future conditions regarding the problem will unfold; there is relatively little uncertainty about the outcome. The issue can be analyzed logically with information capable of predicting future conditions. Decisions made in solving this type of problem prepare and position an organization to meet an expected future.

Simple problems are not necessarily less important than more complicated ones. Rather, decision makers simply find it easier to make the right decision, because there is already agreement on the straightforward nature of the problem, and the issues are well suited to the underlying decision principles of subjective expected utility, as discussed in the introduction to part II. These problems, because of the changing nature of business, are becoming a smaller part of the full range of issues facing the leadership of enterprise.

Divergent-Views Problems

In the upper left corner of the matrix are divergent-views problems, in which the central challenge involves coming to agreement on stakeholders' views or definitions of the problem. This category of problem is relatively simple organizationally and systemically, meaning such a problem does not intersect significantly with many other problems or parts of the organization. However, conflict comes as a result of stakeholders' disparate views about the nature of the problem and its major components. This conflict manifests itself in the following ways:

- Various groups may not have fully formed ideas about what the problem entails.
- It may be difficult to assess stakeholder views with any degree of confidence.
- Decision makers themselves may disagree about what lies at the core of the problem, its scope, and its definition.
- Decision makers may be out of touch with how other groups—particularly those outside their organization—view the problem.
- Various individuals, within the group, may be deeply divided over how they perceive the problem and its effects.

This type of problem is sometimes addressed by Ackoff's concept of "resolution," doing something that yields or comes as close as possible to the best possible outcome. Resolving divergent-views problems involves finding ways to clarify perspectives on the problem throughout the decision-making process, from framing the issue and developing strategy, through implementation and performance tracking over time. Notably, divergent-views problems sometimes occur in an immediate or short time frame, in which there is no time for the environment to change radically enough to affect decision outcomes.

Chapter 8 provides two examples of the effective use of market information to address a divergent-views problem.

Complex Problems

In the lower right-hand corner of the matrix, we find complex problems, in which stakeholders share common, unified views about the definition of the issue, but they struggle with how to handle its extreme complexity. Complex problems intersect with other issues, so they are not straightforward or self-contained. They may involve decisions and implementation steps across many parts of an enterprise, as well as great uncertainty about the future and decision outcomes.

To illuminate complex problems, decision makers need empirically verifiable information that provides insight into the complexity of the problem and suggests alternative solutions. This information should lay out, in systematic ways, all the issues and factors that intersect with a problem, as well as all the levels on which it operates in an organization. Decision makers should identify the uncertain factors that may affect results of the decision and look for ways of minimizing the uncertainty. When this is not possible, decision makers can explore the implications of the uncertainty on decision results and diagnose how the enterprise might respond to the range of potential outcomes. This type of problem is sometimes addressed by Ackoff's concept of solution—"to do something that yields or comes as close as possible to the best possible outcome, something that optimizes."

Chapter 9 shows one approach used to address a complex problem.

Messy Problems

The final quadrant of the matrix involves the most challenging of problems, appropriately named *messy problems*—much like the problem faced by the ABC Company described in chapter 1. These problems require decision makers to operate under extremely difficult conditions, including some or all of the following:

- There is little agreement or comprehension (or both) among decision makers and those affected by the decision regarding the exact nature of the issue.
- The issue cuts across organizational boundaries and levels, complicating both decision making and implementation with its breadth.
- The issue intersects with other processes, problems, and issues in the enterprise, suggesting that a successful solution must be broad and holistic rather than limited and surgical.
- Manifestations of the problem are visible, but the interactions of its parts and causes are not clear.
- The decision must come in the face of unstable, unpredictable conditions that, depending on which condition is activated, may drastically affect the decision outcome.
- Time is a driving force, and its constraints or uncertainties can generate even more complexity.

Key to solving a messy problem is the way decision makers begin thinking about the challenge in the first place. These problems are tough to pin down and isolate, and, given their messiness, isolating individual components would not offer much insight anyway. After all, it is the intersections and uncertainties in messy problems that make them so challenging and potentially rewarding. Trying to simplify these dynamics would yield a solution that was too simplistic. Instead, answers must come out of synthesizing what we learn about how interactions of the pieces affect the whole system. This type of problem is sometimes addressed by Ackoff's concept of dissolution—"to redesign either the entity that has the problem, or its environment, in such a way as to eliminate the problem and enable the system involved to do better in the future than the best it can do today; in a word, to idealize."

Chapter 7 provides examples of different approaches used to address a very messy problem.

7 Solving a Messy Problem

Changing the Way a Product Portfolio Is Developed

Don't do unto others as you would have them do unto you . . . because their tastes might be different.

—George Bernard Shaw

Setting the Right Destination

In 1992, GM's new group of executives decided to develop a strategic car-portfolio plan that made more effective use of a market segmentation model based on customer needs, rather than on the industry-standard product segmentation based on consumer preferences for existing products.

Unlike most vehicle manufacturers that sought to create a single vehicle to appeal to any number of different types of customers in broad product segments (e.g., mid-sized sedans), GM sought to develop different types of vehicles to meet the needs that clustered different customers into needs segments. This approach required a deep understanding of the underlying differences that supported strongly held competing mental models on how to develop a successful portfolio strategy. Although there were strongly held views on the solution, nearly everyone agreed that the current product portfolio had become more of a problem than an asset. This story is how they reached a consensus on a portfolio plan that synthesized market and company knowledge, and also acknowledged the importance of improved quality and a reduction in structural costs. It illustrates the hybrid approach to using the best traits of make-and-sell and sense-and-respond.[1]

The decision process started with review of the full range of alternative portfolio strategies. This intensive review led to the following four alternative positions, each of which represented a participating organization's strongly held divergent mental model of the problem and its solution.

- *Differentiated vehicles.* This alternative was advocated primarily by the marketing organization participants. They believed that GM should make more highly differentiated vehicles in order to win back market share.
- *Fewer but perfect vehicles.* This alternative came primarily from the engineering and manufacturing organizations. They believed that making fewer, nearly perfect vehicles would solve the problem.
- *Reduction of the cost structure.* This alternative came primarily from the finance organization. They argued that the vehicles themselves were not the problem. The problem was the need to reduce our cost structure.
- *Doing in the future what worked in the past.* This alternative was a summation of long-time employees who asked, "Since we have always had it right in the past, why do we need to change now?" Their mental model was to resist any fundamental change. They suggested that we continue doing what we had always done—that we just do it better.

After everyone had a chance to hear the assumptions that supported these strongly held positions, it was clear to the planners that a solution was needed that captured the value found in each of these alternatives and avoided their weaknesses. With the alternatives clearly on the table, the team performed a side-by-side comparison of risk and return for each alternative. The intent was not necessarily to pick the best alternative, but to develop insight into the value embedded in each.

The most compelling finding was that none of the alternatives, on its own, would provide the level of market improvement and financial return required to rebuild GM. In essence, it would take more than a new portfolio of vehicles to rescue the enterprise. As the finance organization had pointed out, GM would have to significantly reduce its structural costs, and, as the engineers had argued, GM would have to improve both actual and perceived vehicle quality. The planners concluded that, after improving GM's cost position and quality, then, and only then, could an improved product portfolio generate billions of dollars in profits. As for the number of products, they realized that GM, as the marketing organization had contended, needed to take advantage of its existing multibrand distribution system to meet customer needs. In this context, GM's broad range of brands was an asset, not the liability that both the engineering and finance organizations had originally assumed.

Even those who felt no fundamental change was needed realized that the rules of the game had changed. In order to ensure enthusiastic customers and segment leadership, GM would have to provide products and services that matched customer needs and offered important attributes, such as quality, reliability, and dependability—all at a value price. And finally, GM would have to communicate to target markets that GM could meet their specific needs better than the competition.

The challenge the team faced was to effectively and efficiently integrate the expertise and insight of each perspective into a unified course of action. It found that each one of the original alternatives was almost right—but not right enough. The decision process allowed all involved to see for themselves that, although their ideas were good, no solution was sufficient by itself for the task at hand.

Eventually, all the shared insights came together in the form of three major findings: a new, hybrid alternative strategy, which combined the best elements of each of the initial alternatives; a concise statement of the underlying rationale for the new plan; and the commitment to allocate resources. Much like the executives of the "hypothetical" ABC Company, the GM executives "came to complete agreement not in principle but in practice." The resulting strategy, based on a market segmentation plan, bore a striking resemblance to an idea developed by Alfred Sloan decades earlier.

Needs-Based Segmentation at GM

Market segmentation was not new to GM. Back in the 1920s, automotive pioneer Alfred Sloan created a segmentation model described as "a car for every purse and purpose."[2] Incorporating keen understanding of market conditions at that time, the segmentation scheme was primarily driven by the extent to which economic status determined the vehicle a person wanted and could afford. The very successful economic hierarchy of Chevrolet, to Pontiac, to Oldsmobile, to Buick, and eventually to Cadillac made both market and business sense. According to business sense, it was an appropriate and very effective segmentation scheme, in that it used GM's understanding of the market to establish a vehicle development system that allowed the production of differentiated vehicles from as many common parts as possible. In 1928, this approach, and Ford's prolonged model changeover, allowed GM to pass Ford in sales volume by meeting different needs, but also to gain economies of scale on the common parts to become cost competitive with Ford's one-model design.[3]

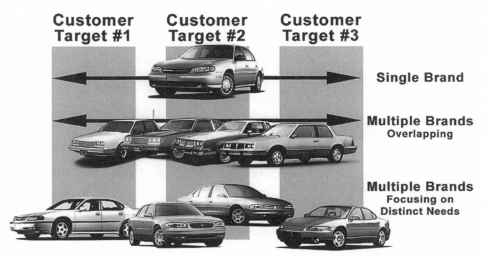

Figure 7.1 Segmentation strategy options for portolio development. Graphic credit: Sam Trella, Trella Productions.

The strategy development team's analysis made it clear that GM, in those parts of the market where each of its divisions had established brands, had the following options in developing a portfolio:

1. Offer a single brand, targeted at the center of a very large segment of customers and have enough options to attract customers at the extremity of the segment. This, of course, is the engineer's dream—a highly focused effort to build as much as is feasible into one vehicle so that customers will "give up" specific requirements in order to acquire a highly valued vehicle.
2. Offer multiple, overlapping brands, targeted at the center of a very large customer segment, off the same platform, to save development costs, and use brand positioning to attract customers at the extremity of the segment.
3. Offer multiple, specific brands targeted at customers with specific needs, off the same platform, but provide sufficient content and performance characteristics to fully satisfy the specific segments. This, of course is the marketing organization's dream. Cluster the customers into segments of sufficient size to warrant the development costs of creating a vehicle for each segment.

Which approach was best? Some GM managers took the position it was option 1. Look at the successes of the Toyota Camry, the Honda Accord, and the Ford Taurus, which were sharing the best-selling car[4] award in the United States in the early 1990s. In the case of Toyota and Honda, their limited product lineup contributed to their very high quality. Using the recently created market research that provided a deep understanding of market conditions, and an assessment GM's current and potential capabilities, including the ability to compete directly with Honda and Toyota, the team agreed on a strategy that was essentially like option 3. The price GM would have to pay to design multiple vehicles to more specifically meet the needs of customer segments was that it would become very difficult to ever be in the race for the best-selling car. The reward would have to be recognized internally as GM's having built and distributed the best-selling platform, upon which highly differentiated vehicles would be developed. The team also recognized that they would have to break the operating paradigm that said you can have a broad product lineup or high quality, but not both.

Although Sloan's original market segmentation based on customers' income levels was successful for many years, it became clear that economic status–based segmentation was now too simplistic for an increasingly complex and fast-paced market environment. The team came to the realization that "a car for every purse and purpose" was not sufficient. What would be required was a portfolio of vehicles based on a full range of needs no longer fully attributable to a person's economic status.

In addition to the need to achieve economies of scale (making more of the same thing less expensively), an enterprise must achieve economies of scope (providing more specific customer products and services from a basic program or platform). Because of the highly personal feelings that many customers have for their vehicles, the team sought a segmentation scheme that captured the dynamics of this more complex market and business.

Choosing the Right Segmentation Approach

During the late 1970s and 1980s, product segmentation dominated the automotive industry. In the late 1980s, needs-based segmentation became an important topic in strategic discussions. The distinction between the two approaches is both simple and profound (table 7.1).

Both systems were based on consumer research (table 7.2).

After careful review of both approaches, GM chose to view the market as segmented into clusters of different types of customers with certain traits and vehicle needs in common and, importantly, not necessarily as based on traditional demographics.

Table 7.1.   Distinctions Between Product and Needs Segmentation

Product Segmentation	Needs Segmentation
Examples: economy sedan, mid-sized coupe, entry luxury	Examples: family affordability, upscale sports
Groups vehicles GM and competitive	Groups people
Driven by shopping consideration (what cars the customer considered while shopping)	Driven by customers' articulated needs
Primarily based on size and price	Primarily based on size, styling, and functionality
Historical perspective (what is available in the market today)	Future perspective (what customers would prefer to be in the market)
Focus on what people buy	Focus on why people buy
Tied to tangible/physical nature of market	Less tangible

The Twenty-First-Century Version of "A Car for Every Purse and Purpose"

CEO Jack Smith had established a clear destination for the firm and set expectations. Among the capabilities required to achieve the goals he set out were the following: (1) understand the voice of the market so well that, with the right product implementation, GM could win back profitable market share (this would require the ability to correctly forecast future customer requirements), and (2) change the decision processes across the organization to be responsive to the voice of the market, reduce cycle time, and create more shareholder value. The report concluded that, assuming the cost and quality problems were remedied, the following would be required to achieve the level of success Smith had called for:

- GM would take advantage of those product categories in which its existing multibrand distribution system was an advantage to meet different cus-

Table 7.2.   Market Research Approach Used for Product and Needs Segmentation

Product Segmentation	Needs Segmentation
This scheme groups vehicles perceived by customers as similar (or substitutes). Vehicles are grouped in product segments based on second-choice market research data derived from the question, "If the vehicle you just purchased were not available, what other vehicle(s) would you have purchased?" If one vehicle is mentioned frequently as the second choice, the two vehicles are assigned to the same product segment.	This scheme groups people according to shared needs or benefits—both physical and psychological—that they are seeking. In accordance with these shared needs and benefits, individual customers are clustered into needs segments.

tomer needs. Properly managed, existing brands could be seen as assets, not liabilities.

- GM's designers and engineers would develop products that ensured enthusiastic customers and segment leadership by providing products and services that not only matched but also exceeded customers' "articulated" vehicle and attitudinal needs. These products and services would also have to possess other threshold attributes, such as quality, reliability, and value pricing. The targets could not be described in broad terms like "baby boomers" and "import buyers."

- Improvements were necessary in productivity and quality. This finding placed significant importance on finding the "right" number of product entries within each product segment, in order to balance the search for market share increase with the ability to provide higher quality vehicles at a profit— in essence, to make sure the company received a greater return on the investment required for each vehicle it chose to develop.

- GM would communicate to target markets that their specific needs would be best met by GM, not by the competition. In other words, GM would have to more effectively and efficiently manage how it communicated the benefits of each of its brands to targeted customers.

Setting the Strategic Direction

The underlying hypothesis of the new portfolio process was based on GM's multibrand ability to distribute highly differentiated vehicles. Therefore, GM must design vehicles to more specifically meet the needs of customers from targeted segments. GM should efficiently and effectively incorporate solutions to those needs into the vehicle, making them so apparent that the targeted customers would choose GM over a competitor whose vehicles met the needs of a broader segment of customers.

All this was based on the premise that GM's quality would equal or exceed the competition and that GM would be able to price its vehicles so they were considered more valuable than the competition.

Meeting Market Needs Better Than the Ford Taurus

The success of Ford's 1986 Taurus is widely known. In its first full year of production, it became the best-selling car in North America, a title it held through

1988, when the Honda Accord surpassed it. An evaluation of its success reveals two important questions: Can market research contribute to new vehicle design? What is the effect of competitive introductions?

In the 1990s, GM was preparing to develop the first vehicle program based on its newly developed portfolio strategy, according, in part, to an extensive market research effort to improve the enterprise understanding of the automotive market. About the same time, in the February 12, 1990, edition of the *Detroit Free Press*, writer Rick Ratliff reported on a market research effort that, allegedly, nearly led to a major error of omission—that is, not doing something that should have been done:

> [Jack] Telnack (vice president of design at Ford) led the team that shaped the Ford Taurus, a car that has reaped many international design awards, spawned a host of imitators and helped Ford become the most profitable manufacturer of the Big Three. This came despite early research which indicated some would react violently against the car's design. Telnack stood his ground, and was rewarded. Today, he believes the future belongs to cars that carry forth new variations of Taurus' so-called "aero look" with smoother corners, low hoods and high trunk areas.[5]

GM's evaluation of Ford's strategy of introducing one vehicle across the entire mid-sized market suggested the vehicle was also successful because it was well proportioned (had the interior size to meet many functional requirements) and looked different and appealing enough to attract people who wanted a distinctive vehicle more than they wanted functionality (fig. 7.2). Its success also seemed to contradict GM's new strategy of multiple vehicles for this core market. As is the case with most successful product programs, success did not happen by accident. There are several versions of the story of the development of the Taurus. What follows is my version, based on published reports and interviews on what was happening in the late 1980s and early 1990s.

The Development of the 1986 Ford Taurus

In the early 1980s, Ford's U.S. car market share and profitability were in decline. Japanese imports appeared to be having a greater impact on Ford than on GM. Some Ford executives felt that that many of its designs were "vanilla"—weak followers of GM.[6]

In Europe, Bob Lutz (then working at Ford of Europe), Uwe Bahnsen, and Jack Telnack had become advocates of the aero look that was evolving in the de-

1986 Taurus

Figure 7.2 1986 Ford Taurus.

signs of European automakers. The Ford Sierra was the first major aero effort and had reasonable market acceptance.

Lutz and Telnack were eventually assigned to Dearborn, Michigan, and brought with them the conviction that Ford needed to establish its own design image in the shape of aero. Initial attempts applied some variant of the aero look to the Tempo/Topaz, then Thunderbird/Cougar, and eventually the Continental. Of these initial attempts, the Thunderbird scored well in the market, and the others did reasonably well.

In the midst of these trial attempts at the aero look, planners were developing the Taurus. An existing Audi influenced the exterior silhouette. But concerns about weight and fuel economy caused Ford to conduct a market research clinic in the early stages. Customers thought the initial concept was too small and appeared to be a poor value.

In their 1988 book *Reinventing the Wheels*, authors Alton Doody and Ron Bingaman reported that the results of the clinic led to specific changes to improve the product. As an example, they pointed out that in April 1981, more than a year after development began, the overall size of the car was drastically changed. They quoted Lewis Velardi, Ford vice president for the Taurus program, as saying "We scrapped the whole car." Their observation of the entire vehicle program, including the basic design and quality standard, led them to condition his statement as follows: " . . . the car was re-engineered to be bigger than originally intended, and this was done because of a perceived change in the targeted market." They summed up the changes by stating "The small prototype of

Taurus was expanded in all dimensions. Its wheelbase was enlarged, its track was widened, and its overall volume was increased."[7]

The *Detroit Free Press* article by Rick Ratliff stated that Ford developed and introduced the Taurus "despite early research which indicated some would react violently against the car's design." The authors of *Reinventing the Wheels* indicate there was more to the study than was provided to the reporter: "Ford researchers also knew that a certain percentage of the American driving population would adamantly dislike the Taurus styling. These would be the types of people . . . who are almost always unreceptive to anything new or different. Ford designers labeled them 'Johnny Lunchbuckets' and, for all practical purposes, these customers were written off as being unreachable—*at least for the first model year or two.*"[8]

Reinventing the Wheels also pointed out that market research not only uncovered the problem but also identified information that led to action plans to overcome it.

Marketing research would go beyond its customary bounds in ferreting out existing consumer attitudes and preferences. It would actually assist in rationalizing attitudes and in changing preferences. In short, the market was to be educated, briefed, and conditioned to appreciate the Taurus and Sable for what they really were, instead of what they merely seemed to be. Doody and Bingaman made the point that market research not only uncovered problems, but also provided insights that led to plans to address them.

Before the Taurus finally reached the market, Team Taurus would disregard or override certain consumer likes and dislikes, even when those likes and dislikes were explicitly revealed through marketing research. Far from reflecting the arbitrariness and arrogance of "old" Detroit, however, these decisions were part of a calculated effort to improve the customers' understanding and appreciation of automotive quality, performance, and aesthetics. It should be recalled that Team Taurus's mission was to build the very best mid-market car that anyone could build. This meant creating a rationally conceived, coherent, functioning piece of equipment; it did not mean tacking together an assortment of features to satisfy any and all of the perceived wants and whims that might emanate from the marketplace. . . . In short, the marketing research role within the team transcended traditional research techniques and parameters. *The objective was not merely to "give the lady what she wants," but to tell the lady why she might want to change her viewpoint or consider an alternative* (emphasis added).[9]

Realizing that it had to overcome some market resistance to the look, but mindful of its objective of getting out from behind GM's designs, Ford went to work *to alter the customer's perception of the aero look*. A massive advertising and public relations effort featuring the even more radically styled Probe, designed in Ford's Ghia Studios, was deployed. The public relations program paid off, as early automotive "buff" magazines gave Taurus high praise for "roadability," package, style, ergonomics, and performance—some rating it the best overall car to come out of Detroit in recent years. Ford was also given credit for "breaking out of the pack" with a dramatic new look.

In this case, Ford listened carefully to its target customers, ensuring that the vehicle was "packaged" right, and took dramatic steps to improve its earlier versions. Regarding the look of the vehicle, however, it did not fall prey to being misled by the average customer response. Instead, it accepted the fact that a portion of its target was uncomfortable with the look, but took action to overcome that reluctance in order to try something new. In this instance, for those who did not initially like the look, the great functionality of the car was sufficiently strong to help Ford convince them that they should try out the look, as well. The balance of these two conditions was managed extremely well and led to a very successful new vehicle program.

GM's Role in the Success of the 1986 Taurus

GM contributed to Ford's success by keeping its mid-sized portfolio of four "look alike" divisional brands in the market longer than it should have (these vehicles were known as the "A" platform). The similarity of these four vehicles can be seen in the Overlapping Multiple Brand option shown earlier in figure 7.1.

Fortune depicted the extent to which GM was actually operating under Option 2, when it was acting as if it was operating under Option 3, in a cover story (published August 22, 1983) titled "Will Success Spoil General Motors?" The *Fortune* cover showed the Chevrolet Celebrity, the Pontiac 6000, the Buick Century, and the Oldsmobile Cutlass in a lineup that visually highlighted the extent to which the vehicles were nearly identical, with the only differentiation being their brand names. Although the cover photograph somewhat exaggerated the similarities, the resulting image was close enough to reality to drive home the point and raise questions about the strategy.

The reason the "lookalike" vehicles stayed as long in the market as they did was due to a string of delays in the design of GM's replacement vehicles, code-name GM-10, which were eventually introduced in 1990, four years after the Taurus. These were the Chevrolet Lumina, Pontiac Grand Prix, Oldsmobile Cutlass Supreme, and Buick Regal. The extent of this problem is reported in a GM publication that chronicles the enterprise's history: "These vehicles proved very expensive to build. They had a long development cycle and were difficult to assemble because of design and engineering complexity; the individual launches were staggered over a two-year period; and sales suffered from quality problems almost immediately after each launch. In addition, at the same time the GM-10 cars were launched, General Motors continued to build and market the older "A" cars. Finally, the initial GM-10 launches were two-door coupes rather than four-door sedans."[10]

So, while Ford was doing some important things right, GM was doing some important things wrong. The extent to which GM's mistakes contributed to Ford's previous successes would not become clear until Ford developed the 1996 Taurus — this time facing a much different GM portfolio of mid-sized vehicles based on its new needs-based segmentation, which was introduced in 1997 through 1999.

The Difference Between the 1996 Taurus and GM's New Mid-Sized Cars

In 1991, Ford set out to redesign its successful Ford Taurus with a single target in mind: not a customer, but the popular Honda Accord, an affordable vehicle best known for its quality, engine performance, and range of features. The Accord had displaced the Taurus as the number-one-selling car in North America.

If Team Taurus made effective use of market research in the development of the 1986 Taurus, the management team for the 1996 Taurus had a different perspective on the value of market research. As reported in *Car*, a book by Mary Walton, who spent three years with the 1996 Taurus design team:

> The stylists hated market research. Did the Vatican recruit Catholics to review Michelangelo's sketches for the Sistine Chapel? Did Frank Lloyd Wright run his architectural plans by a panel of home buyers? Dick Landgraff (1996 Taurus Program Manager) was in their court on this one. He thought the pendulum on market research had swung to an extreme. He was delighted to come across a newspaper article that attributed hard times in the fashion industry to overde-

pendence on a handful of influential consultants, who had believed women when they said they wanted nothing but practical work clothes, which of course was not true. They wanted clothes with pizzazz, just as they always had. It would have been preferable, some said, to rely on the instincts of fashion designers.[11]

With anticipation of the new Taurus mounting within the automotive industry, *Business Week* ran a cover story on July 24, 1995, titled "Taurus: Remaking America's Best-Selling Car."[12] The article revealed additional aspects of how the development team was focusing on competitive vehicles. The development team was under additional pressure because initial reviews of the 1992 Taurus, which was intended as an interim "refresh" before the big changes of 1996, pointed out that, while the update had cost a significant $800 million, Ford had produced a car that was hardly different from its predecessor. Working in this environment, the Taurus design team set out to create a vehicle unlike anything American drivers had seen before.

Although they began by setting their sights on the Honda Accord, by 1991 the Toyota Camry had emerged as an even more popular mid-sized car. The Camry's high-quality premium features, presented for a relatively modest price, was attracting many of the same customers Ford had targeted in its attempt to be better than the Accord. The Taurus team shifted its focus, because it believed Toyota was on to something. Instead of the rallying cry "beat the Accord," the direction switched to "beat the Camry."[13]

The *Business Week* article highlighted Ford's strong desire to have the 1996 Taurus have an even greater impact than the successful 1985 Taurus.[14]

- The new Taurus was to be the first American car that truly matched the quality and engineering of Japanese rivals.[15]
- Ford spent $2.8 billion and five years to develop the new Taurus. It also spent over $100 million in advertising to introduce the new vehicle.[16]
- Ford executives pushed the design team to come up with bold styling. According to the article, Alex Trotman, then CEO, pushed the team to create an entirely unique vehicle. The article reported that, while reviewing early sketches, he told the lead designer, "On the wow scale, this isn't there yet. Give us an absolute grabber."[17]

The article also raised an ominous concern: at the same time Ford was increasing the 1996 Taurus's features, Toyota was cutting back features on its own redesigned 1997 Camry, a vehicle that would come in about $1,000 lower than the previous Camry, thus cutting the price advantage that Ford had been counting on. This left Ford with a mid-sized sedan full of features and with radically new styling, but without the premium quality image of the Camry and the Accord.[18] And the new GM mid-sized cars were about to become a bigger problem.

In the development of the successful 1986 Taurus, Ford made effective use of market information. In the development of the 1996 Taurus it did not use market information as well. Additionally, it targeted competitive vehicles, rather than targeting customers. In essence, it used Honda's and Toyota's old market understanding, which ended up outdated by the time the 1996 Taurus came to market. Ford was skating to where the puck was, not to where the puck was going to be! As reported in *Car*, GM vehicles were not considered a threat: "In December 1994, the advertising agency reviewed its target buyer with Ford for the umpteenth time, 'While imported cars may have seduced them in the past, now they question their intrinsic value,' said a strategy summary. 'They are inclined to buy American this time, but Saturns are too small, *the Lumina and its GM clones too boring*, and the LH [Chrysler mid-sized platform] of dubious quality.' That left, ipso facto, the 1996 Taurus."[19]

GM Uses Market Information Effectively

The first major contributor to GM's current improved market position was the MS2000 program, a major multibrand vehicle program built on the same platform. This program included the Pontiac Grand Prix, Buick Century and Regal, and Oldsmobile Intrigue. The Chevrolet Impala and Monte Carlo were also a part of the program and came out later, again using major components of the existing MS2000 platform.

In addition to not being considered a threat by Ford, these vehicles were almost off the automotive world's radar screen. The replacements for the "too boring Lumina and its GM clones" were not expected by industry observers to wow American drivers.

These vehicles replaced the GM-10 platform vehicles of the late 1980s and early 1990s that were not as well received by targeted customers who purchased the more broadly accepted 1986 Taurus, Camry, and Accord. Each of the vehicles in the MS2000 program, as contrasted with the GM-10 car program, was to be more highly targeted at a group of customers who had expressed their needs

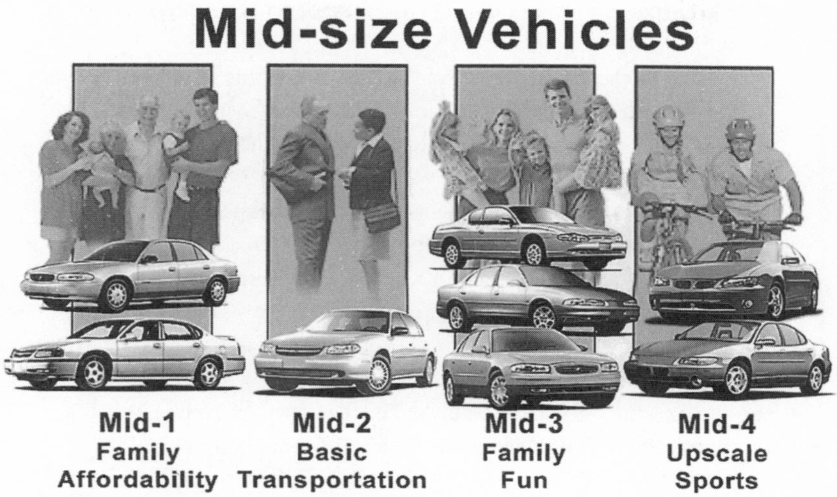

Mid-size Vehicles

Mid-1	Mid-2	Mid-3	Mid-4
Family	**Basic**	**Family**	**Upscale**
Affordability	**Transportation**	**Fun**	**Sports**

Figure 7.3 Mid-sized vehicle segmentation. Graphic credit: Sam Trella, Trella Productions.

in such a manner as to separate them from other customers in the mid-sized market. In this case, each vehicle team was committed to both plan and deliver a product program consistent with option 3.

Program managers for each of these vehicles, given the finding that costs must come down as a basis for future success, were directed to achieve as much commonality across the platform as possible. They were also instructed to ensure that the vehicles were designed with sufficient differentiation so that the customers the vehicle was targeting would be able to "see" and "feel" the differences. The teams established, as an operating principle, that they would focus on exceeding customer expectations, and would maintain a peripheral view of the competition. The vehicle team's interest in the competition, unlike that of the 1996 Taurus program, would be limited to assessing whether their MS2000 vehicle would be able to serve target customers better than the competition.

The vehicles introduced from 1997 to 1999 were targeted to categories of customers as follows (fig. 7.3):

- Buick Century: Consumers looking for value in a practical vehicle. Open, roomy interior with seating for six and conservative, classic styling. We called this mid-1.
- Buick Regal: Consumers looking for a roomy car that did not compromise the appearance and security of a more performance-oriented sedan. It had to

provide the power to pass and merge with confidence. This category was mid-3.

- Oldsmobile Intrigue: Consumers wanting elegant, sophisticated styling (not too sporty) with commensurate performance (premium power train). They would be willing to pay for the right luxury options (the customers were also clustered in mid-3).
- Pontiac Grand Prix: Consumers who were car enthusiasts in the mid-sized market who wanted sporty styling, power, and the feel of the road (a driver-oriented car). They saw the need for a sedan (easier entry for the occasional extra passenger) but preferred a coupe. This category was mid-4.
- Chevrolet Impala and Monte Carlo, to be introduced later, were targeted at mid-1 and mid-3, respectively.
- The mid-2 segment was to be addressed by the Chevrolet Malibu, which was introduced after the MS2000 program off a different platform.

Each of the vehicle development teams immersed itself in the information GM had collected on each of the segments and went into the field to get a better feel for how existing GM and competitive vehicles were meeting the needs expressed by the consumers for whom they were designing their vehicles.

Sometimes the distinctions between segments were quite subtle. For example, the mid-4 "upscale sports" segment epitomized the car enthusiast, the type of person who made it clear that "my car is me!" This type of person felt so strongly about the personalization of his vehicle, that he wanted the driver's area to resemble an airplane cockpit with all the instruments within easy reach of the "pilot." The outward appearance had to be sleek. If the outward appearance compromised the comfort of the backseat passengers, customers in this segment would say, "Too bad; if it is too uncomfortable, don't get in." Customers in the mid-3 "family fun" segment felt the same way about their vehicle, but, because of their family values, they would not compromise the comfort of the backseat for the appearance of the vehicle.

Fred Schaafsma, who at the time was the program manager for the Grand Prix, targeted at the mid-4 segment, exemplified the application of the principle that *the value of information is in how the user reacts to and takes advantage of it*. After spending time understanding what distinguished the customers in his target segment from customers in other GM mid-sized segments, he proclaimed, "I get it— my customers aspire to the equivalent of a four-door Porsche at a Pontiac price." Staying true to the vision in Schaafsma's mind, the roof line on the four-door sedan Grand Prix was exactly the same as that on the Grand Prix two-door coupe.

The intense involvement of the vehicle teams also revealed several unarticulated needs. During market research on-site discussion with customers, the Grand Prix team was able to determine what the customers in its segment meant by the term *performance*. Within the segment, it was primarily about how the vehicle felt when starting out, or, as the engineers described it, "launch feel." The engineers rode with customers to understand the feel that customers actually wanted, instead of trying to translate their words into performance characteristics.

So What Happened?

The underlying hypothesis was confirmed that, if GM designed vehicles to more specifically meet the needs of targeted customers, they would be more likely to purchase GM vehicles than to purchase competing vehicles within the segment.

Of all the customers who purchased the GM mid-sized vehicles at retail, in every instance the highest or second-highest proportion of buyers who bought the vehicle were those in the segment for which that specific vehicle development team designed the vehicle. That is, the Buick Century had its highest proportion of sales in mid-1 (where it was targeted) and its lowest proportion of sales in mid-4 (where the Grand Prix was targeted). The Buick Regal had its highest percentage in mid-3, where it was targeted, and the same was true for the Pontiac Grand Prix in mid-4.

This targeted approach took advantage, to the extent possible, of GM's multibrand strategy. In doing so, GM lessened direct competition among GM entries, resulting in an improved retail market share of 12.5 percent for the GM-10 platform in 1996, to nearly 15.5 percent for the replacement MS2000 in 1999. This increase took place even though the MS2000 program had fewer body styles, was not (at the time of introduction) able to sufficiently reduce the quality-perception issue, and lost sales momentum because of a major autoworkers strike in 1998.

From a broader business perspective, customers saw greater value in each vehicle, which resulted in much higher selling prices for these highly targeted vehicles than for those they replaced. The average selling prices for the GM-10 vehicles were 98 percent of the average selling prices for comparable vehicles in 1994. The MS2000 vehicles selling price rose to 107 percent of the average in 1998. Only the Toyota Camry exceeded the MS2000 vehicles selling prices—another indication of the value of a vehicle's perceived quality.

All this contributed to the MS2000 program's exceeding its program financial targets, leading to a very profitable platform program. As expected, none of the vehicles became the "best-selling" car. In 2001, however, the MS2000 platform was the best-selling mid-sized platform, with annual sales at 641,000 units. At this sales level, the MS2000 program outsold the Camry platform (Camry, Solara, Avalon, and ES300) by 125,000 units, and the Taurus platform (Taurus and Sable) by 185,000 units.

The Flaw of Averages

The success of GM's strategy and the value of the MS2000 program have been mostly missed, because many automotive industry and financial market analysts, in the evaluation of company performance, focus on total GM market share of the industry and pay less attention to segment share, the percentage sold at retail, or the number of entries to achieve that share.[20]

Segment versus Total Share

Given GM's financial condition during the 1992 period, a conscious decision was made to focus on the vehicle segment with the greatest number of customers and where GM had the most brands (mid-sized market) and trucks. The smaller and luxury segments would have to wait for additional funds to become available. Chapter 10 discusses GM's strategy for the luxury segment, which was developed in the late 1990s.

Retail versus Rental and Fleet

The mix of GM's total market share in 1991 was 56 percent retail and 44 percent other (less profitable) sales to rental companies and large company fleets. In the year 2001, it was 67 percent retail. The Ford Taurus had retail share of total sales of 49 percent in 1991 and a 52 percent retail share in 2001.

Market Share Effectiveness

In 1990, GM had a 31.3 percent segment market share. That was the good news. The bad news was that it required twenty entries to achieve that level of market share. At a minimum, an effectiveness goal is to have a firm's market share of entries at least equal the firm's market share. In the 1990 case, GM's twenty entries made up 42 percent of all the vehicles in that segment (versus 31.3 percent mar-

Table 7.3. Market Share Effectiveness

Effectiveness Ratio	GM	Ford	Toyota	Honda
1991	.75	1.73	1.38	2.19
2001	1.10	1.44	1.31	1.36
Differences	+.35	−.29	−.07	−.83

ket share), which is not an effective use of capital and human resources. Table 7.3 illustrates the effect of GM's strategy on not only itself but three major competitors. In this case, GM's 1991 effectiveness ratio of entries relative to market share was .75 (31.3 percent market share divided by 42 percent share of entries). Ford, in 1991, had a 1.73 ratio; Toyota, a 1.38 ratio; and Honda, a 2.19 ratio. This situation was the prime reason that GM's engineers and finance organization insisted that one of the alternatives to be considered in the analysis was to produce fewer, nearly perfect cars. The comparative analysis, however, showed that, although the fewer-vehicles solution had significant merit, it was not sufficient on its own and would have resulted in significant market loss.

In 2001, GM dramatically reduced its number of mid-sized segment entries from twenty to seven, resulting in GM's having just 21.1 percent of the entries. That was the good news. That bad news was GM's market share dropped from 31.3 percent to 23.4 percent of the segment. This market share bad news was tempered, however, by the fact that GM's market share effectiveness had improved dramatically from .72 to 1.1 (23.4 percent market share divided by 21.1 percent of entries). Ford, in 2001, dropped to a 1.44 ratio, Toyota dropped to a 1.31 ratio, and Honda dropped more dramatically to a 1.36 ratio. Although seven entries might not have been the best number for GM to develop, at that time the action was taken, everyone agreed that, "under the circumstances," it was the right choice for GM.

Most important, the long-term systemic benefit of this improvement was the manner in which it addressed the finding that, unless GM became more cost efficient and improved quality, there was little chance of its achieving success with any product portfolio. The effect of reducing the number of entries, along with other interdependent initiatives conducted throughout the entire GM enterprise, contributed to GM's being recognized in 2001 and 2002 as the most improved in productivity among all manufacturers (Harbour Productivity Studies)[21] and among the most improved in quality (J. D. Power and Associates).[22]

Table 7.4.   GM's Performance, Mid-Sized Segment 1990–2000

GM the Segment Leader, 1990	GM the Segment Leader, 2000
Twenty vehicles achieved a market share of 31.3%, which contributed no profits to the enterprise.	Seven vehicles achieved a market share of 23.4%, which led to increased productivity, improved quality, and significantly improved profit.

What a Difference a Decade Makes

This is not to say that the MS2000 lineup of mid-sized vehicles was perfect and could not have been improved. Initial quality was better, but not as good as it is today. Not all the vehicle designs were perfectly executed. Although development and variable costs were improved over previous models, there was room for further improvement.

What it does say is that when GM developed a strategic portfolio approach, based on a diverse distribution system, and improved its execution, the enterprise significantly improved the market share of each of its entries. It also had significant impact on the one-car-fits-all strategy of other companies (table 7.4).

The extent of this impact on other companies is demonstrated by the dramatic impact the targeted strategy had on the Ford Taurus (table 7.5). In addition to the Taurus's dropping from 1996 sales of 515,000 (258,000 retail) to 456,000 (224,000 retail) in 1999, Ford's one-car-for-everyone strategy yielded a reduction in the proportion of its retail sedan sales in the mid-4 (upscale sports) segment, the mid-3 (family fun) segment, and the mid-1 (family affordability) segment, as GM's more highly differentiated vehicles were made available to consumers. The only segment where it increased retail sales was mid-2 (basic transportation), in which the MS2000 program did not develop a vehicle.

In this new environment, Ford faced very difficult pricing strategies. In 1997, Taurus (when sold at retail) had to reduce its selling prices to attract mid-1 customers from the more functionally packaged Chevrolet Lumina and Buick Century. Ford, given its primarily single distribution channel, found itself in the following dilemma: By lowering its price to attract customers in the family affordability (mid-1) segment, it also had to offer the same discount in the family fun (mid-3) and upscale sports (mid-4) segments, where the Taurus appearance and functionality came closest to meeting the needs of the customer in that segment. When mid-3 and mid-4 segment buyers of the Taurus were asked why

Table 7.5.   Impact of GM Mid-Sized Vehicles on Ford Taurus Retail Sales Volume

	Mid-1	Mid-2	Mid-3	Mid-4	Total
1996 Taurus/Sable	90,000	57,000	44,000	67,000	258,000
1999 Taurus/Sable	83,000	58,000	38,000	45,000	224,000
Volume Difference	−7,000	1,000	−6,000	−22,000	−34,000
Percentage Difference	−8%	2%	−14%	−33%	−13%

they purchased the Taurus over the vehicle that was their second choice, price—not the appearance and performance that this segment values highly—was mentioned more often than any other factor. This resulted in the Taurus average selling price dropping from a 104 percent of the average of all vehicles in that market in 1994 to 96 percent in 1998.

Given its multichannel distribution system, GM was able to price the upscale Oldsmobile Intrigue, the more luxurious Buick Regal, and the sportier Pontiac Grand Prix higher than the Lumina and Century. When the customers of these GM vehicles responded to the same questions, exterior styling placed first, and performance and handling placed second. Price as a reason to buy placed third. Significantly, the Grand Prix required no sales incentives for its first two model years.

This situation was an early indicator of the problems Ford would face when it would be less able to rely on profitable truck programs for corporate earnings. Soon, it would face the full force of GM's highly targeted trucks and utilities, the development of which is discussed in chapter 8.

When it became clear that its prime 1996 mid-sized car would not meet its volume and profit expectations, Ford moved quickly to introduce a modified 2000 Taurus. The following description of 2000 Taurus appeared in the October 18, 1999, *Automotive News* article on "2000 Car Highlights" and was accompanied by the caption, "Ford learns Taurus lesson": "The 2000 Ford Taurus, which officially goes on sale Nov. 4, is a sedan with diminished expectations. Ford Division is abandoning the oval styling, football-shaped instrument cluster and tight import-style ride of the current Taurus. A primary lesson Ford learned: Taurus buyers do not want flashy styling that makes them stand out from the crowd. What they want is safety, a quieter car, a softer ride and more conveniences."[23] Ford recently announced that it would discontinue the Taurus in the coming years in favor of an entirely new entry in the mid-sized market.

The description of the "Taurus buyer" in *Automotive News* is very close to the description of the mid-1 and mid-2 needs-based segments that GM came to understand eight years earlier, in 1992. The 1996 Taurus was targeted at the Accord and Camry and was not designed to meet those needs. It did, however, come closer to meeting the needs of mid-3 and mid-4 needs segments. Ford's decision to discontinue the 1996 Taurus, contrasted with the success of the MS2000 platform program, reveals the importance of a multi-brand distribution system that can take advantage of the vehicles that embody the real distinctions between customers across the different needs segments. The story also illuminates the wisdom of Sloan's development of the multifaceted distribution system and common sets of vehicle components to deliver on his promise of "a car for every purse and purpose." Today, of course, we must add to Sloan's wisdom with a vehicle portfolio, distribution system, and effective development and manufacturing processes that provide "a vehicle for every purse, purpose, attitude, need, want, lifestyle, etc."

The MS2000 experience does not mean that understanding customer segmentation leads to improved sales and greater profitability. What it does mean is that information about customer needs, combined with the creative minds of GM human resources, can continue to assist GM management in determining what the future portfolio should be across a full range of possible operating environments.

The lessons from the story of Taurus and GM's battle in the mid-sized market are not unique to the automobile industry. They apply to many other industries in which competition is intense and market segmentation is more complicated than it may have appeared in the past.

The next chapter describes two specific vehicle programs developed under the same significant resource constraints of the early 1990s. These are stories of vehicle development teams that fully applied everything GM knew about the market, its competition, and the consumers, and made difficult decisions that led to great results.

8 Solving a Divergent-Views Problem

Developing the Right Pickup Truck Portfolio and Getting the Right Engine in the Camaro and Firebird

Find out what people like and do more of it. Find out what people don't like and do less of it.

—Kenneth Goode

The previous chapter addressed a messy problem, a problem associated with divergent views across multiple organizations. This chapter addresses problems that also involve divergent views based on different mental models, but, although the decisions are affected by external interests, they are focused within fewer organizations. The role of market research in two examples that will be used here is much more specific than the role of more general market research as applied to the development of the entire car product portfolio. The two examples are (1) an important business issue, the design of a platform for pickup trucks, and (2) an important technical issue, the selection of the right engine for a specific vehicle.

Making a Great Pickup Truck

Immediately after the completion of the design for its car portfolio, GM set out to revamp its full-sized pickup truck program. Although this was another portfolio problem, the complexity of the organizational issues was far less than with the car portfolio, involving two truck-selling divisions (Chevrolet and GMC), rather than six car-selling divisions. There was also a single truck manufacturing organization that would be using a single manufacturing platform, as opposed to multiple car manufacturing organizations using multiple manufacturing platforms.

As pointed out earlier, GM was in the midst of digging itself out of financial disaster. The truck, which had not been refreshed since its introduction in 1987, was targeted for a 1998 rollout. GM did not have enough capital for all the investments that would be required throughout the rest of the decade. The difficult decision had been made, therefore, to refresh ("reskin") the aging CK truck platform rather than design and develop an all-new truck.

Such updates are not uncommon, but, in this case, the Chevy Silverado and the GMC Sierra were already six years old, and the competition, including Ford, Dodge, Nissan, and Toyota, were all scheduled to launch brand-new full-sized trucks of their own in the coming years.

Although the constrained-capital-based decision to not build an all new truck satisfied the requirement to reducing capital spending, a review of the decision would soon make it clear that the proposed solution would create many more problems in the long run, namely a dramatic reduction in GM's truck market share and an even greater loss in long-term revenue and profits.

The truck management team agreed to conduct a significant market research study to not only determine the most beneficial reskin options, but to find out what it would take to maintain truck leadership. The team used the same decision process used successfully in the development of the car product portfolio, because it allowed testing of the mainstream view—that all that was needed was a reskin—against alternatives that some team members were less comfortable considering. Furthermore, it did so in an open manner that engaged all points of view.

The group decided to consider five alternatives:

1. Do nothing (simply bring the truck into compliance with future emissions standards).
2. Update the front-end sheet metal.
3. Reskin the entire truck (the "momentum" strategy).
4. Create an all-new truck.
5. Establish a two-truck strategy, as Ford was expected to do with its new models.

The first two options would have cost less than the proposed reskin, whereas the last two options represented risky, costly investments. Much as was the case in the MS2000 car program, the benefit of the process was that, by weighing all five options equally, the group was able to consider a whole range of possibilities without discounting any of them out of hand.

It is important to recognize that at the time the development began, GM's current trucks were doing extremely well in the marketplace, with approximately half of U.S. truck sales. At the time, GM faced no serious competition. This was about to change. Dodge, Ford, and Toyota were all known to be creating new, innovative trucks certain to give GM a run for its money.

Although a 50 percent market share could not be expected when other manufacturers introduced their own innovative new models, many within GM still felt secure that, even with a simple reskin, GM could not possibly lose too much market share. And furthermore, the company was strapped for cash. Even if it wanted to do more, how could it possibly afford to? This group still felt that a reskin was a good choice. On the other hand, the future was uncertain. What if a reskinned version of the old truck could not hold its own against the competition?

And there were other factors at work in the containing system within which these pickups would be designed, developed, manufactured, and sold. Regardless of the competitive changes, the company would have to update the truck's engines to meet more stringent emissions standards for 1998, the year the truck was slated to hit the market.

GM market analysts had also observed another important trend: the newly introduced extended-cab trucks were becoming extremely popular. In these models, the truck box was still long enough to hold an 8-foot length of wood, but the cab had extra space, either for people or gear. This lengthened cab led to an important new question: Would a third door, located behind the driver's door, be a valuable addition? Would extended cab owners appreciate a third door, or was the present design sufficient? If a third door did matter, the extended-cab version of the truck would require more than a reskin. To produce such a dramatic change, you cannot just cut a new door in the sheet metal; you need to revamp the underlying architecture.

GM also factored into its truck strategy the generally accepted knowledge that Ford was moving into a two-truck strategy, which would split its architecture into heavy- and light-duty categories, thus maximizing the comfort and ride for the light-duty users, while focusing on carrying and towing capabilities for the heavy-duty users. Until that time, truck manufacturers simply compromised on these factors, creating a vehicle that would be acceptable to both types of users but not necessarily perfect for either one.

Realizing the importance of the eventual decision, the truck planning organization worked closely with the market research group to ensure that, whatever the results, they would be accepted as credible by GM management. After a significant review and some preliminary experimentation, the team decided to conduct a major conjoint study using full-sized scale model vehicles.

The conjoint methodology was chosen because it forced potential customers to choose between vehicles described by their features and attributes. By asking the customer to make a series of tradeoff choices, the team was able to quantify the interest level in these features and attributes, including how much the customer valued each part. The team also determined the likelihood that customers would consider or purchase a particular vehicle, according to their summed responses to the features and attributes.

This approach produced two benefits. First, it forced potential customers to make decisions in a more realistic, total-vehicle environment. Second, it reduced the glare of the spotlight on the features or technologies that were being tested, avoiding biases from respondents who might have wished to "please" the questioner with their responses. Researchers asked respondents to weigh numerous attributes, including quality, power train, cab configuration, number of doors, and design, with the understanding that it would be impossible to maximize all factors under all of the alternate strategies.

For the research, GM designers developed realistic, very dense foam models of several alternative designs and illustrated alternative features that could be made available, depending on which of the five strategies GM pursued. The models and the questionnaires were designed to test out regular and extended cabs of various sizes; trucks with two, three, or four doors; and longer and shorter pickup boxes. The foam models were also designed so that the pickup box could be removed and replaced with the rear elements of a utility vehicle. By using this model, the team was able to gain insight into how the different versions would perform both as pickup trucks and sports utility vehicles (SUVs), a step that eventually proved to be extremely valuable. The analysis of the information collected indicated a high level of interest and value in the Dodge Ram's combination of styling and interior-cab roominess.

The assessment indicated that a simply refreshed CK truck pitted against the expected 1994 Dodge Ram introduction would drop GM's share from 51 percent to 35 percent. A similar analysis of the impact of the expected 1996 Ford 150 introduction indicated that it was more likely to appeal to the group preferring the Ram and not cause any further reduction in a future environment that included the reskinned CK truck, the new Dodge Ram, and the new Ford 150. The most devastating assessment took place in an environment that added full-sized pickups from Toyota and Nissan. Toyota, in particular, would be a formidable competitor.

Renowned for outstanding quality in all its vehicles, Toyota was certain to steal a significant portion of the market from GM, which was, unfortunately, perceived as having less than stellar quality in its trucks. The assessment indicated that, although GM would save investment costs, the resulting reskinned CK truck program would lead to a reduction of the company's full-sized truck share from about 50 percent of the market to roughly 25 percent.

As the results of the research began to unfold, cab configuration proved to be a particularly important factor. The research confirmed early results indicating that regular cab users wished they had more room to recline their seats and store their belongings, such as briefcases or toolboxes. Adding 4 or 5 inches behind the seat would solve this problem. In addition, people were beginning to see trucks more as personal-use vehicles. In the past, trucks had been seen as almost entirely utilitarian, vehicles for contractors and tradespeople. They were not usually viewed as personal or family vehicles. In the early 1990s, as GM was conducting its research, this was beginning to change.

This understanding of the value consumers placed on a range of features and attributes was then used by the truck development team to assess the impact of expanding the program beyond a reskin to include attributes consumers valued quite highly, including larger cabs, improved power trains, and better brakes. The conjoint research results indicated that these additional investments would help GM avoid devastating share losses in this critical segment, resulting in a 45 percent market share, even with the advent of newly revised programs from the domestic competitors and two new vehicles introduced by Toyota and Nissan.

Some results were surprising. Asked what they put in their backseats and how often they carried these things, extended-cab owners answered "people" and "daily" most of the time. Clearly, the extended-cab models were being used to move people just as often as "stuff." At the time the research was conducted, most, though not all, of those who used their trucks as personal vehicles also indicated that, from a design perspective, they did not want a more "car-like" vehicle. They wanted trucks that looked like trucks but that drove more like cars.

The results from this conjoint market research were instrumental in assisting the truck organization management team to persuade GM management to significantly increase the investment and scope of the truck program, including specified processes to improve quality, beyond the reskinned CK truck and to the level required to significantly change cab size and power train.

This experience provides an excellent example of a highly focused team that understood customer requirements and incorporated the input into the product. Through extensive effort to better understand the consumer, the truck team identified and prioritized seven key customer focus areas; one of the key areas was comfort and convenience, which included cab size and roominess.

An early follow-on clinic found a surprisingly strong preference for a larger cab. GM market share of clinic respondents nearly doubled with a larger cab. Because several people were skeptical of the results of the first clinic, a different research methodology was used in a later clinic. Mean appeal rating jumped from 2.8 (out of 5) for the old CK cab to 4.2 for a larger cab option. On the strength of this customer input, the team, and the entire GM organization, was convinced to spend the additional $1 billion required to increase the cab size for the new pickups.

With this information in hand, management moved to build an entirely new truck that, although significantly increasing the planned investment, has provided GM with products that have led to truck leadership and improved profits well beyond the incremental investment. The insights the team developed from the market research were extremely accurate in assessing actual consumer behavior in this market (table 8.1).

Cocreation: An Attentive Ear Identifies an Opportunity—Chevrolet Avalanche

In later studies, the group tested whether different combinations of cab size and cargo box length would appeal to different types of customers. During one focus group, an intriguing idea emerged. It quickly became apparent that though customers might want larger cabs, they were mixed in their desire for full-sized box lengths. With the tailgate flipped down, most could still haul lengths of wood, skis, and other long items.

Customers indicated a desire for even more interior space than was currently provided by typical extended-cab pickups. A significant portion indicated a willingness to accept a shorter box to obtain a shorter overall vehicle. One respondent in a focus group first suggested the idea of a "pass through" from the box

Table 8.1.   Comparison of Market Research Preliminary Assessment with Actual Results

Program Alternatives Assessed	1993 Preliminary Assessments	Actual Results (Retail)
GM actual 1993 share	—	52%
GM 1996 share after 1994 Dodge introduction	35%	38%
GM 1998 share after 1996 Ford introduction	35%	36%
GM share after all competitive introductions (Toyota, Nissan), assuming a GM reskin only	25%	—
GM 2001 and 2002 share after all competitive introductions, assuming GM executes larger cab, improved power trains, brakes, and so on (Nissan did not introduce its truck until 2004)	45%	41%

to the cab front, an idea that contributed to the creative design of the innovative Chevrolet Avalanche, first introduced in 2002 (fig. 8.1). This unique vehicle can go from a six-passenger sport utility vehicle (SUV) to a full-sized three-passenger pickup with an 8-foot, 1-inch, protected cargo box in less than a minute, without any tools. When it was introduced, no one had ever seen anything like it.

It is also important to point out that the consumer described the functionality of what he wanted, not the solution. The solution came from the creative and extensive resources of GM's designers and engineers. In 2003, approximately ninety thousand Avalanches were sold. In fact, the availability of the original vehicle has led to a number of successful derivatives, including the Cadillac Escalade EXT.

Overall, the decision process, complemented by the conjoint measurement technology, provided the raw material for the truck organization's keen understanding of the industry and of what was technically feasible to make a very profitable decision. It created and forcefully presented credible assessments of

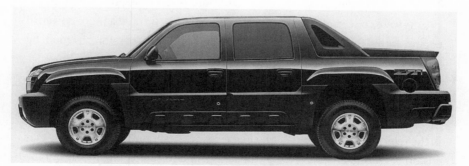

Figure 8.1 Chevrolet Avalanche. Copyright 2003 GM Media Archive.

future behavior, which provided the basis for GM management to make a very expensive investment at a time when there was not a lot of capital to invest. It turned out to be an investment that not only returned a significant financial return, but also positioned the enterprise to increase its position and market share in the SUV product category.

Getting the Right Engine

Another example addressed a problem for which there was a range of alternative solutions, but two functional organizations held different views on their potential.

GM's decision to use a 3800 V6 as the base engine in the 1996 Chevrolet Camaro/Pontiac Firebird illustrates how GM people responsible for decisions—designers, engineers, and those involved in marketing—came to an agreement when they focused their attention on satisfying the customer, as opposed to trying to optimize around the interest of the function they represented.

Before 1996, the base engine for these cars was a 3.4-liter V6. The decision to use the less powerful engine was a financial one, designed to ensure GM was making maximum use of its existing power train production capacity.

Harvey Bell, the chief engineer of the Firebird/Camaro development team, was concerned with the performance of the existing 3.4-liter engine. His impression was that it did not offer a sufficient level of performance or technology for the type of customers that preferred a Camaro or Firebird. Given the sports car appearance of the vehicles and the new aerodynamic design that was being developed, he referred to the vehicles as "sheep in wolves' clothing." In his mind, if GM really wanted to satisfy the customers for whom these vehicles were being targeted, the cars needed a higher performance engine.

But given the competitive pricing conditions of that time, the marketing divisions were concerned that customers, though they wanted a more powerful engine, would find the increased cost too expensive and, therefore, it would be too difficult for the marketing group to sell. In accordance with past experience and market research that supported this view, they believed that customers would not go for the significant price increase.

Faced with differing points of view among the two functional units involved in the vehicles development, Bell sought evidence to support his hypothesis that customers would be willing to pay for a higher performance engine. He put the challenge to the market research community this way: "Don't tell me which engine to use in my car; just describe the performance customers want and let me know their willingness to pay. I'll take care of the details."

Bell's experience acquiring direct customer measurement from the market research group started much earlier. In 1988, as part of an experiment in market research use, Bell attended customer focus groups with the market researchers conducting a study aimed at understanding customer requirements for the sport car market segment. During the discussion, Bell heard strong opinions voiced around the need to be "in control" during the braking process. This emphasis on control differed from conventional wisdom, which held that "stopping distance"—how long it takes to stop from 60 to 0 miles per hour—was the customer's primary concern. As Bell listened to the Camaro/Firebird customers talk about these sporty cars, he understood that the ability to control the vehicle while braking was critical to overall customer satisfaction and confidence. The traditional parameter of stopping distance was a necessary, but insufficient, measure of these customer's concerns.

Using his knowledge of braking systems, Bell was able to translate the targeted customer's need to feel calm and assured while braking into appropriate design requirements. In addition, his team created new measures for braking performance that incorporated this customer concern into subsequent GM brake testing and evaluation. The lesson that he took away from the experience was that people who are responsible for innovation and design need to be directly involved in determining what and how market information is collected. This lesson later played a significant role in the development of the Auto-ChoiceAdvisor discussed in chapter 4.

In the summer of 1992, the market research team supporting the Camaro/Firebird development team used the GM Marketing Dynamics Model (MDM) to attempt to address the challenge posed by Harvey Bell. MDM was based on conjoint methodology, which breaks the vehicle down into a bundle of independent attributes. Customer responses to a series of tradeoff questions generated attribute utility scores and preferences, and provided an indication of how much customers would be willing to pay for these attributes.

The Camaro/Firebird engineers used MDM to evaluate how changes in performance and fuel economy would affect volume and customer satisfaction. In other words, would customers be willing to pay more for the performance of a modified 3.8-liter V6 instead of the existing 3.4-liter V6?

The synthesis of customer and engine-performance data revealed the hypothesis that customers would pay more if engineers could provide simultaneous increases in fuel economy and performance. The basis for this assessment was that many Firebird and Camaro customers could not afford the costs of a V8 sports car, but they still aspired to a higher performance vehicle. The challenge to the engineers was to meet that aspiration at a price the customer was willing to pay.

The proposed solution was found in improving GM's existing 3800 V6 engine's 0 to 60 mph performance from 10 to 8 seconds and simultaneously improving composite fuel economy from 25 miles per gallon to nearly 26 mpg. After a thorough review with all the interested parties, the decision was made, with reasonable confidence, to introduce the 1996 Camaro/Firebird with the modified 3800 V6.

If this was considered an experiment to test out Harvey Bell's hypothesis that customers would be willing to pay for a higher performance engine, in this instance the results supported the hypothesis. After the Camaro/Firebird was launched with the modified 3800 V6 as the base engine in 1996, the early buyer market research compared the satisfaction scores of the 1996 buyers to that of 1995 buyers on engine features. There was a substantial increase in satisfaction scores in both performance satisfaction and fuel economy satisfaction, the precise areas in which the development team had focused their attention and allocated resources to make the necessary improvements (table 8.2).

Camaro/Firebird Percentage of Good Votes

The data virtually spoke for itself. The items the team knew would resonate with these buyers (based on market research) received significantly higher customer satisfaction scores on the new 1996 vehicles than on the old 1995 vehicles.

Harvey Bell, in a review of the program's performance, spoke for the launch team: "The substantial increase in both performance satisfaction and fuel economy satisfaction is confirmation that MDM can be used to establish market-based targets simultaneously for fuel economy and performance, from which a business case can be established."

In this case, deep understanding of customer requirements and willingness to pay for what they really wanted helped overcome significant differences of opinion between engineering and marketing organizations. The key to the

Table 8.2. Customer Satisfaction Before and After Introduction of 1996 Camaro/Firebird

Engine Feature	1995 3.4L	1996 3.8L	Increased Improvement (%)
Freedom from engine noise	69.0	93.0	35
Acceleration/pickup	75.8	98.8	30
Fuel economy	52.7	66.7	27
Smoothness of idle	80.9	94.2	16
Transmission smoothness	81.5	91.8	13
Freedom from transmission whine	81.7	94.4	16
Starting ease	92.7	100.0	4

team's success was the way they discussed the issues and the available information together and then came up with a creative solution—with the customer engaged throughout the dialogue—with a decision tool that synthesized consumer behavior with cost and performance knowledge.

This example, like the truck example, emphasizes the importance of decision processes that ensure a fair and open assessment of alternatives so the eventual direction taken will generate observable customer benefits and a profitable return on capital invested. They also demonstrate the importance of involving the decision makers in the design and use of market information to ensure its relevancy and effective use.

The next chapter addresses a slightly different form of decision-maker involvement—making sure that the true complexity of the problem being addressed is not reduced for the convenience of the information provider and at the expense of the eventual user.

9 Solving a Complex Problem

Averting Unintended Consequences

Everything should be made as simple as possible, but not simpler.

—Albert Einstein

In addition to learning how to better use information in product decisions, GM was also learning how to do the same in the manner in which it marketed its vehicles. This chapter addresses a situation in which the decision makers shared a reasonably consistent view of the problem, but their understanding of the complexity and the manner in which the problem interacted with other aspects of the business, particularly over the longer term, required a significantly different problem solving approach.[1]

The used-car superstores, represented by national chains like AutoNation and CarMax, were able to offer a large selection of nearly new, low-mileage cars with warranties, roadside assistance plans, and services normally available to new-car buyers. Sales for these new stores, only six years old, grew to $13 billion in 1998. Automotive manufacturers were also feeling pressure from dot.com entrepreneurs who were making a strong case that the Internet would soon revolutionize the manner in which new and used cars were sold.

In 1995, Ron Zarrella, group vice president for sales, service, and marketing, was being asked by GM management to respond to press and market analysts' queries regarding the validity of the claims being made by the superstores and Internet companies. In preparation for his response, he asked what information and analysis techniques were available for preparing an answer to these important questions and what it would take to come up with the right strategy to address the issue.

GM, like most of the automotive manufacturers, considered itself in the new-vehicle business, and the sale of used cars was an activity addressed by others.

This attitude was based on the fact that most buyers of new vehicles were keeping their cars an average of more than six years, and given that most used cars offered for sale were over six years old, they were poor substitutes for new cars.

Given the assignment by Zarrella and his commitment to framing the problem, the team gathered all the previous and information and knowledge that was available and put together a simple, working simulation of the market based on the principles of system dynamics—including the ability to observe the interactions of new and used cars and tracked vehicles from production through initial sale or lease, trade-in, the used car market, and, ultimately, scrapping. It also tracked customers moving into and out of the market and included a simple consumer choice model for the new/used purchase decision.

As John Sterman points out in his book *Business Dynamics*, challenging the conventional wisdom, the team expanded the model to include late-model used cars. "Instead of disappearing, trade-ins add to inventories of late model used cars on dealer lots or available for auction. When these cars are purchased, they reenter the stock of late model cars on the road."[2]

As the model was being reviewed, the team was puzzled as to the sources of the superstores' large inventories of attractive late-model cars. It soon became clear that the entire automobile industry had invested in major quality-improvement programs that resulted in late-1990s vehicles being significantly higher in quality and reliability that those produced in the 1980s.

Although insightful, this observation was not sufficient to fully explain the dramatic increase in sales at the superstores. Making full use of the comprehensive nature of the initial simulation model it had developed, the team conducted a further review that revealed an unexpected finding—the effect of short-term leases.

Marketing teams in the early 1990s found that short-term leases were an efficient way to increase sales. These short-term leases, combined with the extent to which vehicle quality had improved, led to these leased vehicles being more valuable at the end of their lease than they had been in the past. This was extremely important because the higher the residual value at the end of a lease, the lower the lease payments. Customers also had the option of buying the car at the end of the lease at a specified price. This was great for the customer because it transferred the risk of a drop in the resale price of the vehicle to the lease-maker. During this period, lease terms were typically 2 to 4 years. Relative to a longer ownership cycle of vehicles bought new, these shorter-term leases stimulated sales by cutting the trade-in cycle time. Leasing as a share of total sales increased from 4 percent in 1990 to more than 22 percent in 1997.

From the marketing department's perspective, leasing was a great way of stimulating sales. Faced with dwindling market demand, the marketing department could increase incentives not by the traditional reduction in price, but by providing a higher fixed resale price for the leased vehicle, resulting in lower monthly payments. As Sterman notes, "If all new car buyers switched to leases with an average term of three years, the trade-in cycle time would be cut in half and new car sales would double—all else being equal."[3]

But not all else was equal. The leasing actions had significant interactions with other elements of the vehicle business. In reviewing this assumption, the team found that in addition to increasing the sales of new vehicles, continuation of short-term leases would also increase the availability of nearly new vehicles, and now there were superstores in the market to sell them as an attractive alternative to many people. The other effect was that as the number of nearly-new used cars increased, used car prices could plummet, leaving people who bought a new car and kept it for six years with a vehicle lacking the trade-in value they had counted on for the purchase of their next new car. If they could not afford the difference between their trade-in value and the price of a new car, they would be able to acquire a leased trade-in vehicle.

The simulations also indicated that when the leases shortened the average trade-in cycle, the average quality of used cars for sale could increase, leading more people to choose off-lease vehicles instead of buying new. The analysis also indicated that the used market could feed back to reduce the number of customers who chose to buy their car when their lease expires. This was a critical observation because when, at lease end, used car prices are higher than the residual value written into the lease, the customer normally purchases the car below market value. If, as the analysis indicated, because of actions being taken in short-term leases, used car prices dropped below residual values, more customers would turn their cars back in and walk away. The number of high-quality, late-model cars would increase, resulting in a decrease in used car prices and creating a vicious, rather than virtuous, circle.

The marketing strategy of short-term leases in the early 1990s led to increased sales, demonstrating that leasing helps "sell" more vehicles. As a result, marketing departments continued to develop and allocate resources to even more aggressive leasing programs. By staying on that course, however, they would eventually find out that the total financial impact of these increased "sales" is only felt after a long delay, and that there was little that could be done to undo the earlier decisions.

The work by the decision support team, though, did provide an early warning signal that that leasing would eventually create a glut of high-quality, nearly new cars, leading to a depression of late-model used-car prices. The synthesis of all information available indicated that new-car sales could suffer as more consumers opted for inexpensive off-lease vehicles. This insight raised the possibility that GMAC, GM's financial organization, would face losses as used vehicle values fell short of the residual value it had booked (and as fewer consumers exercised their option to buy, returning the car instead).

It soon became clear that by the marketing organization's use of leasing to shorten trade-in cycle times and fleet sales, GM and other automakers were creating a glut of high-quality used cars at attractive prices. Superstores were, to some extent, simply the market response to the opportunity the manufacturers had created.

Further analysis suggested GM should de-emphasize leasing, exactly counter to industry trends. Still, even if leasing was a devil's bargain, every automaker felt strong pressure to match the terms and prices of its competitors. Once all major manufacturers were offering short lease terms with aggressive subvention, unilaterally backing away from leasing might risk too much market share —a factor that had to be considered in the model as well.

Once the model was as complete as possible, the decision support team set out to share it with senior management. In doing so, however, the team took further advantage of the dynamic model it had built. But instead of making a presentation, as Sterman describes it:

> They configured the model as an interactive management flight simulator. A "dashboard" contained dials and gauges reporting standard accounting information such as inventory levels, sales volumes, prices, market share, and profitability. Players set production targets, incentives, lease terms, and so on. By clicking a button on the screen, players could get additional information, including the structure and assumptions of the model.
>
> By playing the game instead of listening to a presentation, Zarrella and his management team explored the dynamics of leasing for themselves. They could try various strategies, from aggressive subvention of leases to pulling out of the lease market altogether, and see approximations of the possible impact on sales and profits in the short run and the long run. They came to believe that the full

impact of leasing decisions took up to five years to play out. While leasing did provide a lift to sales in the short run, it often caused problems when the off-lease cars returned to the market.[4]

The effort led to two compelling observations. First, GM would need to shift incentives to favor longer leases. Second, it was imperative to conduct a formal analysis to determine the impact of any pricing or marketing proposal on the used car market and its feedback to the new-car market. The market research organization was directed to develop and maintain research studies to better understand consumer behavior and to design the research program so that data would be continuously available.

These suggestions were met with general agreement. Still, some individuals, particularly those with highly focused functional responsibility, remained skeptical. The following story provides insight into the need to understand and, where possible, modify existing mindsets.

During a progress review, one of the executives who had considerable familiarity with the used-car activities in GM, including the auction process, was shown a chart that showed the behavior of different variables over time.

Since the team was very early in the process it was working with preliminary data and had not fully labeled all the charts. In the case of the chart being reviewed, the units for the time axis were not labeled; as such, the x-axis numbers read from "0" to "120." Early in the review the experienced functional executive informed the modeling team, "This is all very interesting, but you have your time perspective all wrong. It is much too long. It shouldn't be 120 days—it needs to be something in the range of 20 to 30 days to be meaningful."

After an awkward pause, the team informed the executive that the axis was not 120 days, but rather 120 *months*! After an even longer pause of surprise on his part, he stood up and began to walk out of the meeting, saying, "This is way off base, and I'm not going to waste my time any more." Before he got out the door, Nick Pudar, the team leader, asked, "Would you agree that the situation we are all in is a mess?" The response was, "Yes." Nick then asked, "Well, if this is just a 20–30 day issue, then who made the decision last month that put us in this mess? Let's fire him!" The executive replied, "But these decisions were made years ago . . . " His voice trailed off, and he paused, realizing that his narrow focus on the time frame for his functional activity had led him to miss the potential benefit of understanding the time frame and the interactions of the whole system. He returned to the room, sat down again, and said, "OK, I'm listening."

In 1995, GM decided to focus on thirty-six- to forty-eight-month terms and to reduce the number of two-year leases. It also decided not to increase residual values and to move to full accrual of residual risk in calculating reserves. These actions made subvention much more expensive to brand managers and raised lease payments. While these decisions were not uniformly popular, particularly with the marketing organization, they paid off in the long run.

GM acted, in this case, on the wisdom of Ackoff's admonition that "management should be directed at the interactions of the parts, and not the actions of the parts taken separately." As GM discovered, leasing was *not* separate from the used- and new-vehicle markets. Market share today was *not* separate from market share tomorrow.

Sterman reports in his case study the following similar findings.

In 1997 a flood of off-lease vehicles inundated the market. Used car prices fell significantly.

As prices fell, fewer customers opted to keep their cars. The Consumer Banking Association reported that the fraction of vehicles from expiring full-term leases returned to lessor, rather than be purchased by the lessee, jumped from 29% in 1997 to 39% in 1998. Compounding the problem, about three-quarters of all off-lease vehicles returned to lessor incurred losses. The average loss in 1998 was $1878 per vehicle, 220% more than the average for 1993.

GM's early action helped it avoid these losses, while other carmakers found themselves facing huge reconciliation charges. Profits at Ford Credit Corporation fell $410 million in 1997 compared to 1996, a 28% drop, largely due to losses on off-lease vehicles. At GMAC, net income from automotive financing operations fell only $36 million, less than 4%, and overall GMAC profits rose more than 6%.

In 1998 GE Capital dropped its partnership with Chrysler to finance leases because, as *Automotive News* (24 August, p.1.) reported:

> GE Capital Auto Financial Services got burned on residual-value losses in 1997. Much of that was due to off-lease products from Chrysler . . . GE Capital cited residual losses as one reason for the decline in operating profits for Consumer Services, the GE unit that includes Auto Financial Services. Profits fell from $1.3 billion in 1996 to $563 million [in 1997].

In 1998 net income at Ford Credit rose $53 million over the depressed level of 1997 but remained 25% below the net for 1996 (excluding one-time income from asset sales). GMAC's net on auto financing rose $74 million over 1997, a rise of 4% over 1996, and total GMAC profit for 1998 rose $181 million over

1996, a gain of 15%. In 1998 Ford and other carmakers belatedly followed GM's lead and began to move away from short-term leasing.[5]

The possible negative interaction of the forces indirectly involved in and affected by leasing became clear only after the consequences of a current decision were simulated over a longer course of time. By taking the time to understand the impact of the interactions over time, GM was able to anticipate the used-vehicle problem, and take action to avoid a significant unanticipated problem.

The general principle that is illustrated in this example is that complex problems almost always involve interacting elements. Remedying one element does not remedy the problem if it fails to take into account the interacting effects of other elements. Additionally, approximating the potential effects of these interactions over a prolonged time period alerts the decision maker to possible positive or negative unintended longer term consequences.

The next chapter brings together what was learned in the types of problem solving discussed in part II. It brings further clarity and relevance to the principle of "it's not about one approach *or* another, but one approach *and* another."

10 Applying What You Have Learned

Restoring an Existing Brand and Establishing a New One

Indeed it has been said that we are now living in a second industrial revolution; but instead of steam, the new revolution is being propelled by information. And, as in the first revolution, relative success will be determined by the ability to handle the propelling force. . . . There can be little doubt that the need today is for conceptual skills, that is, the ability to process information and make judgments.

—Robin Hogarth

The first four chapters of part II have provided examples of how planners used problem-solving approaches, combined with relevant market information, to develop a new segmentation scheme for addressing a product portfolio problem; met different customer requirements from a single product base; designed a successful repositioning of an aging product line; determined the correct feature to incorporate in a specialty product; and reduced the chances that today's solution would become tomorrow's problem. All of these initiatives were based primarily on the make-and-sell and sense-and-respond business designs and resulted in important incremental improvements in GM's market and financial condition. These initiatives, as well as significant improvements in productivity and quality, positioned the enterprise to take additional risks as it sought to regain its role as industry leader.

But being positioned for greatness does not guarantee it. The world in general and the market in particular are becoming more complex and are changing more quickly than ever. Whatever GM did well in yesterday's business design will not be sufficient to deliver the full promise of its improved position. This chapter identifies two initiatives: restoring a famous brand and establishing a new one. Each example demonstrates the thinking and actions required to take full advantage of the benefits of sense-and-respond. The examples also show how the enterprise began developing the mental model essential to take advantage also of the benefits of anticipate-and-lead. In essence, previous chapters discuss how GM effectively employed the make-and-sell and sense-and-respond business designs. This chapter focuses more on how the enterprise used those capabilities to move closer to some of the traits found in anticipate-and-lead.

Cadillac: Restoring an Existing Brand

In 1992,Cadillac, with sales of 211,000 vehicles, appeared to be the clear leader among luxury brands. The total sales number, was, however, masking the fact that only 148,000 of those purchased were sold at retail, meaning 63,000 (30 percent) were sold through less profitable fleet sales. Among luxury brands, the Cadillac ratio of fleet to retail sales was exceeded only by Lincoln. In 1997, with total sales of 183,000 vehicles, it was not long a question of whether Cadillac was in trouble—it was. The buyer base was aging rather rapidly, and Cadillac needed to do something different to both attract younger buyers and reassure its existing customer base that it was not abandoning them. By 1999, sales would fall to 176,000.

GM faced a critical issue: if Cadillac was still to serve as the flagship for GM, what should the Cadillac brand stand for? The question could be addressed in two different ways, which would lead to entirely different directions for the brand: (1) What is the modern-day expression for Cadillac, and (2) what is a different expression for Cadillac?

Cadillac's managers did not want to shift the focus solely onto younger buyers; rather, they wanted to expand the brand's attractiveness to the luxury consumer—no matter what his or her age. The team led by John Smith, general manager of the Cadillac division (now group vice president of North American Vehicle Sales, Service and Marketing) and Wayne Cherry, head of GM design, decided to answer the first question. Rather than turning Cadillac into something new, the team members chose to bring the brand back to its roots.

In answering the question, they touched on important aspects of anticipate-and-lead:

- Leading by adapting your business design for anticipated changes in business conditions and consumer preferences (some of which you create)

- Growing into new areas of the business and avoiding the zone of discomfort
- Creating the business you want

Given the team's decision to answer the question, What is the modern-day expression for Cadillac?, it started by looking at the things that made Cadillac great in the past. This review was not limited to the obvious items like the tail-fins on the 1959 Eldorado or the first self-starter. Instead, the team dug deeper to identify the aspects of Cadillac that really set it apart from other brands.

Getting to the Essence of Cadillac

As the team began to synthesize what it had found, it soon became clear that what set Cadillac apart was a pronounced risk-taking attitude. The team saw it deployed in styling elements and technological advances. The most memorable Cadillacs of the past boasted bold, distinctive designs and offered technologies previously unavailable in other vehicles. With these findings and observations, the team chose the phrase *art and science* as a modern description of the design and technology characteristics previous designers and developers of Cadillac had introduced by being risk takers.

The team accepted the fact that the current Cadillac vehicles did not truly represent this heritage and therefore were not attracting the type of customers Cadillac had attracted in the past. The Cadillac buyer of the 1980s and 1990s was characterized more by age and income than by devotion to design and technology. And while Cadillac buyers had always prided themselves on owning a premium brand, current owners now had their choice of many more premium offerings than their predecessors.

With this understanding, the team began by focusing not only on what a typical current Cadillac customer would want, but also on what would influence future buyers. Its members looked at the physical environment of their target customers and the things that excited them, and considered how these influences could be designed into vehicles. They accepted the conventional wisdom that "a young man won't buy an old man's car, but an old man will buy a young man's car." Since a younger generation of buyers had grown up using and relying on the advantages computers provide, the visual interpretation of the art and science design theme was edgy and computer-drawn. This design decision was not based, to any great extent, on consumer research.

The team also looked at specific technology characteristics that its members felt would be important to upcoming generations of luxury-vehicle purchasers. In this category, the team was much more influenced by consumer research. The list of possible technologies fell into three categories:

1. Active safety (as opposed to passive safety), technology that enables you to avoid an accident
2. All-wheel control
3. Infotainment

The team realized that Cadillac would have to find a bold and memorable new look and lead in the three technology areas if it was to reestablish itself as a risk-taking leader in automotive design and technology.

Returning to GM's Roots of Anticipating Change

The idea of taking the pulse of American drivers to determine what they might want in the future was not new to GM, though it had fallen out of use over the course of several decades.

Henry "Buck" Weaver, GM's first director of consumer research was a real trailblazer. In a 1932 edition of GM's market research newsletter, "The Proving Ground of Public Opinion," Weaver and his colleagues explored one of the least understood aspects of the business—vehicle design—particularly the issue they referred to as "streamlining."[1] At the time, the roads were filled with box-shaped vehicles, functional transportation with less than exciting design.

But Weaver knew there were people out there who were already thinking ahead of the general population. He called them "motor enthusiasts"—people that today we would call "market mavens" or "early adopters"—and he was hearing from them more and more on "the desirability of straight, rakish lines, low hung construction and a tendency toward the aero-dynamic design." He realized that the signals he was receiving on this issue were "in advance of the industry's offerings to date."[2] By no means did Weaver mean to discount the creativity of GM's designers and engineers. As he said, "It is not the purpose of Consumer Research to unearth new and original ideas on styling, but to afford some indication as to the boundary lines of public acceptance."[3] And this is exactly what he was discovering: the public was ready for something that GM had not yet designed.

Being something of a detective, Weaver speculated on where this preference for streamlining might have come from: "There are few homes in America containing a child under 20 wherein the adults are not stumbling over streamline toy aeroplanes and 'Zeps.'"[4] He noted that, in the past, toy cars had typically been four to five years behind current designs. But, in the early 1930s, the situation had obviously changed. As Weaver realized, toy cars were more likely to have an ultramodern, streamlined design. And he speculated that these toys were influencing public opinion about real cars, because toy shops were selling more than five million toy airplanes each year. Children—and the adults they lived with—were becoming accustomed to the streamlined designs of these cars and planes, and they were ready to see similar designs on the road.

The newsletter report ties Weaver's philosophy of integrating knowledge of human wants and needs with the application of engineering and manufacturing skills. As he wrote, "Streamlining may bring about radical changes in chassis construction over the next few years."[5] He could not have been more right.

Cadillac was undertaking a similar effort as it tried to determine how to position itself for the twenty-first century. The entire positioning effort was completed in less than six months. Cadillac was reenvisioned (not reinvented) in a way that anticipated changes likely to occur over the next ten years, when new generations would become older and have enough income to make a luxury purchase.

The first public visual representation of the art and science concept was the Cadillac XLR (fig. 10.1), introduced at the 1999 North American International

Figure 10.1 2003 Cadillac XLR. Copyright 2003 GM Media Archive.

Auto Show in Detroit. The concept vehicle, a rear-wheel-drive two-seater with a retractable hardtop, was called the Evoq. The positive reaction to the concept was not limited to the younger generation or the North American market. By trying to reach younger buyers, yet staying true to the design and technological risk-taking history of Cadillac in a modern-day way, the team got what they had hoped for: a positive response from younger buyers, plus the reassurance that current luxury owners liked it, as well. Today's buyers of imported luxury vehicles and people who had grown up with Cadillac found the car very appealing.

Though its sights were set on the future, the team still wanted to avoid the zone of discomfort inherent in moving Cadillac in a new direction. As they went through the transition, they still had to focus on the existing business and the preferences of current customers.

Finding the Right Mix of Make-and-Sell, Sense-and-Respond, and Anticipate-and-Lead

Once the team convinced GM management that the art and science theme had the potential to improve Cadillac's position, it was faced with serious questions about what to do between then and when the new vehicles could be designed, developed, and produced. Importantly, much as with the idealized design described in chapter 1, the team's knowing where it wanted to go provided guidance on how to take advantage of opportunities that began to emerge.

The first of these opportunities was not the introduction of Cadillac's first sports utility vehicle based on a truck platform, but the first follow-up to that introduction. The first SUV, the Escalade, was simply a response to a missed opportunity. In 1995, Cadillac decided not to bring out a luxury SUV. It did not take long to realize that was the wrong decision. Other manufacturers, particularly Mercedes, Lexus, and Lincoln, entered—and soon dominated—the luxury truck business. To avoid being left completely out of the market, Cadillac modified the successful GMC Yukon wherever feasible to introduce Cadillac design elements into the stopgap introduction of the Escalade.

In retrospect, this was a smart sense-and-respond move. The Escalade generated significant revenue, for both GM and its Cadillac dealers, and it began to have a positive effect on the brand. It was not what people expected from Cadillac—a big, "bad-looking" SUV, introduced in television commercials with the rock song "Bad to the Bone." Whether consciously or not, many people began to change their perceptions of Cadillac.

From the perspective of appearance, few inside GM appreciated the effect the first generation Escalade was having on pop culture celebrities. The full impact of this effect would become abundantly clear when the second generation Escalade came out just two years later.

From the technology perspective, it is interesting to note the influence of Escalade on OnStar and the influence of OnStar on Escalade. At the time Cadillac approached OnStar about making the service standard equipment on the new Escalade, GM was reconsidering its original strategy of offering OnStar as a dealer-installed option. Offering OnStar as an aftermarket option was not working well, and GM had to find a way to make it more appealing and more readily available to its customers. The Escalade team proposed putting OnStar at the center of its marketing campaign, but doing so would require making OnStar standard equipment on all Cadillac Escalades. Unfortunately, factory installation had not been tested. Although Cadillac was OnStar's biggest supporter, it could not afford to have quality problems tarnish the launch of a new vehicle brand. They had to be sure it would work.

Since Escalade had not yet begun production, GM had a five-month window of opportunity to reengineer the assembly line to include OnStar hardware. No program had ever been put into a GM plant in that time frame. However, if the Escalade program was successful, it would be a huge boost for OnStar and the evidence needed to show that factory installation could work. And, if it worked, OnStar might then be installed on many other GM models.

Once the decision was made to try factory installation for the 1999 Escalade, GM faced the dilemma of managing the interactions of the parts when each of the parts was operating in different time frames. The Escalade program would not provide any meaningful results for months, and a decision had to be made immediately if OnStar hoped to be included on any additional 2000 model vehicles. Even greater questions lingered, such as how factory installation would affect both GM's and OnStar's businesses, and how to successfully reintroduce OnStar to GM dealers. What impact would a significant increase in new technology and the volume of new OnStar customers have on service quality and system reliability?

GM decided to go ahead with factory installation and to use the Escalade experience as a test case for factory installing OnStar in other vehicles. By the middle of 1999, early results from the Escalade pilot test indicated that the program was likely to be a success. According to J. D. Power and Associates, 42 percent of Escalade buyers stated OnStar was a factor in their purchase decision, and 23 percent said it was the reason they bought a Cadillac rather than a competing luxury sport utility vehicle.[6] Escalade helped boost OnStar, and OnStar helped boost Escalade. Taking the option of a promised future return if the electronic functionality was embedded in the vehicle paid off for Cadillac in particular and GM overall, especially considering the then make-and-sell mindset of the enterprise.

If the first Escalade attempted to operate within more of a sense-and-respond design, the second generation Escalade was more a forerunner for the anticipate-and-lead business design. Although the basic structure of the existing truck platform went unchanged, the team had a much cleaner slate when they went to work on appearance and technology. The new Cadillac form vocabulary was introduced, and technology reflected what tomorrow's consumer would want. To satisfy the desire for "active safety," Cadillac offered the following:

- StabiliTrak—a system that helps control the car on a variety of road surfaces, in inclement weather, and in avoidance maneuvers. When Stabili-Trak's sensors determine that the vehicle is not properly responding to your steering commands, the system precisely applies one, or both, of the front brakes to help you keep the car on the course being steered and under control.
- Night Vision—a visual-enhancement system that provides drivers additional visual information beyond what their eyes are capable of seeing. Night Vision helps the driver detect potentially dangerous situations well beyond the normal headlight range.
- OnStar—a system whose benefits were discussed in chapter 3.

All of the decisions to bring individual technologies into the vehicle, either as standard features or as options, were based on management's expectations of what tomorrow's consumer might want—or would want if it were available.

Relevance to a Idealized Destination

The Cadillac leadership team could not have accomplished what it did in any of these examples without having anticipated future customer and market conditions and then taken the measured risks of leading both the internal GM resources and the entire market into a new view of and belief in Cadillac. By reenvisioning the brand and gaining the right level of commitment to that vision, the team was able to learn from its primarily make-and-sell mentality and its

Figure 10.2 2003 Cadillac CTS. Copyright 2003 GM Media Archive.

emerging skills in sense-and-respond. It took the time to understand the history and the characteristics that had made Cadillac great. It sought out and found the "DNA code" that had made the brand great and set about reestablishing it.

The team used existing market information to better understand what tomorrow's luxury consumers might want and how they might want to receive it. All of this researched-based effort reflected the science part of art and science. Insight into the art part came primarily from the intuitive and creative skills of the design team. Wayne Cherry proposed planes and edges as design cues because there was nothing out there like them. He came to his decision in much the same way as the people who made the call to put outrageous fins on the 1959 Cadillac Eldorado. Today, the design is considered classic, but forty years ago it was daring.

The result of this willingness to take chances came through in design and engineering decisions related to the Cadillac CTS sedan, introduced in 2002 (fig. 10.2). With its sheer forms, sharp edges, and crisp intersecting lines, the CTS at once honored Cadillac's past and pointed toward its future. But not everyone was convinced.

Initial consumer research, much like that conducted by Ford for the 1986 Taurus that was discussed in chapter 7, indicated that, while some target customers liked the CTS's starker appearance, others did not. Still, the Cadillac team held fast to its understanding of the future market by following three guidelines:

1. The members trusted the strength of their own convictions. What set Cadillac apart was that it was different. Very different. The current path was very different. It is better to be at one end or the other—never in the middle.
2. The only thing the public had seen was the Evoq. And the response there was cross-generational and global. The CTS was to be that vehicle in sedan form.
3. The automotive media loved the car. They understood why this was the right car to build.

With these beliefs, the team consciously rejected the strategy of taking design elements from the past and going down a retro path. Cadillac was never retro. It was always original. These choices were not made by the customers who were surveyed, although what they said was listened to and considered.

The market research did not deter the team from taking the risk of introducing a bold, new, and somewhat controversial design. The market research did, however, alert the team that there would be some resistance to the appearance of the vehicle, which contributed to their plan on how to introduce, price, and position the vehicle. The actual decisions were made by people anticipating what would position Cadillac to be a leading luxury brand and taking risks to lead the enterprise to actually design, develop, and produce the vehicle.

With the introduction of the Escalade in late 1999 and the CTS in 2002, total sales increased to 194,000 vehicles from the low of 175,000 in 1999. As important, the ratio of fleet sales to retail sales had fallen from 30 percent in 1992 to 13 percent in 2002. With the introduction of the XLR and the XRS in 2003, total sales rose to 216,000 vehicles. Importantly, 167,000 of those sales were for vehicles priced over $40,000, making Cadillac the leader among luxury vehicle sales.[7]

The Cadillac Sixteen: An Extreme Idealized Destination

In January 2003, Cadillac took yet another risk, unveiling the Cadillac Sixteen concept car at the North American International Auto Show in Detroit. The Sixteen was unlike anything Cadillac—or any other manufacturer—had ever created, a new breed of luxury car that defied convention and shattered all notions of what an ultraluxury vehicle should be (fig. 10.3).

The Sixteen is a rear-wheel-drive car powered by an all-aluminum 16-cylinder

Figure 10.3 Cadillac Sixteen concept car. Copyright 2003 GM Media Archive.

13.6-liter engine. In anticipation of environmental concerns regarding fuel economy, Cadillac Sixteen's Displacement on Demand technology allows the engine to run on 4, 8, or 16 cylinders, depending on driving conditions.

Without the new focus on art and science, the Sixteen would have seemed an anomaly, not representative of the real world of Cadillac. In the current climate, however, the Sixteen does what a concept car should. It pushes the envelope on what Cadillac really could produce and encourages the division and its customers to think long and hard about what Cadillac represents.

Although it will take years of experience with Cadillac's new cars and trucks to truly determine Cadillac's standing in the luxury market, there is every reason to believe that the brand has been taken off life support systems and is on the road to recovery.

Hummer: Establishing a New Brand

The Hummer program represents a different type of risk taking, which also required finding the right balance between make-and-sell, sense-and-respond, and anticipate-and-lead.

The Hummer was conceived of just as GM was getting its arms around the sense-and-respond business design. In the late 1990s, after missing out on several new concepts, GM's market research group began to develop the capability to better sense forthcoming product trends. One of the early trends they sensed was an expression of interest, among young people in particular, for military-styled vehicles (fig. 10.4).

Figure 10.4 2003 Hummer H2. 2004 General Motors Corporation. Used with permission of Hummer and General Motors.

In January 1999, a newly formed team suggested creating a smaller Humvee-like vehicle for civilian use, the H2. Rather than attempting to purchase American General, the company that supplies Humvees to the military, GM proposed, in effect, "licensing" the Hummer brand name.

The Cadillac team faced the difficult challenge of restoring a brand. The Hummer team faced a different sort of challenge: positioning a new brand. Fortunately, the team was able to take advantage of Hummer General Manager Mike DiGiovanni's previous assignment as director of GM's market research activity. DiGiovanni spent considerable time working with existing and newly developed market research techniques and information. From this knowledge, he and his team came to the conclusion that the essence of the Hummer brand was captured in one word: *Daring*. This discovery helped the team focus on who the target market would be: rugged individualists and successful achievers—people who were "daring."

Because DiGiovanni was grounded in the world of research, he understood how to properly use data, not just how to collect it. Because he was a risk taker with a clear sense of what customers wanted, he also knew when to trust his intuition. Interestingly, the emergence of the Hummer would coincide with the return to GM of Bob Lutz, another expert in balancing research with intuition about what customers would buy. Lutz's background, and its relevance to the anticipate-and-lead mindset, is discussed in more detail in chapter 14.

DiGiovanni and his team recognized that some of the Hummer's target customers who were primarily rugged individualists would definitely be going off-road. There were, however, other target customers who were primarily successful achievers and probably would not go off-road, but they would be daring. For example, they might make a big stock market play or take an adventurous vacation. But, most of all, they would want to show the world that they were successful.

Upon unveiling a Hummer concept vehicle at the 2000 North American International Auto Show in Detroit, GM knew it had a huge hit on its hands. Response was tremendous. In eighteen months, the vehicle was ready for production. GM had never moved this quickly on a vehicle before.

To sell the Hummer to the public, brand positioning was crucial. GM never positioned the Hummer as a "military" SUV. Though the company fully embraces the vehicle's military heritage, Hummer ads never mention guns and turrets. Rather, Hummer is portrayed in its advertising as tough, rugged, and off-road.

The Hummer represents an initial example of the anticipate-and-lead business design at work. GM anticipated what the market was missing—namely a more affordable militaristic yet civilian vehicle—and then quickly introduced a pathbreaking vehicle. GM was not the only manufacturer to sense this unmet need. Ford also recognized the potential, but it was not as quick to market. By moving quickly and being first to market, GM won the first round in a new game.

Much as restoring the Cadillac brand touched on important aspects of anticipate-and-lead, so did the establishment of the Hummer brand. As the earlier discussion of anticipate-and-lead pointed out, in order to use this business design, an enterprise must be willing to do the following:

- Lead by adapting the business design to accommodate anticipated changes in business conditions (some of which are created by the enterprise)
- Grow into new areas of the business and avoid the zone of discomfort
- Determine the destination it wants

Growing into New Areas of the Business

Hummer helped GM meet all three requirements for successful business design. The ability to grow into new areas of business offers a case in point. Historically, GM has not been a leader in the accessory business. A critical part of the H2 business plan was to develop a leadership position in accessories. In chapter 2, a chart was used to describe GM's anticipate-and-lead business design, illus-

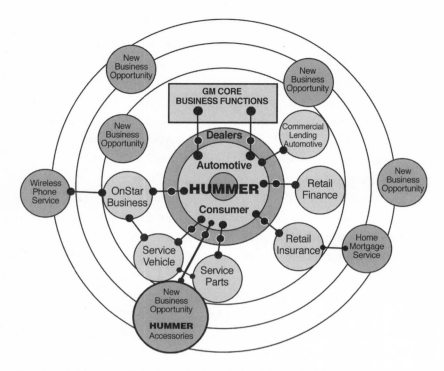

Figure 10.5 Hummer application in GM's extended customer-relationship business design.

trating the opportunity to expand into the more lucrative "related services" business. The Hummer accessory business is highlighted on the chart (see fig. 10.5).

The success with accessories has provided a learning opportunity for the rest of GM. As with the eighteen-month product development cycle, what previously seemed impossible in a make-and-sell world is being shown to be not only possible, but necessary, in an anticipate-and-lead environment. Hummer has become a catalyst for change throughout GM.

The division has also broken all the rules on advertising. Rather than relying primarily on market research to test ads, the Hummer team relied on its instincts. Because its members were so steeped in the brand and what it stands for, their instincts were reliable. This approach is being emulated in other areas of GM, as well.

Moreover, Hummer built its dealer network from the brand up, with new standards of excellence and expectations in terms of customer satisfaction, training, and facilities. Many of these concepts, which mark Hummer as a premium brand, are being used by Cadillac, GM's other premium brand.

Working with AM General

The relationship between GM and AM General is unique, as well. The two companies could not be more different, but, with the best interest of the Hummer brand in mind, everyone involved has managed to make the relationship work, to the benefit of both.

Traditionally, if GM saw a company building a product it wanted, it would go out and buy or acquire significant ownership position in the company. Not this time. As GM has found in other cases when one company buys a controlling interest in another, the buyer has to run the other business and attend to its stresses and challenges.

In the case of Hummer, it made more sense to pay for the brand than to buy the entire enterprise. From GM's perspective, this is an opportunity to learn how to build niche products like Hummer in an all-new plant and hit high quality levels outside the GM system. The Hummer H2 is built in an existing AM General plant, which was retooled for this vehicle. Future Hummers may be built in GM plants, but the learning that occurred during the H2 experience has been invaluable.

From the outset, Hummer represented a new way of doing business within GM. The lessons learned from this anticipate-and-lead experience have begun to permeate other parts of the organization.

Sensing and Responding to Customer and Community Interests

Following its successful commercial introduction, some environmental groups have attempted to raise society's concern over the fuel efficiency of the H2 (11 to 13 miles per gallon). Seeking to find a balance between the very positive consumer response to the Hummer product and the increasing societal concern over the environment, GM developed a future product development strategy that will introduce smaller, more fuel-efficient vehicles. The plan is to still deliver the daring image developed for the Hummer by making sure these smaller vehicle have an authentic off-road capability, as well as Hummer appearance.

Additionally, since there is no question that the Hummer's power and off-road capabilities require a heavier vehicle and more powerful engine than other vehicles, the Hummer team has developed a program to demonstrate the societal benefits of this type of vehicle. For example, the Hummer Helps Web site showcases owners and dealers who have participated in good deeds, including owner club-sponsored off-road environmental cleanups and assisting people and communities in distress where only vehicles with Hummer capabilities could get through. They have also worked with Tread Lightly, an organization created by those who want to cross any terrain, but to do so responsibly, with minimum damage to the ecosystem. Tread Lightly has an extensive education program, and Hummer sponsors the "Guide to Responsible Four Wheeling,"[8] as well as contributing to an endowment fund to be used in providing grants to select outdoor enthusiast clubs that have pinpointed recreational areas in need.

The need for any enterprise to find the right balance between individuals as customers and individuals as citizens is discussed more extensively in chapter 11.

The Importance of the Idealized Destination as the Starting Point

Throughout the period from 1992 to 2002, GM experienced a journey of learning to use the advantages of make-and-sell and sense-and-respond business designs, as well as finding some of the advantages of anticipate-and-lead. Because of its size and the nature of its business, GM's management team correctly chose not to abandon one business design for another but to effect a transition from one to another, keeping those aspects of the business design that still added value and integrating them into the next business design. The application of this thinking at Cadillac and Hummer is both simple and profound.

In *make-and-sell*, the enterprise believes it can predict the future and build its products and services on that belief. Both examples in this chapter show there are still some aspects of this mindset that are of value today. This is no doubt true for most organizations.

In the *sense-and-respond* business design, the enterprise begins to accept the belief that the future is neither predictable nor controllable for some of what it does and plans to do. This forces the enterprise to design business processes that allow it to be better prepared to respond to changing customer, market, and environment requirements. Experience shows that this thinking has been of great value in developing the business design of both an existing brand and a new brand.

In *anticipate-and-lead*, the enterprise also accepts the belief that the future is not predictable, but, in this business design, the enterprise rejects the absolute belief that the future cannot be controlled. Instead, the enterprise operates on the belief that the future will be largely determined by what the enterprise does. It demonstrates that an enterprise can determine, to a great extent, the destination it wants to achieve.

The wise organization is able to adjust its operations while finding the right mix of make-and-sell, sense-and-respond, and anticipate-and-lead business designs. In part III, several thinking and decision tools are presented as travel guides to help the enterprise get to its destination.

MARKETING AS A STATE OF MIND

The customer determines what the business is.

—Peter Drucker

Part III proposes a destination where the enterprise operates as a system of interdependent functions that creates and maintains profitable customers. Each chapter serves as a travel guide to assist management to "get there" in the most effective and efficient manner. This task will be realized mainly when marketing is thought of as an enterprise state of mind, not as activities conducted within a functional organization called "marketing."[1] A 1929 interview with Albert Einstein points to the value of imbedding a systems approach to marketing in the "DNA" of the enterprise. In the interview, George Sylvester Viereck asks Einstein about the value of intuition and imagination relative to the value of in-depth analysis. After some back-and-forth bantering, Einstein tells the following story:

> Perhaps you remember the story of the toad and the centipede? The centipede was very proud of having one hundred legs. His neighbor, the toad, was very much depressed because he had only four. One day a diabolic inspiration prompted the toad to write a letter to the centipede as follows:
>
> Honored sir: Can you tell me which one of your hundred legs you move first, when you transfer your distinguished body from one place to another, and in what order you move the other ninety-nine legs?
>
> When the centipede received this letter he began to think. He tried first one leg, then the other. Finally he discovered to his consternation that he was unable to move a single leg. He could no longer walk at all! He was paralyzed! It is possible that analysis may paralyze our mental and emotional processes in a similar manner.[2]

This parable does not mean that a focused analysis of one part of a system always leads to paralysis. What it does mean is that, without a clear understanding of the properties or behavior of the system under consideration, as well as the system in which it is contained, analysis by itself is less valuable and potentially detrimental.

To create marketing as an enterprise state of mind requires an understanding of the concepts and their distinctions presented in table III.1.

Systems thinking and synthesis are, in many ways, different from how many of today's leaders were trained or gained their experience while starting out in the more mechanistic and analytical world. Attempts to complement the skills acquired in the mechanistic and analytical world with the advantages of systems thinking will require fundamental change in the ways many enterprises currently think, operate, organize, and reward their employees and customers.[3]

Table III.1.   Distinctions Between Mechanistic and Systems Thinking

Mechanistic Thinking	Systems Thinking
The mechanistic approach to solving problems is best described and understood through the metaphor of a simple machine. Most machines operate with a regularity driven by the internal structure and the laws of nature. By taking the machine apart and understanding the behavior or properties of the parts, one can improve understanding of the original item under study. The machine metaphor has led to the belief that even the most complex problem scan be understood through the methodology of science: analysis.	A system is a whole that is defined by its function in a larger containing system, and it has at least two essential parts. The parts must satisfy the following conditions: Each essential part can affect the properties or behavior of the whole, but cannot have an independent effect on the whole; the effect it has depends on the properties or behavior of at least one other essential part, resulting in a connected set. Therefore, a system is a whole that cannot be divided into independent parts, and, when the whole is taken apart, it and its essential parts lose their defining functions.
Analysis	**Synthesis**
Analysis begins by taking the system apart, and the behavior or property of each part is determined. The explanations of the parts are aggregated into an understanding of the whole. When the system is understood, appropriate analytic tools can yield knowledge of its structure, or how the system works. When asystem stops working properly, analysis canand should be used to identify the defectivepart or parts and the way they interact with other parts.	Synthesis begins by identifying the larger system in which the system we want to understand is contained and attempts to explain how both systems and their parts interact. Synthesis has the potential to reveal a system's function, or its role in the broader systems in which it operates. In other words, synthesis can help determine *why* the system works the way it does.

Systems Thinking and Understanding Marketing as a State of Mind

There are a lot of very competent and hardworking people attempting to improve the effectiveness and efficiency of the marketing organization. Unfortunately, much of what is being accomplished is, as Russell Ackoff would say, "trying to do the wrong things righter."

Allocating more scarce human and financial resources to improve the marketing *organization* will not provide a commensurate return. This is true because, given our complex, accelerated, and interacting market conditions, the marketing *organization* as a specialized functional part of the enterprise is, at best, no longer needed and, at worst, detrimental to gaining and maintaining loyal customers efficiently and effectively.

Enterprises need to move away from the traditional sequential business model in which marketing departments determined, effectively using market research, what customers wanted and then other functions of the firm made it. Many enterprises are moving towards a process that incorporates elements of sense-and-respond, with which they build flexibility and adaptability into their system to allow them to respond quickly to changing customer requirements. In this environment, it is *everyone's* job to listen and to understand customers, to sense their needs, and to develop appropriate products and services that either meet or exceed those requirements. This approach is a critical first step, because the enterprise does not have the time to have one function determine what customers want; have another design and build the product or service capability; and then have another sell, deliver, and service when necessary.

It does not mean that the specialized activities currently located in marketing departments (e.g., advertising, sales, and service) go away—these skill sets, with some modification, are still needed. Meeting customer needs has not changed, but available methods and technology allow the entire enterprise to *simultaneously* collaborate with the customer to create a customer experience valued by both the customer and the enterprise.

Peter Drucker said it best: "Marketing is so basic that it is not just enough to have a strong sales department and to entrust marketing to it. Marketing is not only much broader than selling, it is not a specialized activity at all. It encompasses the entire business. It is the whole business seen from the point of view of its final result, that is, from the customer's point of view. Concern and responsibility must therefore permeate all areas of the enterprise."[4] A statement attributed to David Packard is more direct: "Marketing is too important to be left solely to the marketing department."

To move to marketing as a state of mind requires the direct involvement, creativity, and passion of engineers, designers, communications specialists, and planners, all working together with an improved and shared understanding of customers and market conditions. For example, the GM stories told in part II highlight the value of having the market research function interact directly with all functions within the company. The examples demonstrated that there is great value in having engineers, designers, planners and market researchers working together to seek out the "right" solutions to market challenges. This approach increases the chances of choosing the best decision among the available alternatives—and doing so while the market is in a state of dynamic change.

This approach requires everyone in the enterprise to interact, to share information and insights on a regular basis. And that is quite a challenge, because most employees have been educated in specialized disciplines that focus mostly on their functional expertise—sometimes at the expense of the total benefit to the customer and the enterprise. The solution to this problem begins with developing a desire to learn from each other, with adopting a whole "learning" attitude rather than an exclusively functional "knowing" attitude, even in areas where we have the most expertise.

Thinking and Operating Like a System

Today, given the complex and rapidly changing environment, many enterprises need to operate more as a system, looking at systemic rather than structural change and eventually evolving to a system where the strategy is treated as a more interdependent activity throughout the extended enterprise.

Marketing as a state of mind philosophy will move from the current approach of attempting to increase demand to meet production schedules, to developing sensing systems that allow the enterprise to anticipate possible future customer requirements and design solutions that respond directly and quickly to dynamic customer or household intentions—including changes in those intentions.

Marketing as a state of mind does not begin with the simple pronouncement,

"Okay everyone—you're all in charge of marketing now; just internalize it." Instead, there is a need to establish specific processes that allow employees to effectively and meaningfully tap into and make use of the expertise that is imbedded throughout enterprise.

Leading the New Enterprise

Marketing as a state of mind requires the chief executive and the enterprise leadership team to find ways to educate and motivate all employees to embrace the concept. There are three basic steps that, at a minimum, are required.

Step 1: Be Explicit in Defining Marketing

There are at least three separate and distinct meanings that have been attributed to the word *marketing* over the years. For each, there are strongly held opposing positions.

Meaning 1. Marketing is an *activity or function* pursued by the enterprise.

Position A. "The marketing effort behind the product launch was well planned and executed."
Position B. "It takes a lot more than marketing to have a great product launch: it takes a great product."

Meaning 2. Marketing is a type of organization that produces a result.

Position A. "Marketing was able to provide the manufacturing organization a clear picture of what they believed was needed if they were to increase the sales of product *x*."
Position B. "The marketing types really have no idea what it takes to develop a great product at a price people are willing to pay."

Meaning 3. Marketing is a form of knowledge or understanding.

Position A. "What marketing information do we have in support of the current business plan?"
Position B. "Marketing information can sure get in the way of creative and imaginative product concepts."

To overcome the confusion caused by elements of the enterprise speaking a different marketing language, management should establish a single definition that fits the cultural and operating principles of the enterprise. The following definition can serve as an initial draft as each firm ties the definition to its current and expected operating conditions:

> Marketing is a thinking process that brings together the whole business so that the enterprise is seen positively from the point of view of the customer. Achieving this objective requires that we manage the interaction of the key elements of the enterprise to innovatively develop, manufacture, and offer products and customer experiences that current and potential customers believe they must have. The purpose is to ensure that managing effectively the interaction of the parts results in the enterprise's being worth more than the sum of its parts in the mind of its current and potential customers.

Step 2: Establish Principles to Govern Enterprise Operations

A *knowledge-based, proactive enterprise* is the operational response to a decision to become an enterprise with a marketing state of mind. It is knowledge based in that it is distinct from "company forward," "market driven," or "customer oriented," emphasizing that the relationship among customer, community, and enterprise can be best managed by an open, continual, transparent dialogue in which each party learns from the other what works, as well as how and why it works.

It is *proactive*, because it accepts that our ability to predict the future has been drastically reduced, requiring that the enterprise learn how to complement the more traditional approaches by improving its ability to anticipate change and be prepared to innovatively respond to it, or, when possible, cause the change to be favorable to the enterprise.

It is an *enterprise*, rather than a company or corporation, because the boundaries that separate the company from its customers, community, and competitors are becoming less clear. We must think of all the elements that surround how we do our business as an integrated set of interacting parts—that is, a system.

Step 3: Manage Interactions of Functional Organizations So the Whole Is Greater than the Sum of Its Parts

Organization by function did not happen by chance, and it has not persisted over the decades—despite some of its current shortcomings—because of mindless inertia. It persists because each of the functions provides a space in which the core capabilities of the organization can develop and flourish. These functions encourage and nurture the specialized expertise that all enterprises require if they are to improve and innovate. The real challenge for leaders is to retain the benefits of the functional organization while lessening or eliminating its deficiencies—that is, making sure selected portions of a function's specialized knowledge are available in a form from which others can learn.

It is critical for an enterprise's leadership to manage simultaneously the three steps of (1) establishing marketing as a state of mind and not a functional marketing organization, (2) installing the operating principles of a knowledge-based proactive enterprise, and (3) managing the interactions of the functions so that the whole is greater than the sum of the parts. Accomplishing these three steps will take the enterprise a long way in overcoming the reality that breadth without depth is useless, and depth without breadth is paralyzing.

An Idea Whose Time Has Come

In 1990, Kim B. Clark and Takahiro Fujimoto alluded to the need to move toward marketing as a state of mind when they introduced, in a six-year cross-national study of manufacturing firms, the concept *product integrity*, which characterized the more successful firms:

> Product integrity has both an internal and external dimension. Internal integrity refers to the consistency between a product's function and its structure: the parts fit smoothly, the components match and work well together, and the layout maximizes available space. Organizationally, internal integrity is achieved mainly through cross-functional coordination with the company and its suppliers. Efforts to achieve internal integrity through this kind of coordination have become standard practice among product developers in recent years.

> External integrity refers to the consistency between a product's performance and customer expectations . . . [and] external integrity is critical to product competitiveness. Yet for the most part, external integrity is an under-exploited opportunity.

Besides uncovering the value of product integrity and describing its internal and external dimensions, Clark and Fujimoto also identified an important unifying organizational philosophy that underscores the need for a knowledge-based, proactive enterprise: "Of course, there are exceptions. . . . [W]e found a handful of companies that consistently created products with integrity. *What set these companies apart was their seamless pattern of organization and management.* The way people did their jobs; the way decisions were made, the way suppliers were integrated into the company's own efforts—everything cohered and supported company strategy."[5]

Marketing as a state of mind, the knowledge-based, proactive enterprise, and managing the interaction of functional specialties to create product integrity are three important steps that an enterprise can take to increase its chances of emulating the handful of firms that Clark and Fujimoto found over a decade ago. The chapters in part III will demonstrate the extent to which systems thinking, as a complement to traditional approaches, underlies each of the three steps.

Ideas will be presented that will help ensure that the marketing state-of-mind concept is embedded in the "DNA" of the enterprise and not contained solely within any one functional department. The ideas provide insight into taking data and information and, with the proper tools and mindset, transform them into knowledge, understanding, and wisdom; they provide insight into the establishment of goals designed to be consistent with the broader system in which the enterprise operates.

11 Understanding the System in Which the Enterprise System Operates

Management should be directed at the interaction of the parts and not the actions of the parts taken separately.

—Russell Ackoff

Systems thinking demands that you understand more than just the interactions of the interdependent elements within your company. You must also understand how these elements interact with the external environment that influences—and is influenced by—your actions.

This means that you need to understand much more than just the needs your customers are able to articulate through consumer research. You also need to understand their unarticulated needs and ensure that your employees, or members of any part of your extended enterprise, have access to what the organization knows, in order to help them meet these articulated and unarticulated needs more effectively.

In addition, there are other stakeholders beyond your customers that have to know enough about your goals and practices to consider you a company worth supporting. These additional stakeholders include the company, which includes other organizations and companies that deliver the products and services to the customer and community: employees, suppliers, investors, and so forth. Stakeholders also include the community, which is made up of consumers in a societal context, the governmental interests that attempt to represent them, the special interest groups that carry strong views on specific issues, and the competition for customer and community attention and resources.

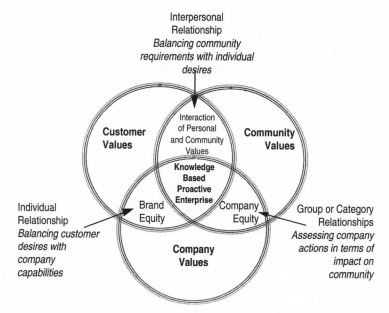

Figure 11.1 Three critical components of understanding and enterprise's encompassing system.

Encompassing System

Figure 11.1 represents these different voices of the market: the customers, the community, and the company. Needless to say, there are plenty of opportunities for agreement and conflict between these different constituents of the market. It falls to decision makers to understand the conflicts and agreements in reaching knowledge-based decisions.[1]

The position of each member of the system's views on issues, as represented in this figure, is not necessarily fixed. For example, vehicle safety used to be solely a community value, reflected in government regulations on safety belts and other features. It is now an enterprise and customer value, as well, to the extent that safety features are a regular selling feature for most vehicles. The same could be said, to a lesser extent, for environmental issues, which began as community values and have begun to take on meaning for both the enterprise and the customer.

Figure 11.1 serves as a visual reminder that customers do not live in a vacuum. Customers live in communities. Thus, we must simultaneously consider the desires both of the individual customer and of the community made up of individuals; people's values in a personal buying situation do not necessarily map to their values in a community situation.

For example, a company making laundry detergent might find that customers want a "whiter than white" wash, which the company knows it can provide by using phosphate-based detergents. At the same time, the community—which includes customers, government regulators, and interested organizations—wants "cleaner than clean" public waters, which are compromised by the introduction of phosphates. Meanwhile, the company (the shareholders and the employees) wants to produce a customer-satisfying and profitable product, one that both meets customer requirements and addresses community concerns about the environment.

But this approach is not as simple as it might appear: there are tradeoffs. Imagine an individual discussing the situation in which a manufacturer has been sensitive to the community concern and reduces dramatically the amount of phosphates in the detergent. The same person could say both of the following:

- *As a consumer:* "Nonphosphate detergents clean my clothes almost as well as phosphate-based detergents."
- *As a citizen:* "I'm not sure how much nonphosphates detergents will clean up the environment, but every little bit helps."

In this case, because of the action the maker of the detergent took, everything seems in balance between customer, community, and company.

Now, let us look at a slightly different product and environmental issue: disposable diapers. In this case, disposable diapers provide real convenience to consumers, and, like phosphate-based detergents, have an environmental cost—the filling of landfills. In this case, imagine an individual discussing the situation in which a manufacturer has not been able to develop a disposable diaper that decomposes quickly enough to minimize the impact on landfills. Again, the same person could say both of the following:

- *As a consumer:* "I find disposable diapers extremely helpful, and the thought of returning to cloth diapers and the mess they create in my house is unacceptable."
- *As a citizen:* "I'm not willing to give up my disposable diapers for the amount of environmental benefit the government or the environmentalists claim. Besides, what happens to all the water that has to be cleaned after I wash the

cloth diapers? How much energy do I use to get all the hot water I need to do the wash?"

In this case, the consumer really likes the product and this bias reduces the chances he or she will "see" the environmental impact to the extent to which he or she sees the impact of phosphates in the water. If you are a manufacturer of disposable diapers, this is not the time to relax. All that has happened is that you have been given some time. In this case, you had better start working on a solution that maintains the level of convenience but provides a more environmentally sensitive solution, because, if some other entity is successful in doing so, it will have a significant advantage if the government and the environmental community decide to support the new product.[2]

Within the company, understanding these relationships can sometimes be quite challenging. Company leadership must create an open environment that allows people to appropriately share their knowledge about customers and communities. These leaders must also promote the right sort of learning environment by asking questions like, "What did you learn from others before starting this project?" and "How has what you have learned impacted others in the organization?"

Leaders also need to constantly look at the system in which specific decisions operate. They need to continually ask, "Am I asking people to work more efficiently at their unit level at the expense of helping the entire system become more effective?" They must also find time to nurture community support by making sure the community is sufficiently aware of the company's behavior.

Consequences of Managing the Parts Independently

These are very important considerations. Systems thinking requires that any enterprise operate as a network of interdependent parts first and foremost. Optimizing at the wrong level can sometimes hinder the effectiveness of the overall system. The following story is an amalgam of experiences incurred when a customer encounters a management decision that has directed parts of the enterprise to optimize the efficiency of their function independently of the actions of the remaining parts—in this case, at the expense of the customer.

Imagine a personal computer (PC) owner (or, for that matter, an owner of any product) who has been a loyal customer and deeply impressed by his experience with the Reliable Computer company's excellent service—a Reliable Computer attribute that has been reinforced by the marketing department's long-term advertising strategy, which communicates that Reliable Computer provides not only the best computers, but also the best service. The advertisement, which has won several awards, closes with the tag line, "You're never more than forty-eight hours away from having your problem solved." The customer has been thinking about replacing his current Reliable Computer PC. Although Reliable Computer computers are among the highest priced, their reliability and service have led him to believe that they are a good value for the purchase price. This would be his fourth Reliable Computer purchase in the last ten years.

The customer is unaware that, a year earlier, under pressure from "Wall Street" to reduce operating costs to "industry" levels, senior management set goals for each major functional organization to reduce its individual operating costs. The Reliable Computer company's service organization, following a major benchmarking study of the lowest cost PC manufacturer, made the decision to outsource field service. The manufacturing organization, under the same pressure, decided to move toward an "order-to-delivery" manufacturing process and reduce parts inventories. The purchasing department, under the same mandate, instituted programs to pressure suppliers to reduce cost and carry some of the parts inventory.

Unexpectedly, the customer, before making his next purchase, suffers a hardware problem with his Reliable Computer. Using the phone number that is prominently displayed on his 2-year-old computer, on a label titled, "You're never more than forty-eight hours away from having your problem solved," he calls the Reliable Computer service organization. The call is intercepted by a switching mechanism that automatically directs him to another number, where he is connected to an automated-response set of screening questions.

The firm that the Reliable Computer service organization selected, the selection being based on the purchasing department's guidelines favoring the lowest cost bid, uses a less sophisticated computer system than Reliable Computer service used. Because of the change in systems, the customer is asked to provide background information he had provided earlier: service contract number, date of purchase, serial number, type, and so forth. After sorting through all the screening questions, the customer is routed to a service agent who represents himself as being from the PDQ service company now handling the Reliable Computer service account. The unavailability to PDQ of any record of previous service requests and past purchases of Reliable Computer products requires the customer to answer questions he has previously answered. After the customer discusses the problem with the service agent, it is determined that the part that is required to repair the computer is back-ordered and it will take two weeks to have the part available for the customer.

The customer expresses his displeasure to the service agent and notes that, after ten years of being a loyal customer and having purchased three Reliable Computer computers, he will for the first time not have access to his computer for more than two days. The PDQ agent expresses concern for the customer's disappointment and transfers him to the Reliable Computer company complaint hotline. After responding to the automated-response screening questions, the customer is put on hold (in part because of the combination of a reduction in service operators to reduce costs and an increase in the number of complaints) to wait for the next Reliable Computer customer-relationship representative. Thirty seconds into the holding period, a prearranged recording of the Reliable Computer company's award-winning advertisement regarding its unparalleled service comes on. When the famous tagline "You're never more than forty-eight hours away from having your problem solved" is played, the customer hangs up and heads out to the local computer store to buy a different computer.

In this instance, following the direction of senior management, each of the functions within the enterprise made decisions that met the cost reduction targets set by management—independent of the actions of the remaining parts. The advertising department continued to receive awards for an advertising campaign that promised a service that was no longer available; the service department, through outsourcing, was able to show that service costs were reduced; the manufacturing organization showed reduced inventories; and the purchasing department showed reduced parts costs. The accounting system, generally managed as an analytic metric of the economic parts of the enterprise, was able to book these savings at the time they were made, indicating the Reliable Computer company met all of its financial commitments for that period. The Wall Street analysts rewarded management's actions by upgrading their recommendation from neutral to buy. What management (and the Wall Street analysts) failed to do was determine the eventual revenue and cost consequences of these actions, how they would be seen by the customer, and the effect they would have on his and similarly affected customers' next computer purchases.

Back to the Future: GM and Thinking in the Broader Context

Peter Drucker spent nearly two years studying GM before writing *The Concept of the Corporation* in 1946. In this book, he addresses the distinction between the corporation as a business and the corporation as an institution, or what we might today call the extended company in relation to community and customer. As Drucker points out, harmony must exist between "the interest of society in a clear and carefully planned corporation policy and the interest of the corporation itself."[3]

GM: Moving Toward a Systemic Alignment Within the Encompassing System

In 1998, CEO and President Rick Wagoner extended GM's vision and values statements by publishing a set of core cultural priorities and modified GM's incentive reward system so that individuals are rated on their performance on each. The cultural priorities were stretching (setting goals that push us to do the very best we can), having a sense of urgency (moving quickly), maintaining product and customer focus (aligning customer needs and wants with innovation and product development), and acting as one company.

The final cultural priority, acting as one company, most affects operating as a system of interdependent parts. It demonstrates the company's awareness that it can succeed only as a unified system, regardless of personal or operational focus. At GM, acting as one company means the following:

- Collaborating proactively on global issues and driving for team success
- Encouraging teamwork
- Leveraging ideas, concepts, products, and processes from GM units around the world
- Leading teams effectively within and across organizations and borders
- Encouraging others to look beyond their individual organizations and focus on GM's success
- Stimulating external and internal exploration, benchmarking, and learning
- Understanding customers, markets, and competitors, and focusing on customer requirements and customer enthusiasm

Much has occurred since GM developed its new vision statement and cultural values. Interestingly, the management team's addition of the phrase "and related services" to the vision statement (see chapters 2 and 16) is at the heart of a systems-based strategy to develop complementary growth in areas beyond GM's traditional core business.

It is no longer acceptable for any enterprise to be seen, as Drucker wrote in 1972, as "increasingly . . . at odds with basic needs and basic values of society and community." GM realized that it must meet the needs of its customers without setting itself up as an easy target for its external critics. It should instead do all it can to be recognized as a positive social force and a global institution consistently seeking to meet the transportation and related services needs of the world's population. Part II and particularly chapter 5 provide evidence of the enterprise's move in that direction.

Metaphorically Speaking

It is important to use appropriate metaphors to describe how a business should operate when applying systems thinking. Although the three intersecting circles discussed at the beginning of this chapter offer a fairly accurate static representation of the relationships between customers, community, and company, they do not adequately reflect the interactive, systemic nature of these relationships.

Figure 11.2 moves away from the more mechanistic Venn diagram of figure 11.1 and uses the more interactive metaphor of a molecular structure to represent the key interactions in this system. Additionally, the term "company"—though it makes for nice alliteration with "customer" and "community"—has been replaced by the term *enterprise*, to reflect the fact that the boundaries between the company and its suppliers, distribution system, and competition have become increasingly blurred.

Every metaphor has advantages and limitations. The strengths of this metaphor are that more parts of the encompassing system are shown and it indicates the interactions. The weakness in this static, two-dimensional version is that it shows a fixed set of interactions, which we know can be altered by changing conditions. For example, as shown in the illustration, the supplier who normally interacts with the enterprise could also interact with the competition or, in some instances, directly with the customer. The key point is that the system of parts we call the enterprise also interacts with the encompassing system in which it operates.

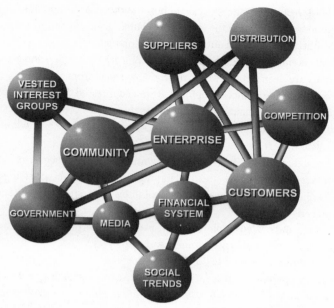

Figure 11.2 Molecular metaphor: Extended enterprise as a system of intacting parts.

This chapter has discussed and raised questions about the need for the management of any enterprise to continuously pursue a dynamic interaction among the parts of the extended enterprise as it explores ways to create value for the enterprise, its consumers, and the communities in which it operates. But what is the objective of this continuous pursuit? The objective is quite straightforward. It is the creation and adaptation of an enterprise not described by its structure but by the following characteristics:

1. An unambiguous sense of direction permeates the organization. The destination of the enterprise is known and understood by everyone; it is the universal premise behind all decisions and tasks, and it is focused on finding better ways to gain customers, develop itself, and—most important—keep customers.
2. Strategic and operational plans reinforce each other. There are no disparities between planning and execution.
3. Employees at all levels of the extended enterprise understand how their roles contribute to the total enterprise, and their accountability is clear. All the arrows are aligned.

4. There are no simplistic ideas about how customers or competitors will respond to the actions of the enterprise. Planning and execution recognize the full complexity and uncertainty of the market.
5. There is empowerment throughout the enterprise. Direction and accountability are clear, but there is no micromanagement from above.
6. Conflict and differences of opinion are not suppressed. When they are revealed, they are channeled into a process that seeks a consensus decision; that is, complete agreement—not necessarily in principle, but definitely in action.
7. The interaction of market knowledge with creative product and marketing ideas results in a steady stream of innovative and customer-satisfying products and services that leverage the capabilities and resources of the entire enterprise.
8. Existing and retired employees of the extended enterprise are the most effective recruiters of new customers and employees.
9. Other enterprises want to do business with you.
10. When employees are asked, "If the enterprise was a school, would you pay tuition for your children to attend?" The answer is an enthusiastic "yes."

This may sound like nirvana has been reached, and practice may fall short of perfection, but it is essential that the enterprise continue to strive for this kind of result if it is to succeed in the short run and long run.

In the next chapter, we will see how any enterprise, whether public or private, can start to achieve these characteristics by challenging the underlying assumptions of existing and proposed business plans and decisions.

12 Challenging Our Critical Assumptions

A fact is an assumption in which our confidence is justified or warranted, whereas an assumption is a doubtful fact.

—Ian Mitroff and Richard Mason

Although there are other definitions of the word *assumption*, defining the term is not the purpose of this chapter. Instead, the purpose is to make clear the importance of revealing, challenging, and making explicit critical assumptions underlying plans and decisions.

The Role of Assumptions in Decision Making

Choosing from among alternative courses of action that have different impacts on interested and involved parties is often hampered by conflicts between equally competent individuals and organizations trying to do what is "right." When these conflicts arise, it usually stems from one of two conditions. In the first condition, people have different views of the explicit underlying assumptions supporting estimates of current and future market conditions. Conflicts of this sort are actually healthy and beneficial to any type of decision making. Skillful interpretation of what is known and an open discussion around differences are the hallmarks of high-quality decision making.

In the second condition, people have failed to establish a common understanding or definition of the explicit assumptions, or they have not revealed the implicit assumptions underlying the estimates of current and future market conditions. Conflicts that result from the lack of an agreed-to set of assumptions can be disastrous. The reasons are simple. There can be no systematic method of comparing alternative courses of actions until those involved have reached some agreement about all the explicit and implicit assumptions that underlie them.

This does not mean that successful actions cannot start on the basis of a doubtful fact or implicit assumptions. However, it does mean that when questions regarding the viability of a plan arise and the underlying assumptions are not fully understood and accepted, and when unforeseen events then occur, support can waver and plans are either shelved or delayed. This is why it is important to reveal and challenge assumptions underlying plans to make sure they are understood and warranted.

Challenging the Obvious

A short trip into world of Sherlock Holmes will introduce a simple procedure for revealing the underlying assumptions that support a proposed plan or decision we need to take, or in this case an assertion we choose to make. In *A Study in Scarlet*, Sherlock Holmes is discussing his deductive ability with Dr. Watson and says, "I have a lot of special knowledge which I apply to the problem, and which facilitates matters wonderfully." Holmes reminds Watson of their first meeting in which Holmes told him that he knew he had come from Afghanistan. When Watson replied, "You were told, no doubt," Holmes snapped back:

> Nothing of the sort. I knew you came from Afghanistan. From long habit the train of thoughts ran so swiftly through my mind that I arrived at the conclusion without being conscious of intermediate steps. There were such steps, however. The train of reasoning ran: "Here is a gentleman of a medical type, but with the air of a military man. Clearly an army doctor then. He has just come from the tropics, for his face is dark, and that is not the natural tint of his skin, for his wrists are fair. He has undergone hardship and sickness, as his haggard face says clearly. His left arm has been injured. He holds it in a stiff and unnatural manner. Where in the tropics could an English army doctor have seen much hardship and got his arm wounded? Clearly in Afghanistan." The whole train of thought did not occupy a second. I then remarked that you came from Afghanistan and you were astonished.[1]

How many times have the readers and viewers of Sherlock Holmes seen him perform his flawless logic, as he uncovers what others were not able to notice?

His deductive powers appear flawless. But how well do Holmes's underlying assumptions hold up in supporting his logical conclusion that Watson had come from Afghanistan?

With all due respect to my favorite crime fighter and his creator, Sir Arthur Conan Doyle, consider the following test of the underlying and, in this case, unstated assumptions of Holmes's assertion, a test that employs some of the techniques found in a logical-consistency model described by Steven Toulmin and colleagues in their book *An Introduction to Reasoning*.[2]

Assumption 1

Holmes first assumed that Dr. Watson was an army doctor, stating explicitly that he was "a medical type" with the "air of a military man." In this case, implicitly, we have to assume that only army doctors show both of these traits, because Holmes has never encountered a nonarmy doctor who demonstrated these characteristics.

Rebuttal: Someone exists with the appearance of a medical type and a military air who has never been an army doctor.

Assumption 2

The assumption that Watson has just come from the tropics because his face is "dark" and is "not the natural tint of his skin" implies that the tropics are the only place that the sun can give such coloration and that Holmes knew of no other location.

Rebuttal: Working in locations other than the tropics—at sea, on a farm, or on a plantation—could produce the same effects.

Assumption 3

Holmes also assumes that Watson has "undergone hardship and sickness" because his face is "haggard" and his arm is held in a "stiff and unnatural manner." This assumption suggests that the only way to have these conditions is to have gone through stress and hardship.

Rebuttal: Perhaps Watson had been through a more recent personal stressful situation, and perhaps his arm's condition occurred at birth.

An Alternative Obvious Conclusion

Holmes's conclusion—that Dr. Watson came from Afghanistan—sounds logical. Indeed, in the fictional story written by Arthur Conan Doyle, it is "true." However, on closer inspection, the underlying assumptions appear weak, because the rebuttal assumptions make as much (if not more) sense than Holmes's original assumptions. And this leads to an alternate conclusion, albeit a less definitive one: Dr. Watson could have come from Afghanistan, but he also could have come from many other places. To find the true answer, one would have to ask Dr. Watson a number of direct questions, not simply draw a conclusion supported by personally held assumptions drawn solely on one person's observations and experiences.

In this fictional situation, the consequences of not revealing and not challenging the underlying assumptions are minimal. However, in the many decisions facing public and private enterprises, the consequences can be enormous. What follows are two examples of how two enterprises, one public and one private, instituted a more formal process to reveal and challenge critical underlying assumptions related to addressing messy problems.

Revealing and Challenging Assumptions:
The Decision Not to Adjust the 1980 Census

The U.S. Bureau of the Census confronts the problem of undercounting every ten years. For a number of reasons, many people are not counted, especially in urban areas, even when the bureau goes to great trouble to find them. How the bureau coped with this in the 1980s is an example of finding and coming to terms with varied, sometimes contradictory, assumptions inside and outside the bureau.

One of the least understood but most important observations on the taking of the 1980 census was that the technical systems that had been invented and designed to help our society deal with complexity were themselves so complex that many felt no one truly knew what was going on. The importance of this observation was heightened when it became clear through the assumption-revealing process that, even among those who claimed to understand, there was strong disagreement. Even worse, it was extremely difficult to get people to admit candidly that this was the case. The systems of politics and judicial process surrounding the census revealed the reality that, although many people acted as though scientific solutions to problems were accomplished with great certainty, in reality that level of certainty did not exist.

The issue facing the bureau was whether to use sampling and other statistical techniques to estimate the number and characteristics of those not counted and to thereby adjust the final count to include people who were not actually counted.

On December 8, 1987, more than seven years after the start of the 1980 census (and after more than fifty lawsuits were filed), U.S. District Court Judge John E. Sprizzo decided that "arbitrary and capricious" action was the appropriate standard of review for deciding whether or not the Census Bureau decision against adjusting the 1980 census should be reversed by the court. Judge Sprizzo went on to say:

Indeed, the extensive testimony at trial overwhelmingly demonstrates that the determination as to whether the use of the currently available adjustment techniques will provide a more or less reliable estimate of the population than the unadjusted census is an extraordinarily technical one, about which reasonable statisticians and demographers can and do disagree. Certainly the Bureau, which has the necessary experience, expertise, and resources to collect and analyze the complex statistical data, is better equipped than the courts to decide whether, in view of this dispute among the experts, the census should be adjusted.

In a footnote to his position, the judge commented:

The court rejects plaintiffs' [City of New York's] argument that the Court should not defer to the Bureau's determination because the Bureau's decision not to adjust allegedly "rested on non-technical, political grounds." That claim is simply not supported by the evidence. The Court finds as a matter of fact that while non-technical consideration played a minor role in the Bureau's decision not to adjust, the Bureaus' decision was primarily based on its determination that it was not feasible to develop and implement an adjustment methodology which would be more accurate than the census itself, a determination supported and confirmed by the evidence at trial.[3]

The Census Bureau actions that led to Judge Sprizzo's comment did not happen by chance. The bureau had gone through a very detailed process of revealing and challenging assumptions upon which the decision regarding adjustment was to be made. This process is fully documented and described in *The 1980 Census: Policymaking amid Turbulence* and "Federal Statistics in a Complex Environment: The Case of the 1980 Federal Census."[4]

How Did the Bureau Decide?

Briefly, the bureau required that the multiple perspectives contained within the decision-making system be represented by different teams that would defend their own positions as part of a dialectic inquiry. In the decision whether or not to adjust the census count, early discussions led to the creation of four teams, each to work on revealing the critical underlying assumptions of the following conventions.

> *Convention A.* Under this plan, only the head count itself would be used, without any adjustment other than imputation to a specific household based on explicit knowledge gained from an independent source (neighbors, lists, and so on), or, in the case of administrative losses and equipment malfunction, imputation based on supporting census records (such as address registers). The crucial issue for this convention was related to the credibility of the Census Bureau: an adjustment could set an unfortunate precedent.

> *Convention B.* Under this plan, the head count would be adjusted with use of all the imputation procedures used in the 1970 census. This would involve not only imputations to a specific household based on knowledge gained from the census about that specific household, but also adjustments to a particular class of households from information collected about that class from the census. For example, the proportion of housing units initially incorrectly reported as vacant in a sample would be applied to all housing units initially reported vacant. This group felt that it was important that the latest state-of-the-art tools be used to assure credibility of the bureau and the census count.

> *Convention C.* Under this plan, census data would be adjusted for undercount by age, race (black/nonblack), and sex. Adjustments would be made with use of a simple synthetic statistical approach. This group felt that the disparity of the undercount was important and should be corrected for, and that estimates of the relative undercount were available for age, race, and sex.

> *Convention D.* Under this plan, the head count and other crucial variables would be modified by experts' using statistical projections in light of all pertinent information. These other crucial variables included age, sex, ethnicity, relationships, income, race, and language. This group felt that, if any adjustment was done to the actual counts, it should correct the undercount as completely as possible. An implicit assumption of this plan is that the bureau is the body best qualified to develop such an adjustment procedure and to perform this adjustment.

The teams then identified key stakeholders who could affect or be affected by that team's convention and listed the assumptions that would have to be held by these stakeholders for the team's position to prevail over the other conventions. More than sixty-one assumptions were revealed, all of which were related to at least one stakeholder. After the teams listed their assumptions, each of them then identified the other teams' assumptions that would be most damaging to their own perspective.

A long and detailed analysis followed about the relative validity and weight of the many assumptions. Many assumptions were deemed important, but in the end the bureau adopted one in particular: that, if an adjustment were challenged in court, the bureau would be adjudged according to whether or not it had acted in an "arbitrary and capricious" manner. Based on the detailed evaluation of all possible alternatives, the Census Bureau assessed and documented the rationale for the each of its decisions against the "arbitrary and capricious" test. This effort resulted in the positive reaction to the bureau's actions, as articulated by Judge Sprizzo later in the decade.

Challenging Assumptions About When a New Technology Could Transform Photography

On February 26, 2002, at 11:06 P.M., in Syracuse, New York, my daughter gave birth to our granddaughter. That evening I used an electronic camera belonging to a friend of my daughter to take the "official" picture, and then used the Internet to send this digital picture to many of our relatives and friends, and to a list of my daughter's fellow teachers at the Skaneateles, New York, elementary school. The next morning, about eight hours after the birth (with no one-hour photo shops open during the intervening period), all the teachers and my daughter's fourth-grade class were able to see several full color pictures of Megan Elizabeth Buff. This was a great application of new electronic imaging technology and the Internet.

The next day, after having somewhat tempered the excitement of becoming a grandfather, I realized that I had used a Sony Mavica camera, and this realization triggered a memory of having run into a Mavica camera twenty years before.

In 1981, Eastman Kodak was struggling with an onslaught of new competitors in its traditional photographic business and was facing nagging questions about the potential impact of digital imaging on its traditional analog, silver-halide-based imaging technology. Various "expert" groups were taking strong and divergent positions on the viability of silver-halide-based imaging technologies. Since the problem was a very complex issue and was surrounded by great business and technical-development uncertainty, Kodak decided to use the same method the Bureau of the Census used in making the decision not to adjust the 1980 census.

The process began with gathering input from many people throughout the company who had diverse backgrounds in imaging technologies, including members of the technical community who were familiar with the capabilities of digital and the silver-halide technologies. Following the process that was used at the Census Bureau, teams formed to take strong positions on whether silver halide or electronics would dominate capturing images by 1990. Each team debated its position with the purpose of uncovering and assessing the most important assumptions that would have to be true for a particular point of view to be accepted. Out of this debate grew a list of critical assumptions upon which Kodak would develop its longer-term strategy. All of this led to a 1981 document, which proposed the following claim:Technological innovation will enhance the growth of personal picture taking, and today's photographic industry participants [Kodak and its business partners using silver-halide technology] will share in that growth in the foreseeable future (1990).

This claim was based on the following assumptions, which were revealed and tested:

1. The science of photography, as we know it (silver-halide crystal), will form the basis of any new, widely accepted amateur still picture-taking system.
2. Electronic enhancements have and will continue in the foreseeable future to benefit industries based on the science of photography.
3. Quality of prints from electronic images will not be generally acceptable to consumers as replacement for prints based on the science of photography.
4. The consumer's desire to handle, display, and distribute prints cannot be replaced by electronic display devices.
5. In-home, personal electronic print systems will not be competitive in terms of price and quality with commercial printmaking services.
6. The incompatibility of electronic-imaging systems to the full range of video-cassette recorders and video disc devices in the market will be a barrier to widespread amateur acceptance of those systems.
7. Electronic systems (camera and viewing input device for television) will not be low enough in price to have widespread appeal.
8. The claim that the introduction of electronic video cameras was a major fac-

tor in the decline of amateur movie camera sales cannot be supported by the facts.

To ensure that assumptions would stand up to internal and external review, the information that not only supported but also rebutted each assumption was made available, as well. For example, see table 12.1, pertaining to assumption 1.

Based on assessment of the supporting and rebuttal information for each of the eight assumptions, the summary chart (fig. 12.1) was developed to determine how important and how plausible each of the assumptions was, compared

Table 12.1. Supporting and Rebuttal Information for the First Critical Assumption

Support	Rebuttal
Portable equipment will require modular optoelectronic scanner (MOS) technology for electronic cameras.	Electronic movie cameras will be readily available in five years. They will be handheld and untethered, and will give images in color. The image on the television set will be very good.
Assuming that electronics continues to advance at the rate of the past twenty years, an all electronic camera will still cost $250 or more in the early 1990s (1981 dollars).	By taking a burst of frames, a movie camera becomes a still camera.
Static memories (a card of magnetic bubbles) will probably not be the preferred method for storing electronic images for at least ten years, which means magnetic tape or disks with attendant moving parts and hence more complexity and cost.	Television is the media of the future—a highly acceptable form of picture viewing, especially for the next generation. Many customers will find that electronic movies meet their picture-taking needs and will take fewer still pictures.
Photography (silver-halide crystals) will be more versatile. Film-type cameras will be more portable for the next twenty years.	Routes can be found for making the occasional print from electronic images: 1,000 × 1000 pixels may be enough to do the job quite well.
Photographic images will have more information than electronic stills for a long time. This will be especially true of traditional photography (as opposed to instant).	Picture taking will be cheaper with electronics—the recording media can be erased and reused when the pictures are not good enough to keep.
Though film images can be easily shown on television, it is more difficult to go from electronic signals to good hard copy.	Cost per bit of information is rapidly coming down.
Electronic technology will be added to film-type cameras and printers to make film images better than those of today.	Electronic technology is newer, earlier in its life cycle and progressing more rapidly than conventional photography.

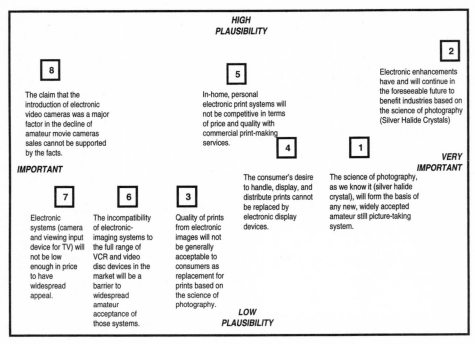

HIGH
PLAUSIBILITY

2

Electronic enhancements
have and will continue in
the foreseeable future to
benefit industries based on
the science of photography
(Silver Halide Crystals)

8

The claim that the
introduction of electronic
video cameras was a major
factor in the decline of
amateur movie cameras
sales cannot be supported
by the facts.

5

In-home, personal
electronic print systems will
not be competitive in terms
of price and quality with
commercial print-making
services.

4

The consumer's desire
to handle, display, and
distribute prints cannot
be replaced by
electronic display
devices.

1

The science of photography,
as we know it (silver halide
crystal), will form the basis of
any new, widely accepted
amateur still picture-taking
system.

IMPORTANT

*VERY
IMPORTANT*

7

Electronic
systems (camera
and viewing input
device for TV) will
not be low
enough in price
to have
widespread
appeal.

6

The incompatibility
of electronic-
imaging systems to
the full range of
VCR and video
disc devices in the
market will be a
barrier to
widespread
amateur
acceptance of
those systems.

3

Quality of prints
from electronic
images will not
be generally
acceptable to
consumers as
replacement for
prints based on
the science of
photography.

*LOW
PLAUSIBILITY*

Figure 12.1 Importance and plausibility of eight assumptions related to the future of photography.
Source: Eastman Kodak Company.

to the claim that traditional photography would be the format of choice throughout the 1980s. For example, as shown, the first assumption was ranked the second most important assumption and at the midpoint of plausibility.

After an in-depth review of each of the assumptions and the supporting and rebuttal information, Kodak management concluded that traditional still photography would continue to grow and remain the predominant form of amateur picture taking throughout the 1980s. Furthermore, it would be at least into the next decade (1990s) before an acceptable all-electronic still camera would become available to the market. The process used made it clear that an electronic camera would happen but that such a camera faced significant and formidable obstacles before it would be appealing to a mass market. It also made the point that technical capability does not necessarily mean mass market practicability.

At about the time the project was finished, Akio Morita, the fabled chairman of Sony Electronics, held a press conference in August 1981 where he announced the Sony Mavica electronic still camera. Although the Mavica was introduced as a still camera, in reality it was, as the technology assessment had assumed, a video camera that took video freeze-frames. While most of the industry analysts were assessing the impact this digital camera introduction would have on the silver-halide-based photography business, Eastman Kodak executives were quite sure that, whatever the impact would be, it would not be significant over the remaining nine years of the decade. What did happen, however, is that, by announcing the camera, Morita put the industry on notice that Sony was ready to move into the still photography business.

What Did Kodak Do with This Insight?

1984: Kodak introduced an 8-mm format video camera to gain experience in electronic imaging channels and gain insight into high-volume electronic devices to capture images.

1986: Kodak research labs developed the first megapixel sensor which could record 1.4 million pixels—somewhat greater than the one-million-pixel sensor the assumption-revealing exercise claimed might be possible to produce acceptable quality prints (in this case limited to 5 × 7 inch prints).

1987: Kodak researchers began exploration into digital printing algorithms and technology to print digital files and bring those benefits to analog (silver-halide-based) files in both commercial labs and one-hour photo labs. These initial efforts have led to Kodak's Perfect Touch Processing, which individually scans and processes each picture and brings together the advantages of both silver halide and digital imaging.

1990: Kodak chose not to participate with other camera manufacturers when they launched the first set of digital cameras. The reason Kodak stayed out was that they believed the cameras would not meet the level of quality consumers would expect. As expected, these initial cameras did not do well in the marketplace.

1991: Kodak became an early participant in developing digital capture, preview, and workflow systems for professional photographers with the Kodak Professional Digital Camera System (DCS). From this early engagement, Kodak gained early understanding of what would be necessary for a transformation from analog to digital photography and how to manage the interim steps. This included working with Canon and Nikon to develop digital sensor backs for professional Single Lens Reflex (SLR) cameras, to allow photographers to take advantage of existing equipment and experience.

In essence, Kodak started to develop technology that would go after its own very strong silver-halide-crystal business, instead of waiting for others like Sony to do so. It also used this same technology to improve its existing products, which still stand today as an element of its overall business design. Questions regarding whether it took its actions as quickly and as effectively as it could have do not obscure the fact that this deep understanding of future possibilities based on the revelation of critical assumptions provided great insight toward its correct destination.

Both the Census Bureau and Eastman Kodak addressed a significant problem by first looking to the encompassing system in which they were operating, and synthesized a considerable amount of information into actionable knowledge and wisdom to determine the options available before making critical decisions. The next chapter addresses the issue of ensuring that the knowledge and wisdom that is developed from facts and information is made available throughout the interdependent parts of an organization attempting to apply systems thinking.

13 Leveraging Knowledge Across the Enterprise

I keep six honest serving men
(They taught me all I knew).
Their names are What and Why and When,
and How and Where and Who.

—Rudyard Kipling

Ah, if it were only that simple!

Most companies and institutions in one way or another organize around functional "silos," such as marketing, finance, manufacturing, and engineering. Generally, this type of organizational structure has one "silo," or group of people, determine what it thinks customers want; another group designs the product; other separate groups handle the engineering, manufacturing, and promotion; and still other groups sell and service the product and determine the terms of trade.

Unfortunately, too few of these groups share knowledge with each other in a systematic way. The fault for this has less to do with individual employees than with the silo thinking and structure of most organizations, which affects the way work processes link—or fail to link—people together technically *and* emotionally.

There are reasons, of course, why silos exist. The depth of knowledge in these functional parts of the enterprise is extremely important. The purpose of moving to a more systemic way of running the business is to tap into this deep level of facts, information, knowledge, understanding, and wisdom to identify and synthesize those portions necessary to gain a comprehensive look at the markets in which the enterprise currently does, and potentially could do, business.

A Taxonomy Is Required

What should we call what is known? Is it *data* or *information* or *knowledge* or *understanding* or *wisdom* or any other of the hundreds of words that have been used over time? The issue is not, however, about *or*; it is about *and*.[1]

One of the major obstructions to organizational learning is the extensive focus and reliance on specific information—as in management information systems—or even the more recent extension of information systems to knowledge management. Information and knowledge do not exhaust the content of the human mind and are not even the most important types of "knowing." The mind can go beyond using *data*, *information*, and *knowledge*; it can comprehend understanding and wisdom, as well.

In the development of solutions to simple, divergent-view, or messy problems, information is more valuable than data; knowledge, more valuable than information; understanding, more valuable than knowledge; and wisdom, more valuable than understanding. Nevertheless, the attention and effort that most organizations spend acquiring and using these elements is sometimes inversely related to their importance. This is in part because many are not aware of the differences between them, let alone the differences in their values.

What Are the Distinctions?

There are many ways in which the following terms are used in both the practice and the study of decision making. The purpose of what follows is not to provide the sole "correct" manner in which the terms should be described. Instead, the terms are presented to help explain the critical distinction between them as they are used in this book.

Data consist of symbols that represent the properties of objects and events. In general, data (like iron ore) are useless until processed into information (like iron). Only when data are put into context, to make their meaning clear or relevant to the current use, do they become information. If we do not know what data mean in context, they are uninformative. Not all data are incorporated into information; they are incorporated when they are deemed relevant by those who will make decisions (or those who support the decision makers).

Information is contained in *descriptions*—as in finding answers to four of Rudyard Kipling's "six honest serving men" contextual questions, which begin with words like *who*, *where*, *when*, and *what*. The decision team, by drawing inferences about how the information relates to a specific issue or decision, needs to certify information for it to become knowledge.

Knowledge is contained in *instructions*, or answers to *how* questions. Knowledge is:

- Clear, because it is understandable by those who must use it
- Timely, because it gets to them when they need it
- Reliable, because diverse observers using the same procedures should see it in the same way (although they may draw different conclusions)
- Valid, because it is cast in the form of concepts and measures that can capture congruence with established knowledge or independent sources[2]

It is in the generation of knowledge that policy makers and information providers must work to jointly ensure that their inferences relative to the application of information are shared, sufficiently analyzed, and considered to be "certified" for use as knowledge. When knowledge is synthesized by decision makers, it contributes to understanding and wisdom.

Understanding is contained in *explanations*, or answers to Kipling's sixth serving man, *why* questions.

Data, information, knowledge, and understanding are concerned with efficiency—the likelihood of attaining one's objectives, or the amount of resources consumed in obtaining them—but not effectiveness.

Wisdom incorporates effectiveness, as well. Effectiveness also takes into account the value of the outcome of one's behavior. Should we be doing this at all? This synthesis of what we know with the context of the decision is what wisdom does.[3]

The value of wisdom is lost when the distinctions are presented with a "refinery" metaphor: data is distilled into information, information is distilled into knowledge, and so on.[4] The flaw in the refinery metaphor is the implication that wise decisions can be made by understanding how to apply knowledge condensed from information distilled from data analysis: it ignores the effect of the complex external conditions and internal relationships existing throughout the hierarchy. When decision makers do not capture and make explicit the underlying assumptions of decision making and do not understand the role of the "in-between" stuff, they place a severe limit on their opportunity to truly learn.

Think of the relationships this way: data distilled into information reveals the properties or behavior of a system, knowledge reveals how it works, understanding reveals why it works the way it does, and wisdom reveals whether we should even be working on the problem. Learning should focus on understanding and wisdom, as well as on information and knowledge. But, as was pointed out in the introduction to part III, understanding and wisdom are rarely generated by analysis alone. Synthesis is also required.

Ensure the Free Flow of Information

If the mindset is focused on systems thinking and knowledge use, the first requirement of the knowledge-based enterprise is an open decision "life-support system" that pumps a free flow of information among employees and across functions in support of a full range of decision processes.

Its nervous system is a network of market-based decisions that encourage and reward the sharing and application of information. The development, sharing, learning, and application of information contributes to the critical ability to anticipate and adapt to changing conditions. This informational advantage is a critical component that helps give the enterprise a competitive edge in the marketplace.

Like a cardiologist with an angiogram, management must examine the organization to find blockages to the free flow of information. Externally, these blockages may exist in any number of forms:

- Inadequate or passive market research capabilities
- Intermediaries that stand between the customer and the entire enterprise
- Lack of direct feedback mechanisms between customers, suppliers, distributors and the enterprise
- Information systems that fail to detect and properly classify data coming from the marketplace

Internally, information blockages are usually found between the functional silos. Silos are much better at designing information systems to serve their own needs than at designing systems to circulate information to other areas.

Once it is accepted that information is a critical asset, it naturally follows that some people will want to possess and control it. Among the ancient Mayans, priests controlled information about the changing seasons. They alone knew when it was time to plant and to harvest, and control of this vital information gave them control over the agrarian society in which they lived. Most corporations, too, have information priesthoods, and their control of vital information invests them with status and organizational power. It should not be surprising that some information handlers feel threatened when senior managers go looking for ways to free up the movement of information within the enterprise.

Yet this sharing is an absolute requirement of the knowledge-based enterprise, so management must drive the information priests from the temple, so to speak. Information professionals have an important and honorable place in a knowledge-based, adaptive enterprise, but they cannot stand between employees and the accumulated information of the organization. There can be no keepers of enterprise information; there can be only stewards. Information stewards act as facilitators and as coaches for others in finding and using the right information, and in developing enterprise knowledge and understanding.

The use of information handlers works well only from a mechanistic viewpoint, which accepts the enterprise as a machine of independent parts. Its negative aspects are more obvious today, particularly as we attempt to move to greater cross-functional activities. Since most information handlers are bound to particular functions of the enterprise, they inadvertently maintain barriers to cross-functional information sharing. Their tradition has been to collect, order, and analyze information for the particular uses of their parent functions, not to make it available or meaningful to "outsiders." And just their being part of a function skews what they listen to toward what the function is keen to hear.

In his book *Marketing Organisation*, Nigel Piercy reinforces the point that functional information handlers also serve as absorbers of the uncertainty surrounding their organization's information base. They do this by drawing inferences from a body of evidence and then communicating the inferences instead of the evidence itself.[5] For example, designers and salespeople might come to an information handler and say, "You've seen all the customer studies, so what do you think of our new product concept?" There is a great deal of uncertainty in all of the new-product studies, but they ask this question because they want the information handler "to be left holding the bag" of all uncertainty and give them a straightforward answer, such as, "Generally, the product concept is all right," or "Customers won't accept it for these two reasons." Neither of these responses transmits the complete richness of customer feelings or the ambiguities that naturally exist in most product markets. The questioners know intuitively that these answers are underpinned by uncertainty, but the range of that uncertainty—from low to high—cannot be communicated in the answer they seek.

As was shown in part II, there are decision process tools that improve the communication of the range of informational uncertainty.

It is this absorption of uncertainty that has led some individuals and organizations to hold implicit power over portions of their function's decision making. The information handler is in a position to tip the scales in favor of one product or project over another. The symbolic ways in which we recognize this power are several. For example, we tell individuals with ideas, especially junior people, "You'd better check the information that supports your idea with Charlie if you are to gain its acceptance," or "We are going to accept Bill's insight on this issue because he knows more about that subject than we do." It also occurs when staff functionaries make forecasts or price estimates in such a way that the specific relationships of underlying assumptions are implicitly, not explicitly, tied to outcomes.

What is needed is a process that makes possible cross-functional decisions, optimized at the enterprise level, without disrupting or giving up the benefits of strong functional management and information systems. To allow this to occur requires the creation of a networked organization and infrastructure capability that improves the quality of cross-functional decisions at the enterprise level, without giving up the benefits of strong functional management and information systems.

If we are to achieve these benefits, we need to design decision-making processes that encourage trust, information sharing, knowledge creation, and institutional learning.

Synthesizing Functional Knowledge

From an organizational standpoint, an enterprise is better off as its individual members increase their storehouses of knowledge. Knowledge is more than information, though it is based to a large extent on information. Knowledge comes from synthesizing and understanding a wide range of information and personal experience. By connecting knowledgeable individuals or functional departments through shared, synthesized knowledge (i.e., an integration of data, information, knowledge, understanding, and wisdom), we enhance the organization's ability to create greater customer value over time (fig. 13.1). An example of this value is the way Harvey Bell, mentioned in chapter 8, went through stages of listening to customers, using market research, suggesting changes in

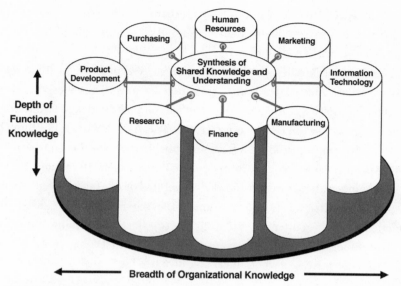

Figure 13.1 Synthesis of shared knowledge and understanding.

market research procedures, and playing a critical role in the design of Auto-ChoiceAdvisor (chapter 4). And, throughout the process, he continued to integrate what he was learning with his deep functional understanding of engineering the design of a vehicle.

The general challenge is to create an environment where all the functional organizations' experiences are viewed as contributing essential and deep knowledge of their functions so that this knowledge can be effectively synthesized with similar information and knowledge from other functional areas. This requires an environment in which this functional perspective enhances the understanding of the broader issue being addressed, without being diminished by the perception that functional representatives hold biased positions based on their functional ties. That type of perception precipitates behavior that inhibits the function's contribution as the enterprise attempts to determine what it knows and needs to know.

This is not a recommendation to inhibit the collection of deep, specific functional knowledge. On the contrary, the continued development of deep functional knowledge is critical to the enterprise's desire to innovate. What is necessary is to develop this knowledge in a manner that allows decision makers access to what Reid Smith and Adam Farquhar have coined as a "knowledge hub,"[6] which is more valuable than the sum of all the specialized functional knowledge to which it is connected.

This principle applies whether it is in business, education, health, or any other specialty affecting the human condition. Even by themselves, these isolated bits of knowledge are valuable, but, when combined with knowledge from other sources, they can take on even greater value. In the extreme, like threads in a tapestry, single threads of information are of little value. When woven together properly, however, they form a coherent image of greater value.

Just as internal and external knowledge captured by one function tends to be trapped within that function, by the same token, the tradition of organizing by functional activities often leads to decisions or external communication that make it difficult for customers or constituents to form a coherent picture of what the enterprise, as a whole, is capable of delivering.

Relating Information Technology to Business Designs

How a knowledge system is developed and managed will be determined by the enterprise's predominant business design. The framework for making this decision is found in the matrix that shows the characteristics of the three business designs, make-and-sell, sense-and-respond, and anticipate-and-lead, as they relate to traits of the enterprise (tables I.1 and I.2). The traits in table I.3 are most relevant to this discussion: *information architecture* and *knowledge-management perspective* are repeated in table 13.1.

A review of management's operating requirements under each of the three business designs indicates why each design has a significant effect on information architecture, storage and retrieval, and accessibility across functional departments. When the enterprise is operating according to a make-and-sell business design, it is likely more information resources will be allocated primarily to the functional departments, because every one is working on an accepted, predicted-future plan, which reduces the need to share information when changes occur. When the enterprise is operating according to an anticipate-and-lead business design, resources are more likely to be shared between the functions. In this business design, a cross-enterprise activity is responsible for sharing of information that is constantly changing and synthesizes the knowledge gained in understanding the effect on each function caused by the changes. The important point is that one formula for allocating resources is not inherently bet-

Table 13.1. Effect of Alternative Business Designs on Enterprise Information Architecture and Knowledge Use Systems

Trait	Make-and-Sell	Sense-and-Respond	Anticipate-and-Lead
Information architecture	*Functionally managed*, for use by people in the function. Each function creates its own view of "what's going on out there" and has its own processes for "how we do things around here." Focus is on providing the information needed to execute the function's business plan.	*Enterprise management* of information to represent the current status of the environment and of organizational context. Supports decentralized decision making using role-specific manage-by-wire support based on common data storage and use.	*Web-based open system.* Enterprise and customer share access to what is needed for each to gain maximum benefit from the other. Transparency will require established privacy and security procedures acceptable to all parties.
Knowledge management	The most efficient knowledge management is to store precise measurements of what the enterprise knows and what it will need to know in an efficient and accessible warehouse.	Primary knowledge is know-why (systems knowledge) as opposed to know-how (process knowledge). It must be available to all those who need it.	The goal is not management: it is quick acquisition. The enterprise needs knowledge about the future it wants to create. Storing what worked in the past is less useful. Design a system that will adapt as strategy develops, based on prior success in changing the way things happen

ter than the other. Success will be determined by the extent to which the information architecture and knowledge use systems are tied to the business design.

The Problem Is the Same in the Private and Public Sectors

One of federal statistics' most knowledgeable observers, James Bonnen, highlighted the need to organize relevant knowledge around the decision makers' need to understand the broader system, not to focus on the workings of a functional organization. The debate was whether the Census of Agriculture should be collected at the U.S. Census Bureau or at the U.S. Department of Agriculture.

While almost everyone in government was focusing on the bureaucratic question of who should collect the information, Bonnen pointed out that society needed to know and understand both the specific knowledge and how it interacted with the knowledge of the rest of the system, regardless of who collected it—a system that started with the growing of agricultural products and ended with the products being eaten at the consumer's table (fig. 13.2).

This meant the federal statistical agencies needed to integrate the data, information, knowledge, understanding, and wisdom collected about the inputs

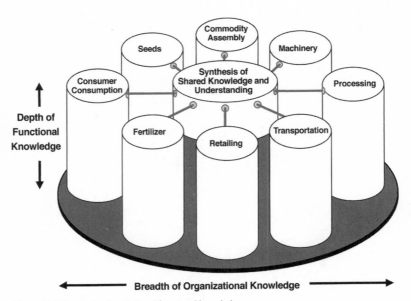

Figure 13.2 Synthesis of agricultural functional knowledge.

(that is, seed, fertilizer, machinery, etc.) through agricultural production, commodity assembly, initial processing, further manufacturing, wholesaling, retailing, transportation, and eventually to consumer consumption.

With this systems view in mind, Bonnen recommended that the Census Bureau commit resources to identifying and integrating the different pieces of food-sector statistics scattered throughout several economic censuses and surveys, and relate them to the agricultural census. In essence, he suggested alignment of our statistical practices around the user's needs, not around the existing organizational structure. Today, the same issue exists on a much larger scale in both the public and the private sectors.

It's Not in the Collection, It's in the Use!

Looking at the problem from the standpoint of the user illuminates some fundamental issues regarding how individuals interact with government. A single, working parent does not view the problem of raising a family as various independent activities of getting a job, staying healthy, getting to work, getting the children to school, and improving the children's chances for success by improving their education. To that person, these are all interdependent activities, the interaction of which must be managed if the person is to survive. The government does that person a disservice by forcing her to go to independent units and figure out how to get these units to interact on her behalf.

Instead, a responsive government would bring together congruent agencies and their areas of deep knowledge to provide the constituent a holistic view of the resources available and allow the person to choose among the alternatives— even if such action might affect the efficiency of an agency. This can be accomplished only when government leaders accept that the well-being of their constituents can be positively affected when these specialized areas function as a system and, from the constituent's perspective, when they are therefore more valuable than the sum of the government's parts.

When Things Are Perceived as Real

Whether in government or in business, it matters little that participants of a decision-making team do not actually hold a functional bias, if their colleagues in other functions incorrectly perceive that they do. The Thomas theorem, "If men define situations as real, they are real in their consequences," expresses well the significance of this traditional bias toward those who are in other functional organizations.[7] In other words, if one functional member of a decision team perceives another team member from a different function as presenting information biased in favor of his function's objectives, the team is likely to reject the information—even if it is unbiased and reliable—for the wrong reason.

This, like many other traditional problems, is not a new phenomenon. In Plato's *Republic*, a magnificent discourse takes place between Socrates and others in their attempt to envision the perfect political state. It turns into a discussion about what people are able to know from what they can observe. In an allegory about a cave, the acquisition of human knowledge is likened to the shadows and reflections seen on cave walls. People and objects passing outside the cave may have different appearances because of the way the light shines into the cave at any given point in time. For people sitting inside the closed walls of the cave, it would be naive to interpret the shadows as the real world.[8]

For today's decision makers, the point is still relevant: while we strive to move closer to reality, our knowledge is based on our understanding of the images or reflections we see. We must remember that both synthesized and analytic approaches that support decision making, like the cave images, can provide no more than a *reflection* of reality.

What we are searching for is an environment that enhances our ability to make—if not *perfect* business decisions—at least the *best possible* decisions, decisions based on all that we know to be relevant to the decision.

In today's complex world, the challenge for a manager in decision making is not to seek *the* right decision based on a single-point forecast of what the conditions will be at the time the decision in implemented. Rather, it is to manage the process in a way that increases the chances of choosing the best decision among the available alternatives, given all the circumstances at that time, and considering circumstances that can occur in the future—doing all this in a manner that gains consensus among all those affected by and affecting the decision.

What is needed is a decision system that provides the appropriate tools, expertise, and innovative momentum to facilitate this decision making. The decision system must be adaptable to the environment in which it will operate and be considered an appropriate place for the decision maker to inquire.

Much as Plato's cave had an implied structure of walls, a floor, and a ceiling, which can be perceived as a three-dimensional space, we can similarly form a three-dimensional approach to increase systems thinking–based decision making.

The first two dimensions, which also served as the basis of the matrix for problem definition discussed in chapter 6, are the *extent of complexity* and the *extent to which there is a shared vision of the problem to be solved.*

The third dimension is the ability to access quality information relating to the problem.

Choosing the Right Tools to Clarify the Images
Seen on "Cave Walls"

Experience has shown that no single decision tool is sufficient to address the types of problems facing management. At GM it was necessary to put a full range of decision support tools, such as decision and risk analysis, multiattribute utility technology (conjoint measurement), system dynamics modeling, linear programming, game theory, and other approaches, into the toolkit of decision making. As in any selection process, when choosing a decision process, an enterprise must predict what kinds of answers the process will likely produce and, just as important, what observations or possible answers it will likely overlook. A traditional system dynamics model, for example, will focus on aspects of the problem that vary over time but will be of less help in dealing with uncertainty, whereas a traditional decision and risk-analysis approach will emphasize uncertainty but minimize time dynamics. Ultimately, understanding the nature of a given problem should determine which analytical approach (or combination of approaches) is most likely to provide the ability to address the problem. What follows is a thinking tool that will assist in this process.

A Checklist to Determine the Appropriate
Decision Support Tools

Answering the following questions will help the decision team members to provide any internal or external decision support organization with the direction and decision support services it needs to address their problem. The first two sets of questions were derived in developing the matrix for framing the problem (fig. 6.1).

The first set of questions assesses the extent to which there is a perceived shared understanding of the problem.

- How do various stakeholders inside and outside the enterprise view the problem under consideration, at both a rational level and an emotional level?
- Do stakeholders inside and outside the enterprise have well-formed ideas about the nature of the problem, or are their views only partially formed and impressionable?
- Do those involved in the problem hold very similar views about the nature of the problem, or are their perceptions varied and disparate?
- Do decision makers understand clearly the views of stakeholders outside the decision circle who will be affected by outcomes: customers, investors, constituents, or staff members? Or, alternatively, are decision makers "out of touch" with these "external" audiences?
- Have members of the decision team worked with each other before, or are they unknown to each other?

The second set of questions assesses the extent of complexity according to the nature of the problem.

- Is the problem self-contained, or does it interact heavily with other problems that also need to be addressed? To what extent can we understand these interactions?
- Do decisions and actions regarding the problem take place within a single work group, or must they cut across multiple areas inside—or even outside—an organization?
- Are the timing and sequence for dealing with the problem clear and flexible, or are there other factors that introduce uncertainty, rigidity, and immediacy to solving the problem?
- Can we ascertain with confidence what will probably happen as a result of our decisions, or is there a great deal of uncertainty regarding how stakeholders may react? In other words, to what degree can we predict decision outcomes?
- Is the short-term effect of our planned intervention likely to be different from the long-term effect?

The third set of questions assesses the extent to which the knowledge necessary to address the problem is available. The overall assessment is based on answers to the following questions:

- Is the knowledge in a consistent digital format that can be easily transferred into the decision process being used? Or is it in a variety of formats, both digital and printed, that will be difficult to access and apply?
- Is there sufficient documentation on how the original data was collected and the assumptions that were made when it was distilled into information and eventually presented as knowledge? Or is there limited documentation and open questions about the way the knowledge was originally acquired?
- Are there secondary sources of data and information that can be used to glean further insight into the issue? Or will the team be required to conduct special studies of difficult-to-reach respondents?
- Considering previously strongly held positions, will those who might have to change their positions accept the information? Has the knowledge ever been taken out of context and misapplied by others, casting a cloud over integrity?
- Have all the functions involved in the decision provided access to all they have that is relevant to the decision? Or have they held back information that could be perceived as devaluing their points of view?

As simple as these questions appear, answering them is not always easy. But answering them will take you a long way toward addressing the right problem the right way.

Putting It All Together

One of the main premises of this book is that the effective use of all these elements requires an approach that takes, depending on the situation, some of its cues from the realm of synthesis and systems thinking—and is not limited to the realm of analysis and traditional, hierarchical management procedures.

For a synthesis to occur and work efficiently and effectively, management needs to ensure that all members of the enterprise have access to what the organization knows, which can help them do their jobs more effectively. This requires that the enterprise's leaders create an environment where people are encouraged and rewarded for sharing what they know with others. It also requires leaders who promote the right sort of environment by asking the following three important questions:

1. What did you learn from others before starting this project?
2. How has what you have learned impacted others in the organization?

3. Have you shared what your have learned with others who might benefit from this new knowledge?

Leadership needs to be constantly looking at the system in which specific decisions operate. It needs to be continually asking, "Am I asking people to work more efficiently at their unit level at the expense of helping the entire system become more effective?"

Getting any organization to think and act more systematically will, of course, require the organization to go through varios levels of transformation. The level of transformation required is succinctly described by the Office of Force Transformation within the Office of the Secretary of Defense, which is led by Vice Admiral (ret.) Arthur K. Cebrowski.

> Transformation is foremost a continuing process. It does not have an end point. Transformation is meant to create or anticipate the future. Transformation is meant to deal with the co-evolution of concepts, processes, organizations and technology. Change in any one of these areas necessitates change in all. Transformation is meant to create new competitive areas and new competencies. Transformation is meant to identify, leverage and even create new underlying principles for the way things are done. Transformation is meant to identify and leverage new sources of power.[9]

In the next chapter, I identify the importance of applying intuition and imagination to the information, knowledge, and wisdom developed and made available throughout the enterprise.

14 Combining Imagination and Market Knowledge

Imagination is more important than knowledge.

—Albert Einstein

Knowledge is Power.

—Sir Francis Bacon

Although the quotations that introduce this chapter appear to place two distinguished thinkers apart, the extent to which these thinkers do disagree can be tempered by putting their comments into the contexts from which they were extracted.

The Albert Einstein quote, "Imagination is more important than knowledge," comes from an in-depth interview by George Sylvester Viereck in the *Saturday Evening Post*.[1] After an interesting discussion of the problem of excessive analysis (an excerpt of which led off the introduction to part III), Viereck asks two questions: "If we owe so little to the experience of others, how do you account for sudden leaps forward in the sphere of science? Do you ascribe your own discoveries to intuition or inspiration?" Einstein replies as follows: "I believe in intuition and inspirations. I sometimes feel that I am right. I do not know that I am. When two expeditions of scientists, financed by the Royal Academy, went forth to test my theory of relativity, I was convinced that their conclusions would tally with my hypothesis. I was not surprised when the eclipse of May 29, 1919, confirmed my intuitions. I would have been surprised if I had been wrong."

Viereck then asks, "Then you trust more to your imagination than to your knowledge?" Einstein replies: "I am enough of the artist to draw freely upon my imagination. Imagination is more important than knowledge." Often left out of the quotation is the basis on which he made this judgment: "Knowledge is limited. Imagination encircles the world."[2] In this context, Einstein recognizes that knowledge still has value but it is limited in scope.

The phrase "knowledge is power," attributed to Francis Bacon, is usually used to mean that by controlling knowledge one gains power. That is not, it turns out, what Bacon had in mind. The phrase was presented in the context of a position that Bacon had developed on the relationship of knowledge of God to God's power. In fact, what he actually said was, "For Knowledge itself is Power," which, in the context of sixteenth-century England, was more likely to imply that knowledge is the power though which humankind can create a better life here on earth. For Bacon and his contemporaries, knowledge was a resource that made it possible for other good things to happen.

By putting both quotations in their original contexts, we see that these two insightful people were not in deep disagreement. For example, if further questioned on the *relationship* of knowledge *and* imagination, it is not a stretch to imagine Einstein's replying, "Although limited in its scope when compared to imagination, knowledge is a resource to be used by imaginative people to cause good things to happen"—with which Bacon would probably have agreed.

The Power of Research and Imagination

In chapter 13, we saw the importance of a consistent taxonomy of terms. So it is important to what follows to remember that knowledge comes from an understanding and synthesis of information. We will see that "market research" yields *information*, and that market research leads to *knowledge* when the relevant actors have come to understand the meaning of the information derived from market research.

In *USA Today*, James Healy and David Kiley comment on GM's improved position: "The buzz around Detroit is that GM is 'finally acting like the world's biggest car company.' It's asserting its strengths, fixing its weaknesses, tooting its own horn and striding confidently ahead of competitors."

The review goes on to quote David Cole, president of the Center for Automotive Research: "It's a market-based system. It's mean. It's tough. And it's very painful right now for Ford and Chrysler." The reviewers finish by further commenting on GM's comeback during harsh market conditions: "GM trudged through backstage improvements, enduring catcalls and hoping it was on the right track. Cole says GM began remaking itself in the early 1990's when it 'had its close walk with the grave.' Results have not come sooner, Cole says, because 'you can't just throw a switch, or take next year off to change the production system. It's like rewiring a house while the current's still on.'"³

Despite this type of review by veteran reporters and longtime industry observers like David Cole, as well as the overwhelming evidence contained in part II, stories about the limitations of knowledge based on market research continue—stories framing the argument as market knowledge *or* imagination.

Looking Beyond the Obvious

If the facts presented in part II did not convince you of the value of using market research effectively, then consider the following principle: To use market information effectively—and, in fact, to truly understand its market—an enterprise must nurture a strong and effective relationship between and among those who provide the wherewithal for knowledge development (e.g., market researchers), and imaginative and creative people (decision makers) who are capable of using the developed knowledge. This is a necessary requirement if your goal is to be able anticipate market needs as you strive to determine your destination.

This principle applies whether you are in a make-and-sell, sense-and-respond, or anticipate-and-lead business design. There is, however, a continuing battle regarding this principle between two broad categories of people:

- Those who prefer to come up with creative solutions unfettered by the requirements of "proving" their ideas right—the "just do it" point of view
- Those who believe the right answer will come forward from a deep understanding of market information collected through market research techniques—the "you must prove they will buy it before you make it" point of view

The trouble with much of the debate around this issue is that participants on both sides of the argument tend to suffer from selective perception, hearing only that part of the available evidence that fits their point of view. For example, let us take a more in-depth look at two individuals who have had memorable careers in applying their creative and intuitive skills in making decisions and who are held up as champions by those who support the "just do it" point of view.

David Ogilvy

Legendary advertising executive David Ogilvy understood the balance between collecting information and using it to make effective decisions. His research background—unknown to most that saw him solely as a creative genius—prepared him to trust his creative instincts. His experience reflects a deeper truth found in any industry that designs products for its customers. Still, it was his creativity that was most well known, as reflected in his following comments:

> The creative process requires more than reason. Most original thinking isn't even verbal. It requires "a groping experimentation with ideas, governed by intuitive hunches and inspired by the unconscious." The majority of businessmen are incapable of original thinking, because they are unable to escape from the tyranny of reason. The imaginations are blocked.
>
> I am almost incapable of logical thought, but I have developed techniques for keeping open the telephone line to my unconscious, in case that disorderly repository has anything to tell me. I hear a great deal of music. I am on friendly terms with John Barleycorn. I take long hot baths. I garden. I go into retreat among the Amish. I watch birds. I go for long walks in the country. And I take frequent vacations, so that my brain can lie fallow—no golf, no cocktail parties, no tennis, no bridge, no concentration; only a bicycle.
>
> While thus employed in doing nothing, I receive a constant stream of telegrams from my unconscious, and these become the raw material for my advertisements. But more is required: hard work, an open mind, and ungovernable curiosity.[4]

It should not be surprising that many individuals involved in creative functions, such as design, product development, marketing communications, and the like, identify with the notions in these comments, because the comments reinforce their perception of the type of environment most conducive to the creative process. It is also not hard to understand why someone who wants "total freedom from the tyranny of market research" would interpret Ogilvy's comments to mean that the rather structured and logical procedures required to measure customer attributes and behavior are significant barriers for creative solutions to the problems they are asked to address.

But, as with the Einstein and Bacon quotations, one must be careful in using selected comments from such an incredible talent as David Ogilvy. For example, in an interview in *Viewpoint*, Ogilvy is asked, "David, to what do you owe your success?" In partial response to the question, he says, "I came into advertising from [market] research and that gave me great advantage. . . . A lot of creative people fight research and don't want much to do with it. I was the exact opposite. I came at it from research and suddenly I was doing very good campaigns."5

Ogilvy, who was a part of the pioneering group that formed the Gallup Poll organization in the early 1930s and who served as the director of the Audience Research Institute, understood that decision makers need to learn how to *use* market research. In his book *Ogilvy on Advertising*, he reinforces the need to ensure an appreciation of both the intuitive approach and the logical approach:

> Advertising people who ignore research are as dangerous as generals who ignore decodes of enemy signals. Before I became a copywriter, I was a researcher. I delivered the first paper on copy-testing in the history of British Advertising.
>
> The best fun I ever had was in the early days of Ogilvy & Mather, when I was both Research Director and Creative Director. On Friday afternoons I wrote research reports to the Creative Director. On Monday mornings I changed hats, read my reports and decided what to do about them—if anything. In due course I was able to afford the services of Stanley Canter, a far better researcher. It took Stanley only ten days to get me out of his department. Like I always say, hire people who are better than you are.6

Ogilvy closes the chapter on the "Miracles of Market Research" as follows:

> Few copywriters share my appetite for research. The late and great Bill Bernbach, among many others, thought that it inhibited creativity. My experience has been the opposite. Research has often lead [*sic*] me to good ideas, such as the eyepatch in the Hathaway campaign.
>
> I have seen ideas so wild that nobody in his senses would dare to use them— until research found that they worked. When I had the idea of writing headlines for French tourism in French, my partners told me I was nuts—until research revealed that the French headlines were more effective than the English headlines. Research has also saved me from making some horrendous mistakes.
>
> I admit that research is often misused by agencies and their clients. They have a way of using it to prove they are right. They use research as a drunkard used a lamppost—not for illumination but for support. On the whole, however, research can be of incalculable help in producing more effective advertising.7

Ogilvy was a great user of information, and it contributed to his ability to move beyond the realm of facts and analytical thinking to the higher altitude of vision and intuition.

Bob Lutz

Bob Lutz, GM chairman for North America, with responsibility for product development, provides further insight into the breadth and depth of creative people.

The legendary Lutz is known for much he has said about the automotive industry. Among his most quoted statements, many are found in his book, *Guts*, in which he outlines "Lutz's Immutable Laws of Business," beginning with "The Customer Isn't Always Right." Many people have interpreted this law to mean "The Customer is Never Right." Because of this misinterpretation and many other comments Lutz has made, almost every automotive press writer has determined that Lutz's success is based on his possession of what has been referred to as the "Golden Gut of Automotive Design." They go even further to contend he is strongly opposed to the use of market research. For example, in a 2002 *Fortune* article, "Finally GM Is Looking Good," Alex Taylor III, quoting Lutz, writes as follows: "'One critically bad thing at GM has been the subordination of design,' says Lutz, with characteristic directness. 'People who rent our cars at airports look at them and say, "Isn't this depressing?"'" Following this quote, Taylor concludes, "Lutz is deemphasizing research and encouraging designers to create more appealing models."[8]

Much like David Ogilvy, however, Bob Lutz actually uses market research extremely well in confirming his many creative and sometimes intuitive decisions. In recent correspondence, he nearly mirrored the comments of Ogilvy: "I have this reputation for being anti-research. Well, I am not. I just prefer that we use it the right way. And the wrong way is to use it before you have the big idea that eventually becomes the vehicle. You use it after you develop your idea, to fine-tune it and to make sure the rest of the public shares your enthusiasm."[9]

In this comment, Lutz correctly puts emphasis on making sure the market research does not get in the way of the initial creative process. This position, however, needs to be considered in the context of his almost unique forty-year career in the automotive industry. During this period, Lutz has learned much from introducing big ideas, fine-tuning them, and then closely observing how they are received in the market. So, although he may not make extensive use of explicit market research studies to come up with the big idea, his keen sensitivity to what he has had the opportunity to learn undoubtedly contributes to his ability to develop, and encourage others to develop, creative ideas—ideas that

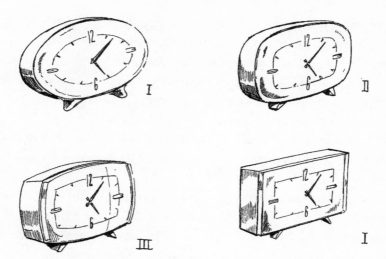

Figure 14.1 Drawings of different clock faces used in Bob Lutz's MBA thesis.

will actually sell for a profit! Others, without the benefit of his experience, might do well to be aware of one of his earliest endeavors.

As with Ogilvy, it was Lutz's experience in his early years that led him to understand the value of balancing his intuitive and analytical sides to become an effective user of market research. In his 1962 MBA thesis at the University of California at Berkeley, "An Exploratory Study of the Influence of Design on Product Image,"[10] Lutz personally conducted market research on how customers reacted to different clock faces (fig. 14.1).

Lutz was able to relate the physical differences among the clocks to differences in customer reactions—an early indication of what would be his quest to better understand the relationship between the product's design and the customer's reaction to that product. As he stated in the purpose section of his thesis,

> [M]y study hopes to be able to say something meaningful about the way consumers' perception of the *product's qualities* change as a function of changes in the style or package. This should be of interest to the marketer as well as to the stylist, for it means that the product should be styled not only in the manner which will evoke a favorable aesthetic responses from the socio-economic class at which it is aimed, *but should also be such as to evoke in the perceiver the product image which the manufacturer desires his product to evoke.*"[11]

In seeking to prove his hypothesis regarding the role of design elements in changing customer perceptions of a product, Lutz used what was then a somewhat new technique called the "semantic differential," a method to plot the differences between individuals' connotations for words and thus map the psychological "distance" between words.[12] At the time of his thesis, this was on the "cutting edge" of market research's capability to understand the deep meanings of words and concepts. Interestingly, it was an approach Richard Wirthlin (mentioned in the preface) and I used in political research in the late 1960s and is an approach that has been adapted and is used extensively at GM today—the results of which have assisted Bob Lutz in making product decisions.

Lutz's research demonstrated two principles that led to the effective use of the market research he conducted. First, each of the designs of the clocks in his study was carefully chosen to elicit specific differences. Because the designs were sufficiently differentiated, he developed a questionnaire able to elicit measured differences in customer reaction to something long considered to be limited to the intuitive realm: design. Second, although not the practice generally considered appropriate for an enterprise trying to overcome concerns of functional bias, a seamless connection existed between two roles: much as Ogilvy had the jobs of both research and creative direction, Bob Lutz was the information provider—he designed and executed the study—and Bob Lutz was the information user. Since, in this case, Bob Lutz represented all the functions of a company, the research provided precisely that information which he needed to test his hypothesis. As important, that experience set him on a journey of many experiences that have allowed him to appreciate the limits, as well as the potential value, of market research. This understanding has also contributed to his ability to be a *constructive* critic of market research use.

The discussion of Ogilvy and Lutz illustrates the importance of understanding the interactions of creativity and analytical thinking when you use consumer and market information. It is also interesting that the two men have both collected information and used the information they collected. There is some merit in having individuals from both sides of the aisle share more time with each other to gain an appreciation of what the other person does and, more important, what each needs to do to perform his or her respective assignments more effectively.

GM's attempt at an organizational integration started in 1992, when Wayne

Cherry became GM Design Center director. In accordance with his experience in Europe, he offered to have the market research organization move into the GM design center. Additionally, he encouraged the market research unit to transfer Jeff Hartley, one of GM's more "creative" market researchers, to the design organization so that he could work on a day-to-day basis with the designers. Hartley is now back in the market research organization and provides keen insight into the way GM has modified many of its market research practices to provide more meaningful and acceptable information to the designers. Additionally, Andrew Norton, the director of GM's market research department, worked for many years in the design center and a vehicle division before he was selected to lead the market research department. Also, Mike DiGiovanni, architect of the Hummer brand discussed in chapter 10, preceded Norton as the director of market research.

It is hoped that this discussion of the "unseen" side of two well-known and respected visionary people, together with the examples described in this section, has provided further insight concerning the important question, "Can market research techniques help consumers provide meaningful information that can support decision makers in the development of products or services?" This question is, in essence, the same question that Jack Smith asked in 1992, when he wanted to be assured that the market research we were using reflected what was going on the in the market. The answer today is *yes*—the same as it was in 1933, when Alfred Sloan discussed with GM stockholders where market research should fit into the organization and what its effective use was: "To discuss consumer research as a functional activity would give an erroneous impression. In its broad implications it is more in the nature of an OPERATING PHILOSOPHY, which, to be fully effective, must extend through all phases of a business—weighing every action from the standpoint of how it affects the goodwill of the institution, recognizing that the quickest way to profits—and the permanent assurance of such profits—is to serve the customer in ways in which the customer wants to be served."[13]

The strength of the positive answer, however, is still conditioned on assurances that *the information be focused not solely on any single organizational function, that it be available at the time it is needed, and that it be listened to.* These conditions can be achieved only if there is a jointly developed and approved process designed to foster a shared belief: that the information is correct, and that the value of the knowledge it yields to those for whom it was developed is greater than the cost of the development.

Up to this point in the book, I have offered evidence of the importance of systems thinking and the development of useful knowledge. The next chapter discusses methods to help you create the business design most appropriate to the business conditions you face today and most appropriate to those you will face in an uncertain future.

15 Creating the Right Business Design in the Face of Uncertainty

One cannot make decisions for the future. Decisions are commitments to action. And actions are always in the present, and in the present only. But actions in the present are also the one and only way to make the future.

—Peter Drucker

It's tough to make predictions, especially about the future.

—Yogi Berra

This chapter presents a thinking framework to help business and public-sector leaders decide what kind of enterprise they want to become in the face of an uncertain future. This type of strategic thinking is crucial to helping an enterprise find ways to get to where it wants to be from where it is now. It also requires the leadership team to take into consideration, as was pointed out in chapter 12, changes in the broader societal environment, including customer needs, political realities, economics, and many other factors.

The Impact of Digital Technologies on Business Design

Throughout this book, it has been pointed out that customer needs change rapidly and are difficult to predict. The digital economy's primary effect has not been change itself, but an increase in the rate of change. Just as an organization begins to understand customer wants and needs, those wants and needs change, in both subtle and dramatic ways.

As computing and communication technologies improve, along with the understanding of their applications, so will the ability for businesses to acquire deep and broad external knowledge of *current* and *potential* markets, thus allowing companies to better sense changes in customer requirements and begin to anticipate additional changes. These technologies will also help reconfigure and make better use of internal knowledge of a company's capabilities as an extended enterprise, enabling it to innovatively serve these markets. Technology is redefining the nature of competition. Businesses are expanding their radar screens, realizing that the Internet and other nontraditional technologies present a type and scope of competition that is unfamiliar to most enterprises.

There is no doubt that the business environment today is changing at exponential rates. At the same time, the response to these changes with the use of established methods just cannot keep pace. This is why it is so important that businesses learn to approach transformation in a different way.

Lacking a crystal ball, one can assume only that the future will be different from the present. The degree of difference is, of course, what every enterprise would like to know. Pursuit of a single answer to this question, however, has led to approaches that require a significant amount of simplification of the future's true complexity, such as point estimates of the growth of the gross national product, price indices, population growth, competitive actions, cost of raw materials, and so on. The inherent futility of these approaches requiring specific point estimates of what will be is that the more point estimates one lists, the higher the probability that one or more of those assumptions will be wrong. Yet, despite such faulty reasoning, this is the approach that underlies the long-range planning and thinking of many enterprises. A more realistic approach is to accept the reality that we cannot know with precision what the future holds and to learn how to design business plans and strategies to deal with that uncertainty.

This understanding, in the context of a shared corporate business design, can enable a company's decision makers to decide how to "craft a business model that is not only superior, but *unique*," as Adrian Slywotzky and David Morrison suggest.[1]

One approach is to choose from among alternative business designs by determining which of those designs is robust over a range of possible alternative future scenarios.

First Step: Identify Realistic Alternative Business Designs

A business interacts with customers in at least two ways: it makes offers to them, and it responds to requests from them. All businesses do some of both, but the mix and match of each type of behavior calls for particular business designs.

To demonstrate the process. we will use the three business designs discussed in previous chapters: make-and-sell, sense-and-respond, and anticipate-and-lead. As a reminder, the three designs can be quickly described:

- A make-and-sell design does just that: it predicts what the market will demand, makes a product, and then goes out and sells it.
- A sense-and-respond design says to selected markets, "Help me to identify your needs and let's work together to satisfy them."
- An anticipate-and-lead design leads the consumer to new ideas based on identified unarticulated consumer needs gleaned from direct observation of the consumer's behavior as he or she chooses from among existing products and services. The focus is on creating the future you want.

Hybrid Models

As we saw earlier, it would be foolish to assume that one model is inherently better than the other. I will demonstrate later in this chapter that, depending on the business conditions that exist, the leadership team is more likely to determine that a hybrid model, taking advantage of the positive traits of each design, is most beneficial.

Many enterprises grew successful by using customer research to efficiently predict and then make and sell products in cadence with changes in customer needs. In many cases, they even defined these needs by creating innovative products and then communicating the benefits of these products to prospective customers. In those instances when the enterprise did not "get it right," the discrepancies were generally resolved by adjusting prices. The brand-new widget is not exactly what the customer wanted? Let us "deal" with this discrepancy by marking its price down—until someone buys it.

On the other hand, some companies, including Cemex, Cisco, and Dell, have grown successfully because they organized themselves to respond flexibly and economically to individual customer requests in the required time frame.

Thinking Strategically

Currently successful companies are notorious for believing that they know what is best, regardless of how the world is changing around them. Central planning staffs and long-range business plans based on a long list of single-point assumptions have traditionally been the norm.

However, discontinuous change has raised questions about the value of forecast-based long-term plans. Hence, a framework for strategic thinking is more important than ever to help approach options with intelligence and insight. But instead of expressing the results as a plan, the enterprise must, instead, consider a range of alternatives linked to a set of possible responses. Strategic thinking, in contrast to traditional planning, can operate only within a business design that is knowledge-based and adaptive to unexpected change.

Second Step: Envision Alternative Future Scenarios

To make good decisions in the face of the longer term, during which the unexpected is to be expected, requires a decision process that evaluates how robust a business design would be in an uncertain future.[2]

This is no small challenge. For example, although everyone agrees digital technology will definitely influence the way businesses will operate, there is little agreement on precisely the extent and timing of its impact. Dealing with this uncertainty requires an envisioning process that senses and interprets a broad expanse of technological, societal, and demographic trends, in order to gain understanding about what could occur in the future and the implications it may have for current decisions

The envisioning process enables better interpretations of possible future business environments, especially in areas in which one has only some or very little control but which still impact—and are impacted by—the decisions made. It is most important to remember that the scenarios are not developed to limit the range of possible actions. Instead, the benefit of the process is in revealing actions that could be taken to create future conditions more conducive to the actions you want to take.

Envisioning Process

The envisioning process begins by gathering together experts from a variety of key fields and providing them with available foresight to develop a set of scenarios—plausible, challenging stories about what might happen in the future. These are not forecasts. They do not predict by extrapolation. Instead, these scenarios reveal a state of understanding possibilities, allowing for the condition of not knowing exactly what the future might hold.

Many business decision makers like to sort out and simplify things and get to know the things (problems) themselves. But, in doing so, you must be cognizant that what we "see" is based on images and reflections of personal and, many times, functional organizational experiences. These images, like those on Plato's cave walls (discussed in chapter 13), provide no more than a reflection of market reality. Although decision makers must stay close to reality, they must do so by understanding the interaction with the broader system that contains the reality they are attempting to address. Breaking things down into their parts is about analysis, not synthesis. To operate as a system, we need to remember the definition of a system: A system is a whole that is defined by interdependent parts in which the function of each essential part affects the functions of the whole, and the system as a whole cannot be divided into independent parts or it will lose its defining function.

The envisioning process attempts to maintain as much of reality's complexity as possible, while allowing management to make decisions in the context of an uncertain future. The possible scenarios that emerge from the envisioning process, combined with the appropriate decision process, help prepare for, not avoid, discontinuities and sudden change, and help one recognize and interpret important events and new developments as they occur.

For purposes of description, a set of alternative scenarios designed to reflect what could be the outcome of an envisioning process is found in table 15.1. It is important to reemphasize that, as used in this process, a scenario is not a prediction of what will happen. Scenarios are descriptions of *possible* futures that *could* occur. Several are presented to ensure a high likelihood that whatever may occur is captured in one of the scenarios.

Table 15.1. Possible Alternative Scenarios

Key Element	Scenario "A" Manufacturing Economy (Today's Dominant Model)	Scenario "B" Hybrid Economy (Scenario "A" Manufacturing Convergence with Scenario "C" Digital)	Scenario "C" Digital Economy (Digital Achieves Promise)
Buyer and seller role relationship assumptions	*Tilting slightly toward seller power:* Product differentiation minimizes overcapacity. Product information concentrated in firm. Difficult for buyers to interact with sellers. Mass-market advertising is main format for customer communication. Tailoring products is expensive.	*Tilting toward buyer power:* Greater buyer diversity leads to oversupply of specific goods and services. Improved buyer access to information and contact with sellers in placing orders. Enhanced ability for sellers to communicate with previous owners of enterprise products. Ability to tailor products	*Buyer power dominant:* Market fragmentation leads to oversupply of goods and services. Widespread information. Enhanced ability to interact with sellers and buyers in placing orders. Significantly enhanced ability to communicate with previous owners of enterprise products. Enhanced ability to tailor products.
Enterprise direction	*Firm driven:* In accordance with the firm's assets and skills, marketing forecasts future customer demand tempered by assessments of emerging regulatory and societal concerns. From forecasts, management specifies products the firm designs and manufactures and which of its existing outlets shall distribute them. Marketing uses mass-market advertising to persuade customers to buy the product.	*Customer-based:* Buyers assess availability of products and services promoted by all firms. By networking with trusted individuals and assessing other information sources, buyers specify the product attributes they want, and when they want them distributed. They propose a price and preferred financing arrangements.	*Web-driven:* Web tools rapidly screen all products based on the attributes of relevance to the customer. The customer orders the "best match" delivered either to his or her location or a nearby outlet. Executives focus on creating best-in-class products and on creating a trusted Web interface for customers. Enterprises develop alliances to ensure they have access to products wanted by buyers.
Definition of marketing	Marketing *organization* forecasts customer needs, persuades customers to buy the firm's products, and distributes them in the most effective manner.	Senior enterprise executive uses the marketing concept and oversees all the functions of the firm in delivery of what the customer ordered.	Enterprise develops systems that allow an interactive trusted relationship with each customer. Information is gathered to allow the firm to tailor its offerings to that customer's specific needs and interests.
Places of customer contact	Firm has many established outlets in all the locations in which it sells products. Customer must come to one of those outlets to buy product.	Firm has outlets to enable customers to physically experience the product. But firm distributes the product globally, using whatever distribution channels the customer prefers.	Sells the product to the customer and delivers it to the customer anywhere, any time, any way the customer desires.
Primary method of communication to customers	The firm advertises its products, using mass media or mail campaigns without the customer's consent and presumes that it represents a main source of product information.	The firm invites the customer to ask it for further information and requests permission to send the customer ads. The firm recognizes that it is only one source of product information.	Interactive trust-based communication with customer (customers can easily detect false claims). Information delivered when the customer is interested. Reduced conventional advertising.
Pricing practices	Firm sets an initial price to attract customers and then offers higher priced options. In some cases, firm makes certain options standard to make the base product more appealing.	Customer proposes a price and interacts to determine the price that will be paid. Enterprise might reduce price in return for customer's signing up for additional services (e.g., insurance, wireless service, maintenance plans).	Firm specifies a mechanism by which the customer's price will be discovered (e.g., auction, dynamic pricing). The buyers use that mechanism to set price they are willing to pay.

Putting the Scenarios to Good Use

The scenarios allow decision makers to consider which combination of the three business designs (make-and-sell, sense-and-respond, and anticipate-and-lead) to adopt in case any of these scenarios actually occurs. To appreciate the risks and rewards associated with each of the alternative business designs, the decision team can map possible outcomes of the three business designs under all three scenarios in a decision-tree format, as seen in figure 15.1. It is impor-

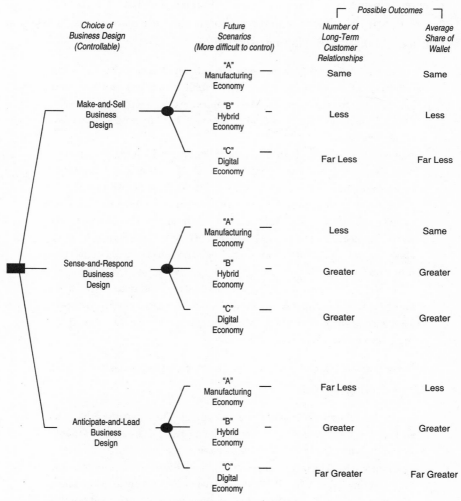

Figure 15.1 Simplified decision tree for developing business design mix.

tant to point out that, if the decision tree were completed by others, then the interpretation of the expected results could very well be different. The value of the process is to assist the decision team in reaching a consensus decision based on a synthesis of all that the team members have available at that point in time.

For this hypothetical analysis, the decision involves choosing between the make-and-sell, sense-and-respond, and anticipate-and-lead business designs. The criteria for selection is limited to two items: (1) which business design will increase the number of customers with whom the enterprise will have a long-term relationship, and (2) which business design will increase the enterprise's "share of their wallet." If the enterprise chooses the *make-and-sell* business design, it could expect the following to occur.

- Under the "A" scenario, a manufacturing economy: The enterprise is likely to end up with the same customers, given its ability to forecast customer needs, and continue to take advantage of economies of scale. It will likely achieve the same share of wallet, since it will continue to limit its product portfolio to the same products.
- Under the "B" scenario, hybrid economy: The enterprise is likely to end up with fewer customers. This would be the result of developing products for which the demand is less likely to meet enterprise forecasts. This would drive operating costs up and require price reductions to convince consumers to buy products that do not meet all their requirements. The share of wallet will be less because the customers will see the enterprise as dealing on price alone and not capable of providing additional products or services the customer prefers.
- Under the "C" scenario, digital economy: The same conditions as the "B" scenario are likely to occur, except that they would be exacerbated by the speed at which customers would be able to determine alternatives to the enterprise's products and services.

If the enterprise chooses the *sense-and-respond* business design, it could expect the following to occur.

- Under the "A" scenario, manufacturing economy: The enterprise is likely to end up with fewer customers, given that it may have added costs to achieve flexibility, which is of relatively little value since the firm can actually forecast future sales. The increase in costs could put the firm at a price disadvantage resulting in lost sales. Share of customer wallet is likely to be the same, with the possibility of a slight increase if customers seek additional services.

- Under the "B" scenario, hybrid economy: The enterprise is likely to end up with a greater number of customers. This would be the result of developing products for which the enterprise is more likely to meet consumer requirements. Although the investment in flexibility could drive operating costs up, the ability to meet customer requirements will allow the firm the opportunity to price for having the right product. The share of wallet will be greater, because the customers will see the enterprise as being more responsive to their needs, and they may therefore be willing to entrust more of their expenditures to the firm.
- Under the "C" scenario, digital economy: Since predicting customers' future needs will be extremely difficult for everyone in the industry, the enterprise is likely to experience a competitive advantage if it moves to sense-and-respond before major competitors, thus allowing it to gain more understanding about each customer's unique profile of preferences and the value that the customer attaches to each preference.

If the enterprise chooses the *anticipate-and-lead* business design, it could expect the following to occur:

- Under the "A" scenario, manufacturing economy: The business is likely to face results similar to those of the sense-and-respond business design—only worse. This occurs because competitors that maintain the make-and-sell business design could be at a significant cost advantage, because they do not invest in the digital technologies and flexibility. By contrast, this enterprise will have spent considerable sums on equipment and on training people to accomplish unnecessary tasks.
- Under the "B" scenario, hybrid economy: The enterprise is likely to face the same improvement in number of customers and share of wallet as under the sense-and-respond business design.
- Under the "C" scenario, digital economy: The enterprise is likely to gain far greater numbers of customers and share of wallet. It could provide the full range of products required by these customers, and, because it anticipated their requirements early, it could meet these requirements where, when, and how the customers desired, creating, in effect, the environment conducive to the products and services the enterprise had introduced.

Although limited in scope, a review of the expected outcomes of this hypothetical analysis clearly shows that the decision surrounding which business design to choose is affected by which of the possible future scenarios is expected to emerge.

Decision makers, under these circumstances, are left with several choices: (1)

to do what they want to do and hope the future environment goes their way, (2) to try to develop a business design that is robust for all scenarios, or (3) to see what they can do to encourage the desired future environment.

If the decision makers choose to encourage the desired future environment, they must first determine, given their current and potential competencies, which of the future scenarios they would prefer. They must then determine the likelihood that they and potential alliance partners could cause that scenario to occur.

When an enterprise is reviewing alternative strategies for addressing a problem in this manner, a hybrid strategy generally emerges that is superior to the initial strategies used in conducting the analysis. In this case, one might choose to create an anticipate-and-lead organization with sense-and-respond characteristics, or vice-versa. In the future, it will not be wise to strictly choose one over the other. There is great value in developing a business design that avoids the tyranny of "either/or" and takes advantage of the opportunity presented by "and."

GM's introduction of the OnStar mobile communication system in 1996–1997 is an example of operating within three business designs. If the automobile is the epitome of the make-and-sell offering, how does an auto company create a customized sense-and-respond or anticipate-and-lead value proposition for the customer? As discussed in chapter 3, when faced with this question, GM created OnStar, an onboard computer connected via cellular phone to a satellite system and a central customer service center. Vehicle owners who purchase OnStar receive the ultimate sense-and-respond add-on to their make-and-sell-designed vehicle. OnStar customers can call for directions, information, or personalized music. An OnStar service representative can unlock a car door by phone, order flowers, or dispatch emergency help if the air bag deploys.

The sense-and-respond aspects of OnStar work because the basic vehicle was specifically designed to satisfy individuals clustered in a customer segment: the best of the make-and-sell model. Rather than attempting to make the basic vehicle in a sense-and-respond business design that would be so costly that it would put the vehicle beyond the reach of most customers, GM designed an electronic infrastructure into the vehicle that allows the customer to switch on and pay for those features he or she wants.

The introduction of XM Radio, the first satellite radio systems in vehicles, was more of an anticipate-and-lead business design. In this case, GM determined that satellite radio would be successful only if sufficient numbers of vehicles had radios that could receive the satellite signals. The availability of these radios would provide enough potential subscribers to warrant the investment required to develop and deliver the appropriate programming at an acceptable price. By creating a strategic relationship with XM Radio, GM changed the environment by installing satellite-compatible radio in a large percentage of its vehicles. In doing so, GM was able to "kick start" the industry to such an extent that its strategic partner, XM Radio, is currently the market leader in satellite radio, with over one and a half million subscribers.

Recent experience has shown that, regardless of how much analysis is conducted, one still cannot always predict which future will emerge. It could be one of the scenarios envisioned or another entirely unexpected alternative. However, if the enterprise knows what conditions could occur, it is then faced with at least two options: it can determine how much it wants to spend to ensure its plans are robust across the range of possible scenarios, or take action to allocate resources to try to bring about the scenario that offers the best competitive position.

Although planning for a certain future may have worked in the past, this chapter has provided a way to choose among business designs so that the negative impact is minimal if the future turns out to be different than expected.

16 Starting with Your Destination

Knowledge resides in the user and not in the collection. It's how the user reacts to the collection of information that really matters.

—C. West Churchman

All this strategic thinking is well and good, but it is insufficient without the proper competencies that lead to effective implementation. There are two competencies that are critical for the leadership of an enterprise that desires to determine its destination:

- First is the ability to understand and anticipate not only changes in customer preferences, but also changes in the broader system that encompasses the enterprise.
- Second is the ability to communicate these observations in such a manner that they are accepted throughout the enterprise. Given a clear direction, individuals and organizations can move quickly and consistently within enterprise guidelines to incorporate these changes in their strategic direction and operating plans.

To fully benefit from the experiences and recommendations found in this book, the enterprise must accept the notion that "even if we improve on doing what we have done in the past, we may never know what future opportunities we missed by not doing things—not just better, but *differently*."

It is important to remember that neither of these business designs is superior to the other. The benefit of one over the other can be determined only by understanding the context of the encompassing system and the business strategy with which the firm is operating. Additionally, it is likely that a firm will find itself applying aspects of all three business designs, depending on the uncertainty and complexity of the business environment within which it operates. It is also important to keep in mind that one design is not any more exciting or rewarding than another to those involved in its development and use.

For example, the Corvette automobile is unquestionably one of the more exciting and emotionally rewarding products that GM produces. The Corvette development, design, and production teams love their work. Corvette customers are extremely loyal and have formed Corvette Clubs around the world. The Corvette has its own museum. It also epitomizes the make-and-sell business design. Although other companies claim to have a superior sports car, there is little argument that the Corvette delivers the most value to its customers; that is, given its design and performance, it costs less than comparable cars. With the consistent positioning of the Corvette since its creation in 1953, GM can predict with reasonable certainty the number of Corvettes that can be sold within a specified price range. With this deep understanding of the current and potential Corvette customer, GM has invested in a factory and in distribution systems capable of interacting to handle any minor discrepancies between actual volume and the planning staff's volume predictions.

Another distinction between the business designs is the extent to which they are established. Make-and-sell is firmly established and understood, sense-and-respond is understood and in the initial stages of implementation, and anticipate-and-lead is an emerging state (fig. 16.1).

From 1998 to 2000, many of the firms that made up these industries had a long way to go to complement make-and-sell designs with the additional advantages of a sense-and-respond business design, much less the benefits of anticipate-and-lead. Industries such as oil and gas, utilities, airlines, chemicals, and automotive were deeply entrenched in the make-and-sell business design.

The potential of digital technology to cause and accelerate the rate of change

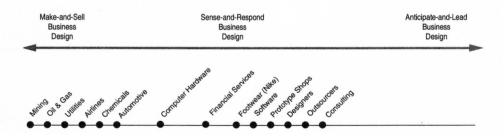

Figure 16.1 1998–2000: State of American business compared to business designs.

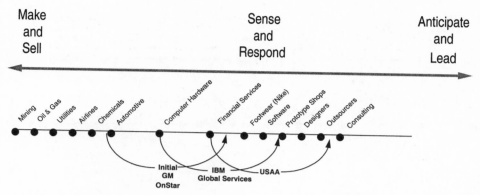

Figure 16.2 How enterprises have adapted their business designs to changing conditions.

should alert everyone not to be fooled into looking at competitors (either within their own industries or outside) solely on the basis of where their industry is represented on the continuum of adaptive business design change (fig. 16.2).

Figure 16.2 illustrates how, toward the end of the 1990s, firms began taking advantage of sense-and-respond, even though the industry in which they were categorized did not.[1] Some enterprises like USAA, a worldwide insurance and diversified financial services association serving the military community since 1922, have conceptualized their business designs more like sense-and-respond. IBM reversed its strategy of having each of its divisions operating as independent companies and had them come together in a more systemic manner to offer customer-specific solutions that cut across the divisions. GM used make-and-sell vehicles, complemented by the initial version of OnStar, to provide limited sense-and-respond capabilities, thus demonstrating the importance of not discarding make-and-sell as a part of overall strategy.

Using an Idealized Destination to Transform GM

Throughout this book, the point has been made several times that, although we may not be able to predict the future, by using systems thinking methods, we can help make our future happen. To do so, everyone throughout the enterprise must have a consistent idealized notion of where the leadership of the enterprise wants to be, and they must understand why the leadership wants to be there. This shared vision, along with an understanding of the assumptions that un-

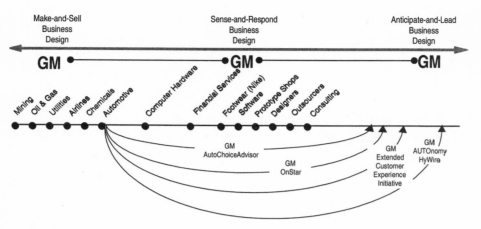

Figure 16.3 GM's attempt to improve mix of alternative business designs.

derlie all the most likely alternative future environments, provides the basis for a highly efficient and effective enterprise.

Figure 16.3 illustrates how some anticipate-and-lead applications have been implemented without abandoning those sense-and-respond and make-and-sell business designs that are still applicable. In this way, the enterprise is now positioned to take advantage of all three business designs, and did so, while minimizing the impact of the zone of discomfort during transformation.

At a senior managers' meeting in 1999, GM's CEO Rick Wagoner articulated a future vision for GM. The vision had GM continuing to develop vehicles but, in addition, enhancing existing services and developing additional products and services that would be seen as valuable by existing automotive consumers and their households. These new services would generate growth and create greater profits and loyalty than GM was currently creating with existing individual GM transactional relationships.

His rationale for selecting this goal was quite clear: there was about twice as much revenue and profit opportunity in moving "downstream"—selling and servicing products after the vehicle had been sold for the first time—than there was in developing, manufacturing, and selling vehicles new.

Reviewing how other companies had successfully moved "downstream" made it clear that the most efficient and effective approach for GM was to do so by improving on GM's current core businesses. Wagoner also made it very clear that this strategy did not relieve anyone from improving the way he or she currently performed current responsibilities, which were to create satisfied automotive consumers by using make-and-sell and sense-and-respond.

This direction was developed with many of the principles of anticipate-and-lead, but it was not described under that term (see chapter 2). It evolved as GM was uncovering an unarticulated customer need for well-managed everyday experiences with automotive companies, a need to save time and energy, and enjoy personal attention, privacy, and personal safety—all issues that customers had identified as important and not yet satisfactorily addressed by the industry. By reviewing the needs and reviewing GM's ability to address them, GM concluded that it should attempt to package existing products and services, and create new products when necessary. A synthesis of all existing information led to the belief that, by so doing, GM could increase not only its market share, but also its share of the disposable income of its customers.

It was noted with some interest that this customer-centric approach was remarkably consistent with the question that was asked by Alfred P. Sloan's management team in 1923. Then, as today, the question was, "What does General Motors mean to me [the consumer]?" In 1923, the answer, as it appeared in an advertisement, was fourfold:

1. By uniting the purchasing power of many companies, General Motors buys more economically, whether the material purchased be tiny lock washers or tons of steel. You benefit by these economies in the price you pay for General Motors products.

2. Many minds are better than one. No American automobile company is more than 29 years old, but the car and truck divisions of General Motors have an aggregate experience of more that 100 years, which is available for each separate division in the development of its cars.

3. You can pay for a General Motors car out of income, just as you pay for a home. The General Motors Acceptance Corporation makes this possible, through resources which place it among the nation's principal institutions.

4. In Detroit and in Dayton, General Motors maintains the largest automotive laboratories in the world—two cooperating organizations of scientists and engineers, working constantly for progress in the automotive industry.

Thus, General Motors, the family, is more than the sum of its members, for it adds a contribution of its own to the contributions made by each individual company. And these united contributions, crystallized in added value, find their way to you.[2]

It is interesting to note that when these answers were written, the automotive industry was deeply entrenched in the mechanistic, machine-age, mental model and a make-and-sell business design. Yet Sloan and his team actually articulated a visionary systemic statement. First, it was a clear description of the importance of managing the interaction of the parts, not the parts taken separately, because the goal was to have the enterprise provide a service that was greater than the sum of the individual parts. It was a business design at the forefront of its time, and it led to long-term prosperous growth.

In today's systems thinking age, the answer is also fourfold.

General Motors, the enterprise, offers the customer more than the sum of its parts:

1. By constantly monitoring the needs, behavior, and satisfaction of millions of current and potential customers, we can anticipate and provide products and services to meet the broadest range of your requirements and desires.
2. Our full range of products and services, combined with our global team of people and technological assets, enables us to translate those requirements and desires into the precise combination of products and services that are most valuable to you and your household today. Additionally, basing our actions on these relationships, we will anticipate and develop products and services to meet your future requirements as your household needs change over time.
3. Our purchasing power and capability allows us to acquire the right mix of components, at the best possible price. We can then provide the components and services you want, in a manner that allows you to configure them to meet your specific requirements, at a price you can afford.
4. Our global reach ensures that these services are designed, developed, and delivered to you when, where, and how you want them.

Although the question is the same as Sloan's, GM's more current answer is at once both profoundly similar to and dramatically different from the 1923 answer.

It is similar in that it still develops a proposition of consumer value in which what GM in total (the system) offers its customers is greater than the sum of the products and services of its individual business units.

It is different because of radical changes in consumer requirements and in the technologies and processes that define GM's individual parts and their interaction in the greater GM system.

The ideas and approaches discussed in part I and part III have provided examples of idealized designs and various ways of achieving them.

The systems thinking way of approaching the future builds on what is already known (that is still worth knowing), identifies the interdependencies of the whole and its containing system, recognizes the uncertainty of what we do not know (but need to know), and perhaps most significantly improves our understanding of uncertainty by helping develop the most likely assessment of the future. In this way, the enterprise is positioned to create an idealized design of what it wants to be and understands the possibilities and consequences of its actions before important decisions are made and resources are irrevocably allocated. By gaining competency in this type of systems thinking, any enterprise will be better prepared to start with the destination it prefers. Whether it will be successful in arriving at that destination depends on the enterprise's ability to learn, and on the quality and commitment of its leadership in determining the destination and providing its employers and partners the travel guides and resources for the journey to get there.

Notes

Chapter 1

1. The idea for the "Zone of Discomfort" is drawn from the executive summary of the *Report on the Jumping the Curve Consortium* (Oslo, Norway: Performance Group, 2000).

2. Russell Ackoff, *Re-Creating the Corporation* (New York: Oxford University Press, 1999), 87.

Part I

1. Adrian Slywotzky, *Value Migration* (Boston: Harvard Business School Press, 1996); Adrian Slywotzky and David Morrison, *Profit Zones* (New York: Times Books, 1997).

2. Slywotzky, *Value Migration*, 4.

3. C. K. Prahalad and Venkat Ramaswamy, *The Future of Competition: Co Creating Unique Value with Customers* (Boston: Harvard Business School Press, 2004); Philip Kotler, Dipak Jain, and Suvit Maesincee, *Marketing Moves* (Boston: Harvard Business School Press, 2002); Jerry Wind, Vijay Mahajan, and Robert Gunther, *Convergence Marketing* (Upper Saddle River, N.J.: Prentice Hall, 2002); Adrian Slywotzky and David Morrison, *How Digital Is Your Business?* (New York: Crown Business, 2000).

4. Stephan Haeckel, *The Adaptive Enterprise* (Boston: Harvard Business School Press, 1999).

5. David Riesman, *The Lonely Crowd* (1950; New Haven, Conn.: Yale University Press, 1961), 15–16. In his penetrating review of twentieth-century social character, Riesman identified a range of personality types. Among them was a group he described as "inner-directed," which had "one thing in common: the source of direction for the individual is 'inner' in the sense that it is implanted early in life by the elders and directed toward generalized but nonetheless inescapably destined goals." Riesman used the metaphor of a psychological "gyroscope" that, once set by external forces, keeps the inner-directed person on course. In discussing the metaphor, Riesman commented: "This metaphor of the gyroscope, like any other, must not be taken literally. It would be a mistake to see the inner-directed man as incapable of learning from experience or as insensitive to public opinion in matter of external conformity. He can receive and uti-

lize certain signals from outside, provided that they can be reconciled with the limited maneuverability that his gyroscope permits him. His pilot is not quite automatic."

6. Stephan Haeckel, recent correspondence.

7. Riesman, *Lonely Crowd*, 21. Riesman uses the metaphor of radar to distinguish between the "other-directed" and "inner-directed" personality types: "What is common to all the other-directed people is that their contemporaries are the source of direction for the individual—either those known to him or those with whom he is indirectly acquainted, through friends and through the mass media. This source is of course 'internalized' in the sense that dependence on it for guidance in life is implanted early. The goals toward which the other-directed person strives shift with that guidance; it is only the process of striving itself and the process of paying close attention to the signals from others that remain un-altered throughout life."

8. Much of the original thinking regarding the make-and-sell and sense-and-respond business design descriptions grew out of collaborative work with Stephan Haeckel. This table benefited from continuing that collaboration. Jeff Hartley contributed greatly to the personality traits of all three business designs.

9. Nicholas Negroponte, *Being Digital* (New York: Alfred A. Knopf, 1996), 11–13.

10. Clay Christenson, *The Innovator's Dilemma* (Boston: Harvard Business School Press, 1997).

11. Jacob Bronowski, *The Ascent of Man* (Boston: Little, Brown, 1973), 19.

12. Adrian Slywotzky, Foreword, in Haeckel, *The Adaptive Enterprise*, xi.

13. Slywotzky, Foreword, xiv.

Chapter 2

1. John Hagel, III, and Marc Singer, "Unbundling the Corporation," *Harvard Business Review* (March–April 1999), 133–41.

2. Adrian Slywotzky and David Morrison, *How Digital Is Your Business?* (New York: Crown Business, 2000), 8.

3. *The Incumbent Response* (Washington, D.C.: Corporate Executive Board, 1999), 16.

4. Michael Porter and Nicolaj Siggelkow, "Contextuality Within Activity Systems," Harvard Business School Working Paper (Feb. 20, 2001); Nicolaj Siggelkow, "Change in the Presence of Fit: The Rise, the Fall, and the Renaissance of Liz Claiborne," *Academy of Management Journal* 44 (2001): 838; Nicolaj Siggelkow, "Misperceiving Interactions: Organization Consequences," Wharton School of Management Working Paper (2001).

Chapter 3

1. General Motors news release (Detroit, Mich.), January 28, 2004.

2. Keith Crain, "Maybe Cars Are Getting Simpler," *Automotive News* (Aug. 12, 2002), 12.

3. Todd Lappin, "The New Road Rage," *Wired* (July 1999), 126–132.

4. Reported by WRAL-TV5 (Raleigh-Durham-Fayetteville) on March 31, 2003.

5. A detailed documentation of OnStar's development can be found in two case studies:, Clayton M. Christensen and Erik Roth, "OnStar: Not Your Father's General Motors," Harvard Business School, (A) N9-602-081and (B) N9-682-082 (Nov. 15, 2001); and Vincent P. Barabba, Chet Huber, Fred Cooke, Nick Pudar, Jim Smith, and Mark Paich, "A Multimethod Approach for Creating New Business Models: The General Motors OnStar Project," *Interfaces* 32, no. 1 (Jan.–Feb 2002): 20–34.

6. Anjan Chatterjee, Hans-Verner Kaas, T. V. Kumaresh, and Philip J. Wojick, "A Road Map for Telematics," *McKinsey Quarterly* no. 2 (2002), 100–109.

7. Larry Downes and Chunka Mui, *Unleashing the Killer App* (Boston: Harvard Business School Press, 1998).

Chapter 4

1. Robert A. Lutz, "An Exploratory Study of the Influence of Design on Product Image" (MBA thesis, Graduate School of Business Administration, University of California, Berkeley, 1962), 7.

2. Glen L. Urban, *Digital Marketing Strategy* (Upper Saddle River, N.J.: Pearson Prentice Hall, 2004), 2.

Chapter 5

1. Matt Daily, "Dow, GM Launch Largest Commercial Fuel Cell," Reuters news release, Feb. 10, 2004, 6:08 P.M.

2. This can be found under the innovation tab at www.gmev.com.

Part II

1. Printed with permission from General Motors Corporation.

2. For a more thorough discussion of these competencies, see Vincent P. Barabba, *Meeting of the Minds* (Boston: Harvard Business School Press, 1995), chaps. 5–7.

3. *General Motors: Priorities and Focus—Yesterday, Today, and Tomorrow* (General Motors University, November 2000), 3.

4. Barabba, *Meeting of the Minds*, 51.

5. General Motors Corporation, "White Paper: Clinic Effectiveness," 1992.

Chapter 6

1. Ian I. Mitroff and Tom R. Featheringham, "On Systematic Problem Solving and the Error of the Third Kind," *Behavioral Science* (Nov. 1974), 383–93.

2. Arthur D. Little, Inc., "Report to International Business Machines Corporation: Investigation of Two Haloid-Xerox Machines as New Product Opportunities in the Office Reproducing Equipment Field," mimeo (Dec. 1, 1958), C-61613.

3. Douglas K. Smith and Robert C. Alexander, *Fumbling the Future: How Xerox Invented, Then Ignored, the First Personal Computer* (New York: Morrow, 1988).

4. National Academy of Sciences, *Research Briefings 1986: Report of the Research Briefing Panel on Decision Making and Problem Solving* (Washington, D.C.: National Academy Press, 1986).

5. Satisficing is a hybrid term coined by Nobel Prize-winning economist Herb Simon in the 1950s that refers to the satisfying and sacrificing that occurs when a difficult decision is made reached by a group with conflicting goals. Satisficing is an alternative to optimization in cases where there are multiple and competitive objectives, in which one gives up the idea of obtaining a "best" solution.

6. Russell Ackoff, *Re-Creating the Corporation* (New York: Oxford University Press, 1999), 13–14.

7. Ian I. Mitroff, *Stakeholders of the Organizational Mind* (San Francisco: Jossey-Bass, 1983).

8. Robert J. Waller, "Knowledge for Producing Useful Knowledge and the Importance of Synthesis," in R. H. Killman et al., eds., *Producing Useful Knowledge for Organizations* (New York: Praeger, 1983), 284.

9. Vincent P. Barabba, with Gerald Zaltman, *Hearing the Voice of the Market* (Boston: Harvard Business School Press, 1991), chap. 11.

Chapter 7

1. See Vincent P. Barabba, *Meeting of the Minds* (Boston: Harvard Business School Press, 1995), 186–205 for a description of the decision process used to develop the portfolio.

2. John Whysner, *Every Purse and Purpose* (Mich.: Wilderness Adventure Books, 1994), 1.

3. Arthur J. Kuhn, *GM Passes Ford, 1918–1938* (Pennsylvania State University, 1986), 313. The strategy that led to this change is more broadly reviewed in Daniel M. G. Graff, "Making Cars and Making Money in the Interwar Automobile Industry: Economies of Scale and Scope and the Manufacturing Behind the Marketing," *Business History Review* 65, no. 4 (Winter 1991): 721.

4. The title *best-selling* reflects the total number of vehicles sold, including vehicles sold to relatively less profitable rental car fleets.

5. Richard Ratliff, *Detroit Free Press* (Feb. 12, 1990), E4.

6. Richard T. Pascale, *Managing on the Edge* (New York: Simon and Schuster, 1990), 144–45.

7. Alton F. Doody and Ron Bingaman, *Reinventing the Wheels: Ford's Spectacular Comeback* (New York: Harper and Row Perennial Library, 1990), 50.

8. Doody and Bingaman, *Reinventing the Wheels*, 54, emphasis added.

9. Doody and Bingaman, *Reinventing the Wheels*, 56.

10. William Pelfrey, *General Motors Priority and Focus—Yesterday, Today and Tomorrow* (Detroit, Mich.: General Motors Corp., 2000), 3.

11. Mary Walton, *Car: A Drama of the American Workplace* (New York: Norton), 51.

12. "Taurus Remaking America's Best-Selling Car," *Business Week* (July 24, 1995), 60–66.

13. *Business Week*, 63.
14. *Business Week*, 61.
15. *Business Week*, 62.
16. *Business Week*, 63.
17. *Business Week*, 64.
18. *Business Week*, 65.
19. Walton, *Car*, 315; emphasis added.
20. The "Flaw of Averages" term was coined by Sam Savage, senior research associate at Stanford University.
21. "Harbour: GM Outpaces Competition with 4.5% Overall Gain," *Automotive Intelligence News* (June 19, 2002), available at www.autointell.com.
22. "Auto Quality Improving," available at cbsnews.com, last accessed May 31, 2002.
23. "2000 Car Highlights," *Automotive News, Insight 2000 Cars* (Oct. 18, 1999), 4i, quotation at 8i.

Chapter 9

1. The content of this chapter draws on a GM case study found in John D. Sterman, "Automobile Leasing Strategy, Gone Today, Here Tomorrow," *Business Dynamics* (New York: McGraw Hill Higher Education), 42–55. All Sterman material here has been reproduced with the permission on The McGraw-Hill Companies. The case study goes beyond this chapter in that it provides a more detailed discussion of the systems dynamics process used in addressing the problem.
2. Sterman, *Business Dynamics*, 44
3. Sterman, *Business Dynamics*, 46
4. Sterman, *Business Dynamics*, 50
5. Sterman, *Business Dynamics*, 54–55.

Chapter 10

1. Henry Weaver, "Streamlining from the Consumer Viewpoint," *The Proving Ground of Public Opinion* (Detroit, Mich.: General Motors, Dec. 1932), 1–3.
2. Weaver, *Proving Ground*, 1.
3. Weaver, *Proving Ground*, 1.
4. Weaver, *Proving Ground*, 1.
5. Weaver, *Proving Ground*, 2.
6. Todd Lapin, "The New Road Rage," *Wired* (July 1999), 126.
7. John K. Teahen, Jr., "In the 2003 True Luxury Sales Race, Cadillac Beat Mercedes by a Nose," *Automotive News* (Feb. 2004), 17.
8. "The Tread Lightly! Guide to Responsible Four Wheeling" (Ogden, Utah: Tread Lightly! Inc., 2000).

Part III

1. The idea of moving from marketing as a functional organization to marketing as a state of mind comes from Everett Rogers, Future of Marketing Conference, Offices of Strategic Decisions Group, Menlo Park, Calif., Sept. 1991.

2. Albert Einstein, interviewed by George Sylvester Viereck, *Saturday Evening Post* (Oct. 26, 1929), 7, 110–17, quotation at 116.

3. For a concise and comprehensive discussion of systems thinking, see the first two chapters of Russell Ackoff, *Creating the Corporate Future* (New York: Wiley), 3–50.

4. Peter F. Drucker, *The Practice of Management* (New York: Harper and Row, 1954), 38–39.

5. Kim B. Clark and Takahiro Fujimoto, "The Power of Product Integrity," *Harvard Business Review* (Nov.–Dec. 1990), 108–18, quotation at 108; emphasis added.

Chapter 11

1. Abraham Maslow, *Eupsychian Management: A Journal* (Homewood, Ill.: Richard D. Irwin and Dorsey Press, 1965). Abraham Maslow elaborates on the internal and external conditions that affect these interactions. His 1965 observations still have merit.

2. I am indebted to Pam Pudar for her work in developing the examples used here to delineate the concept of individual as consumer versus individual as citizen.

3. Peter Drucker, *The Concept of the Corporation* (New York: John Day, 1946), 211.

Chapter 12

1. Arthur Conan Doyle, *A Study in Scarlet* (New York: Oxford University Press, 1994), 20–21.

2. Steven Toulmin, Richard Rieke, and Allan Janik, *An Introduction to Reasoning* (New York: Macmillan, 1978).

3. New York City v. United States Bureau of the Census, 80 Civ. 4550, 1987.

4. Ian Mitroff, Richard Mason, and Vincent P. Barabba, *The 1980 Census: Policy-making amid Turbulence* (Lexington, Mass.: Heath), 139–96; Vincent P. Barabba, Richard O. Mason, and Ian I. Mitroff, "Federal Statistics in a Complex Environment: The Case of the 1980 Federal Census," *The American Statistician* 37 (Aug. 1983).

Chapter 13

1. The concept of a taxonomy relative to organizational learning is presented in Vincent P. Barabba, John Pourdehnad, and Russell L. Ackoff, "Above and Beyond Knowledge Management," in Chun Wei Choo and Nick Bontis, eds., *Strategic Management of Intellectual Capital and Organization Knowledge* (New York: Oxford University Press, 2002), 359–69.

2. Modified from the original found in Harold L. Wilensky, *Organizational Intelligence: Knowledge and Policy in Government and Industry* (New York: Basic Books, 1967), viii–ix.

3. Vincent P. Barabba, *Meeting of the Minds* (Boston: Harvard Business School Press, 1995), 154–55.

4. The original work on the hierarchy of elements that go from data to wisdom is more fully described in Vincent P. Barabba, with Gerald Zaltman, *Hearing the Voice of the Market* (Boston: Harvard Business School Press, 1991). An information pyramid and Haeckel's hierarchy are presented at 54–56.

5. Nigel Piercy, *Marketing Organisation: An Analysis of Information Processing, Power and Politics* (London: George Allen & Unwin, 1985), 13.

6. Reid G. Smith and Adam Farquhar, "The Road Ahead for Knowledge Management: An AI Perspective," *AI Magazine* 21 (Winter 2000): 17–40, subject discussed at 23.

7. Robert K. Merton, *Social Theory and Social Structure* (Glencoe: The Free Press, 1963), 421.

8. Plato, *The Republic*, Book VII, trans. and ed. Richard W. Sterling and William C. Scott (New York: Norton, 1985), 209–34. The author is grateful to Dr. Karl Joseph Does, who originally brought the idea of using the allegory to my attention.

9. Vice Admiral (ret.) Arthur K. Cebrowski, *Military Transformation: A Strategic Approach* (Washington, D.C.: Force Transformation, Office of the Secretary of Defense, 2003), 8.

Chapter 14

1. George Sylvester Viereck, "What Life Means to Einstein," *The Saturday Evening Post* (Oct. 26, 1929), 110–17.

2. Viereck, "What Life Means to Einstein," 117.

3. James Healy and David Kiley, "GM's Rivals Eat Its Dust," *USA Today* (April 4, 2002), B2.

4. David Ogilvy, *Confessions of an Advertising Man* (New York: Atheneum, 1963), 20.

5. "David Ogilvy at 75," *Viewpoint* (Sept.–Oct. 1986), 9.

6. David Ogilvy, *Ogilvy on Advertising* (New York: Vintage Books, 1985), 158.

7. Ogilvy, *Ogilvy on Advertising*, 166.

8. Alex Taylor III, "Finally GM Is Looking Good," *Fortune* (April 1, 2002): 68–74; quotation found at 72 and 74.

9. Robert Lutz, personal correspondence, Jan. 2004.

10. Robert Lutz, "An Exploratory Study of the Influence of Design on Product Image," Report to the Faculty of the Graduate School of Business Administration for partial fulfillment of MBA thesis, University of California, Berkeley.

11. Lutz, "An Exploratory Study," 10.

12. C. E. Osgood, G. T. Suci, and P. H. Tanenbaum, *The Measurement of Meaning* (Urbana: University of Illinois Press, 1957).

13. Alfred Sloan, letter to the stockholders, Sept. 11, 1933.

Chapter 15

1. Adrian Slywotzky and David Morrison, *How Digital Is Your Business?* (New York: Crown Business, 2000), 8.

2. A more detailed description of the process is presented in Vincent P. Barabba, "Revisiting Plato's Cave: Business Design in an Age of Uncertainty," in Don Tapscott, Alex Lowy, and David Ticoll, eds., *Blueprint to the Digital Economy* (New York: McGraw-Hill, 1998) 34–59.

Chapter 16

1. Figures 16.1 and 16.2 were first introduced in Vincent P. Barabba, "Revisiting Plato's Cave: Business Design in an Age of Uncertainty," in Don Tapscott, Alex Lowy, and David Ticoll, eds., *Blueprint to the Digital Economy* (New York: McGraw-Hill, 1998), 58.

2. William Pelfrey, *General Motors Priority and Focus—Yesterday, Today and Tomorrow* (Detroit, Mich.: General Motors Corp., 2000), 8.

Index